STALINGRAD • Paul Carell

Paul Carell

STALINGRAD

The Defeat of the German 6TH Army

Schiffer Military/Aviation History
Atglen, PA

Translated from the German by David Johnston
Photo captions translated by William Warda Sr.

First English Edition
Copyright © 1993 by Schiffer Publishing Ltd.
Library of Congress Catalog Number: 92-62188

Printed in China
ISBN: 0-88740-469-3

This book was originally published under the title,
STALINGRAD-Sieg und Untergang der 6.Armee
by Verlag Ullstein, Frankfurt/Main © 1992

We are interested in hearing from authors with book ideas on related topics.

Published by Schiffer Publishing Ltd.
4880 Lower Valley Road
Atglen, PA 19310
Phone: (610) 593-1777; Fax: (610) 593-2002
E-mail: Schifferbk@aol.com
Please visit our web site catalog at **www.schifferbooks.com**

In Europe, Schiffer books are distributed by Bushwood Books
6 Marksbury Avenue Kew Gardens
Surrey TW9 4JF England
Phone: 44 (0) 20-8392-8585; Fax: 44 (0) 20-8392-9876
E-mail: Bushwd@aol.com
Free postage in the UK. Europe: air mail at cost.

This book may be purchased from the publisher.
Include $3.95 for shipping. Please try your bookstore first.
We are always looking for people to write books on new and related subjects.
If you have an idea for a book please contact us at the above address.
You may write for a free catalog.

CONTENTS

Foreword

Describing the battles of a war which was lost and which has gone into the history books as a criminal war of aggression is not an easy undertaking. In particular this applies to the 180-day Battle of Stalingrad, which ended with the annihilation, the death and ruin of an entire German army. Far in excess of 100,000 men went into captivity. Only 6,000 returned.

Repeatedly the question is asked, what meaning does this battle, this "turning point in the course of the war," have from today's perspective and what lessons are to be derived from this event. This state of affairs alone would be reason enough to examine this battle, to present it in the sense of a historical event: how it really was, how it came about and how everything turned out.

In addition, many evaluations have changed in fifty years and much new information has been gained by exploiting previously unknown sources, including some from the Soviet side.

For example, the memoirs of Soviet military figures and the publications of Russian historians have revealed how desperate was the Soviet situation – including at Stalingrad – during the German summer offensive of 1942, what decisive lessons the Soviet High Command drew from the German blitzkrieg strategy, how and with what means tough, young Russian Generals mastered strategic crises and how the Soviet soldier kept fighting in spite of appalling conditions and huge losses.

How was it possible that Stalin's Red Army and its soldiers and officers fought with such devotion and passion? How was it possible that the units of Hitler's Wehrmacht, soldiers and officers, fought so fearlessly in the third year of the war, obeyed and went to their deaths?

After the war sons eagerly asked their fathers what it had been like. Today grandsons associate the Battle of Stalingrad with terrible sacrifices in Hitler's "war of conquest," but in many cases the real story and the details of the battle are as foreign as the Battle of Waterloo, which led to Napoleon's downfall, was to the author in his youth.

But should not Stalingrad the military event, which is a fateful name in German and world history, be deserving of a more factual assessment? Because the story of this battle is part of the history of our people. "We can't compensate for it through inquisition," is how eminent Second World War historian Walter Görlitz formulated it. Using the lost battle and the brutality of this war to judge soldierly actions and virtues is dishonest and contrary to history.

Therefore it is important that we not just see Stalingrad as the result of Hitler's utopian strategy, but that we bring home what the units of the Wehrmacht were capable of even in hopeless situations fifty years ago. What those 19-, 20-, 30- and 40-year-old soldiers, corporals, sergeants and officers went through, what they endured and suffered, is inconceivable to many today, but it deserves respect not criminalization.

The soldierly abilities demonstrated in Operation Blue – in the marches and battles in the burning steppes in plus 30 degree temperatures and in holes in the snow in minus 30 degree temperatures; in the battles in the passes of the high Caucasus and on the old high-mountain roads of Asia; in the assaults through the subtropical valleys, the crossing of raging rivers while under fire and in man-against-man struggles in the labyrinths of fortress works and ruined buildings – was only possible through the acquired and conduct-determining maxims like duty and obedience, courage and readiness for action, team spirit and comradeship. Are these still realizable in our age? The fact that the highest-ranking of these soldierly virtues, namely a sense of duty and obedience, tragically became the key problem, indeed the cause for the annihilation of the Sixth Army at Stalingrad, lay not in these virtues themselves, rather was based in the dictatorial structure of the national-socialist state and the Wehrmacht command.

The photo section illustrates the operational conditions described in the text. The photos, taken by German soldiers and Soviet correspondents, often say more than any written account could. One must see the vastness of the steppes to comprehend the trials endured by the soldiers as they marched across them. One must see the mighty Russian rivers if one is to measure what it means to cross them at blitzkrieg speed. The photos show the gorges of the forested areas of the Caucasus and the glaciers of Elbrus. The Don, the Volga, the Terek. The treeless Kalmuck Steppe. They bring to life the elementary obstacles in the endless spaces which set boundaries before even the greatest bravery and prevented the final push to the decisive objective. Anyone who examines the photographs of the tangle of rubble of the Stalingrad factories can understand why every step had to be paid for with blood.

All of this is reason enough to consider a fateful battle, its mistakes and brutalities, in order to see, as Clausewitz said, "how it all happened and how it will always happen."

PART I

THE ROAD TO STALINGRAD

CHAPTER I

Case Blue: The Caucasus and the Oil

Generaloberst Halder Drives to the "Wolfsschanze" – Führer Directive No.41 "Case Blue" – Opening in the Crimea – A Failed Dunkirk by the Russians – Kleist's One-armed Armored Pincer – The Road of Death – 239,000 Prisoners

Generaloberst Halder's car drove out of the East-Prussian Mauerwald forest, in which, well-hidden, lay the headquarters of the OKH, and turned onto the road to Rastenburg. A late-winter storm swept through the crowns of the mighty beeches. It whipped the waves of the nearby lake into foam and caused the clouds to sail low over the land, so low that it seemed as if they might be slit open by the tall stone cross which topped the Lötzen military cemetery.

It was the afternoon of March 29, 1942. *Generaloberst* Halder, Chief of Army General Staff, was driving to see Hitler at his *"Wolfsschanze"* Headquarters, which lay hidden in the forests of Rastenburg.

The executive officer held the briefcase on his lap. At that moment it was the most valuable briefcase in the world. It contained the German General Staff's war plan for 1942, the offensive on the southern front which was to crush the Red Army once and for all: Case "Blue," Führer Directive No.41.

Halder thought over his proposals once again. It had taken weeks of work to create a plan from the ideas, thoughts and wishes that Hitler, as Commander in Chief and Supreme Commander of the Wehrmacht, had developed during the recent situation briefings. They principal element of the campaign plan for 1942 was a major offensive in the southern sector to the Caucasus. The offensive's objectives were to destroy the main Russian forces between the Donets and Don Rivers, capture the crossings into the Caucasus and then deliver the huge oil region on the Caspian Sea into German hands.

The Chief of the General Staff was not happy about the plan. He was full of doubts as to whether a major German offensive was justifiable at all after the bloodletting of the winter. At the end of March there were many dangerous crisis situations still weighing heavily on the German High Command and the Army General Staff.

In the final days of March 1942 General Vlasov's army on the Volkhov had not yet been completely smashed.

Graf Brockdorff-Ahlefeldt and the divisions of his II Corps were still stuck in the Demyansk pocket.

Battle Group Scherer had not yet been freed from the Kholm pocket.

At the end of March an atmosphere of crisis still reigned in the Dorogobush-Yelnya area, only forty kilometers east of Smolensk. The Soviets were conducting operations there with elements of an army, a guards cavalry corps and an airborne corps.

But these were not the only worries afflicting the Chief of the German General Staff at the end of March 1942. In the Crimea Manstein and the Eleventh Army were bogged down before Sevastopol and the Russians had even recaptured the Kerch Peninsula in January. But the situation was especially critical at Kharkov; heavy fighting had been raging there since mid-January. The Soviet High Command was making every effort to take Kharkov in a pincer attack. The southern arm of the pincer, the Soviet Fifty-seventh Army, had burst open an eighty-kilometer section of the German Donets front on either side of Izyum. The Soviet divisions had already established a bridgehead 100 kilometers deep. Their attack spearheads were threatening Dniepropetrovsk, the supply heart of Army Group South (see map on page 20).

Whether the Soviet penetration would develop into a bursting dam with incalculable consequences depended on whether or not the two corner posts north and south of the break-in point, Balakleya and Slavyansk, could be held. For weeks the battalions of two German infantry divisions had been fighting what had already become an almost legendary defensive battle there. On its outcome hung the entire development of the southern front. The 257th Infantry Division from Berlin held Slavyansk, the Viennese 44th Infantry Division Balakleya.

The Berlin regiments defended the southern edge of the Izyum salient in bloody fighting. A battle group under *Oberst* Drabbe fought for the wretched villages, collectives and farms with such flexibility and bravery that even the Soviet war communiques, which were usually extremely reluctant to recognize German successes, were full of admiration. The village of Cherkasskaya became a bloody symbol of the battle. In eleven days of fighting there the Drabbe group lost nearly half its one-thousand men. Six-hundred fighting troops held a circular front of fourteen kilometers. The Soviets lost 1,100 men known killed attacking the German nest. They finally took the village, but by then their strength, that of five regiments, had been consumed.

Before driving away from his quarters for the *Wolfsschanze* on the afternoon of March 28, *Generaloberst* Halder had reviewed the infantry division's combat reports on the battle which had been going on for seventy days now. The division was to be named in the Wehrmacht communique: the regiments had wiped out three Soviet rifle divisions and a cavalry division. However the division's own losses reflected the severity of the fighting: 652 dead, 1,663 wounded, 1,689 cases of frostbite, 296 missing – a total of 4,300 men, half of all the casualties suffered by the division in ten months of war in Russia: Slavyansk!

Fighting on the northern edge of the Izyum penetration was the Viennese 44th Infantry Division. It held a front of one hundred kilometers. And attacking this one hundred kilometers was an entire Soviet corps, reinforced by armored forces and rocket batteries.

Here, too, the battle groups and their commanders were the soul of the defense. What the battle group under *Oberst* Boje, commander of the 134th Infantry Regiment, which carried on the *Hoch- und Deutschmeister* tradition, went through in the vital sectors on the wind-swept banks of the Balakleya belongs among the most extraordinary chapters of the eastern war.

The battle was fought for possession villages and farms, or for shelter. A house and a warming stove for a few hours sleep were a matter of life and death in minus forty degree temperatures. The Germans clung to the villages and the Russians tried to drive them out, because they too wanted to get out of the castles of snow behind which they assembled for their attacks, wanted a warm corner under a roof where they could get a night's sleep without fear of freezing to death.

For the soldiers the war was once again over the elementary things of life. Germans and Russians fought with everything they had. Both wanted Balakleya and the villages to the north, because of the houses and because of strategy. Had Balakleya and the heights commanding the roads leading west been lost, Timoshenko would have been able to turn the Izyum penetration into a major breakthrough toward Kharkov.

But Balakleya held. To the north, however, Strongpoint 5 came under such heavy attack that it could not be held. The German battalion there defended to the last man against Soviet tank attacks. Among those killed was *Leutnant* von

Hammerstein, a nephew of the former Chief of the Army GHQ, von Hammerstein-Equord.

These young officers like Hammerstein, ready for any mission and any sacrifice, were a prominent element in the terrible defensive battles. Together with the battle-hardened, fearless corporals and sergeants they formed small fighting teams which performed almost unbelievable feats.

The bitterness of the fighting in the Balakleya sector is reflected in the fact that, on more than one occasion, *Oberst* Boje and his staff were themselves forced to participate in close-quarters fighting with pistols and hand grenades.

These were terrible battles. Typically they were decided by individual fighters. The successful German defensive actions in the winter and spring of 1942 were largely the result of the efforts of individual soldiers. At that time the German soldier was still superior to his Russian counterpart in experience and fighting morale. This is the only explanation for the amazing feats performed by the German soldier, often left on his own, against a numerically superior and better equipped enemy, in every sector of the front between Schlüsselburg and Sevastopol.

The fiercely-contested Kharkov area may be seen by all as an outstanding feat of courage, of fearlessness and of tactical skill. In March the 3rd Panzer Division from Berlin fought there as a mobile fire-brigade for the constantly threatened front. *Feldwebel* Erwin Dreger held a two-kilometer-wide strip of terrain with fifteen men. Of course this was only possible thanks to a special tactic conceived by Dreger and the iron nerves of his men, all "old foxes" of the Eastern Front. Dreger equipped each of his men with a machine-gun from captured stocks and kept three more in reserve to meet any eventuality.

Dreger's machine-gunners were positioned in a wide arc with their front facing the tip of a wood, from which the Russians attacked repeatedly. Because it was there that the Soviet advance forces had chosen to make their breakthrough, and it was supposed to happen on March 17. At about 1030 the Russians began advancing in battalion strength. Dreger had gone into position in the center, which was the deepest point in the defensive line. The Russians came nearer and nearer. Not a shot was fired. Dreger had impressed firmly upon his men: "Wait until I open fire." The enemy point forces had approached to within about 50 meters when Dreger fired the first burst with his machine-gun. As the enemy assault was aimed at the center of the defensive line it was possible to "outflank" the attackers. Under effective fire from both flanks the Russian advance collapsed after twenty minutes.

The Russians attacked five times in fourteen hours. Five times their battalions collapsed under the massed machine-gun fire of the Dreger group. Sixteen determined men defied an enemy force which outnumbered them more than one hundred fold.

Three days later, however, the war demanded the ultimate of Dreger. He and his platoon had finally been forced out of the village. In the freezing cold of the night his men needed at least a few hours in a house, a room, a cellar, to escape from the cold and especially the icy wind. Dreger launched a surprise attack in an attempt to recapture a collective farm, but he was hit by a burst of submachine-gun fire. His men dragged him to the rear and bedded him down behind a haystack. Dreger clapped his ice-cold hands together as if to warm them and listened to the still, ice-cold night. Softly, he said to his men: "Listen, Friend Hein is knocking!" Then he died.

Generaloberst Halder was unaware of the story of *Feldwebel* Dreger, but on March 28, 1942 the combat report concerning the action near Balakleya was very much on his mind. He had sent it to Jodl on February 13 for inclusion in the Wehrmacht communique. The Viennese unit had been mentioned for the first time on February 14. Six weeks had passed since then. Thanks by and large to the astonishing performance of the troops, the Soviet assault had broken on the corner-posts of the Izyum salient. But even if one was optimistic and concluded that this trouble spot, like all the others, would soon be cleared up, there still remained the legitimate question: in view of the heavy losses on the entire Eastern Front, including Army Group South, would it not be better to call a pause and let the Russians come so as to wear them down from the defensive, let them attack and thus deplete their reserves?

This was the question which was raised repeatedly by Halder and his officers during the planning for 1942.

But the head of the operations department, *Generalmajor* Heusinger, had suggested that by doing so they would lose the initiative and with it a great deal of time. Time, however, was working for the Russians and the western allies, who were in the process of mobilizing their great sources of strength – not just for themselves but for the Russians as well. If it was to be done at all, according to Heusinger, they had to try to force the Red Army to its knees as soon as possible.

Halder accepted this argument, but in his opinion the new offensive should once again have been carried out against the heart of the Soviet Union, against Moscow.

But Hitler resisted this notion fiercely. He seemed to be terrified of Moscow.

He wanted to do something completely different. After the unpleasant experiences of the previous year on the central front, he now wanted to seek a decision in the south, wanted to take away from Stalin the Caucasian oil and then drive on to Persia. Rommel's Africa army was also incorporated into this plan. The "Desert Fox," who was just preparing his offensive from Cyrenaica against the British Gazala position and the North African heart of the British defenses, Tobruk, was to drive across Egypt and through the Arabian desert to the Persian Gulf. Then Persia, the sole point of contact between England and Russia, and next to Murmansk the second major supply base for American aid to the Red Army, would be eliminated. Furthermore, the rich Arabian oil resources would have fallen into German hands along with the Russian: Mars had been appointed the god of war economics.

Halder's car stopped before the entry bar at Gate I to Security Zone I of the *Wolfsschanze*, the actual Führer camp. The guard saluted and raised the bar. The car drove down the narrow paved road into Hitler's wooded citadel. The squat concrete barracks with their camouflage paint and planted flat roofs lay well-hidden between tall beeches. Even from the air they were invisible. All around the area was hermetically sealed, protected by barbed wire obstacles and minefields. The roads were blocked. The small switch-line had been shut down and was now used only by Göring's rail car. Göring had his command post south of Rastenburg, near Spirding Lake, in the Johannisberger Forest.

Generaloberst Jodl once said that the *Wolfsschanze* was a combination of concentration camp and monastery. In any case it was a spartan field camp, with only a single difference from military life in that Hitler made night into day, working until two, three, even four in the morning and then sleeping late the next day. His closest associates had to adjust to this rhythm whether they liked it or not.

Halder drove past the Reich press chief's communications center. On the right was the radio and telephone center, beside it the quarters of Jodl and Keitel. Beside the road on the left were the quarters of Bormann and the Reich Security Service. Finally, at the edge of the forest, came the Führer barracks, again cordoned off by a high wire fence. Together with Hitler's German Shepherd bitch "Blondi," this wire mesh was the last obstacle before Hitler's spartan hermitage in the Rastenburg Forest.

Hitler had asked only a small circle to the March 28 conference, the senior commanders of the Wehrmacht: Keitel, Jodl and Halder and a half-dozen high-ranking military men from the three branches of the armed forces. They stood or sat on wooden stools around the oak map table. Hitler sat in the middle of the long

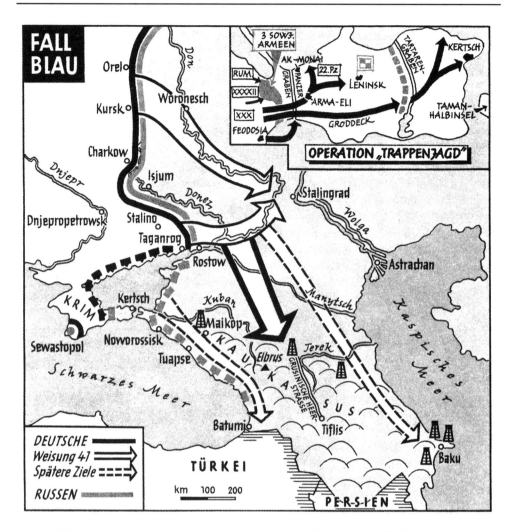

Map 1. Hitler intended to force the decision on the southern front with his 1942 summer offensive, "Operation Blue." A gigantic pincer was to surround the Soviets west of Stalingrad, to be followed by the drive into the oil region. Inset map: The offensive began with "Operation Bussard Hunt," the recapture of Kerch.

side; diagonally across from him, on the narrow side, sat the Chief of the General Staff.

Halder was allowed to speak and began presenting his plan. It bore the code-name "Case Blue." It was originally supposed to have been called "Case Siegfried." However, Hitler wanted no more mythical figures as patrons for his operations, since Kaiser Redbeard (*Barbarossa*) had proved somewhat less than propitious.

Hitler repeatedly interrupted Halder with questions. The talk went on and on, but after three hours Hitler gave his endorsement to the basic concepts of the plan:

Act I: two army groups form a huge pincer. The northern arm of the pincer advances out of the Kursk-Kharkov area southeastward along the middle Don, while the right arm of the pincer races directly eastward from the Taganrog area. The two arms meet west of Stalingrad, close the pincer around the main Soviet forces between the Don and the Donets and destroy them.

Act II: Subsequent advance into the Caucasus, the 1,100 kilometer mountain range between the Black and Caspian Seas, and capture of the Caucasian oil region.

According to "Blue" the city of Stalingrad was not a strategic objective. It was left open, "to reach" the city "or at least bring Stalingrad under the effect of our heavy weapons, so as to eliminate it as an armaments and transportation center."

It was midday when Halder left the *Wolfsschanze* and drove back into the Mauerwald. The chief of the German general staff was tired and worn out, full of doubt and cross over Hitler's arguments. But he nevertheless believed that he had at least won Hitler over to a workable plan. A plan which was economical with German forces and approached the chosen objective on the southern front step by step with clear points of main effort. If it worked Stalin would lose all of Caucasia, including Astrakhan and the mouth of the Volga, which meant the land bridge and waterway to Persia. The southern objective of Operation "Barbarossa" would then be reached.

All that was left now was to put the whole thing into a clear order for the commanders of the individual branches of the Wehrmacht.

Seven days later, on April 4, 1942, *Generaloberst* Jodl presented the draft order. The Wehrmacht operations staff had completed the task according to traditional general staff practice: the situation was described briefly, the objectives formulated as "missions." In this way the conducting of this huge operation was left to the responsibility of the Commander-in-Chief of Army Group South, *Feldmarschall* von Bock. This was a proven general staff tradition going back 130 years, from Scharnhorst through Schlieffen to Ludendorff.

But it was on this corner that the OKW version of Operation "Blue" foundered. Hitler had lost confidence in his Generals in the winter crises. Commanders-in-chief and corps commanders had shown to some extent that they carried out his orders only reluctantly. Now Hitler had assumed supreme command of the army himself. He was not prepared to allow his authority to be limited to such a degree by "flexibly formulated missions."

After Hitler had read the draft he declined to give it his approval. The plan gave the Commander-in-Chief South far too much of a free hand. He – Hitler – wanted to hear nothing of the flexible assignment of missions.

Hitler demanded the detailed issuing of orders. He wanted the carrying-out of the operation laid down precisely. When Jodl rebelled Hitler took the documents from him with the words: "I'll work the thing out myself." The next day the results appeared on ten typewritten pages: Führer Directive No.41 of April 5, 1942. Next to Directive No.21, the "Barbarossa Plan," it was the most fateful paper of the Second World War, a mixture of operations order, fundamental decisions, execution regulations and secrecy instructions.

Since this directive was not only a gigantic campaign plan, but above all the time-table which was to lead to Stalingrad, we will quote the most important parts of the paper, contained in which was a turning-point in the war.

A risky thesis was advanced in the preamble: "The winter battle in Russia is approaching its end. The enemy has suffered the heaviest losses in men and materiel." That was correct. But the conclusion that: "In endeavouring to exploit apparent initial success, he has this winter also largely used up the bulk of his reserves earmarked for later operations," was false. Because as the groundwork of the great offensive was being put down on paper, Stalin was busy conjuring up new armies and a series of independent large formations – in total about 80 divisions – from within his giant empire.

The order developed on this dangerous error: "As soon as weather and terrain conditions provide the necessary pre-conditions, the superiority of the German command and troops must regain the initiative in order to impose their will upon the enemy."

"The objective is to finally destroy the remaining military power of the Soviets and to the extent possible deprive them of their most important military-economical sources of strength."

The plan was to be carried out as follows: "Adhering to the original basic concepts of the eastern campaign, it is important that, while holding in the army center . . . to initially assemble all available forces for the main operation in the southern sector with the objective of destroying the enemy forces forward of the Don, in order to capture the oil region in the Caucasus area and the crossings over the Caucasus itself."

His directive for the operational command of the campaign stated: "The first task of the army and air force following the conclusion of the muddy period is to create the preconditions for the carrying-out of the main operation."

"This will require the mopping-up and consolidation of the entire Eastern Front and in the rear army areas."

"The next task is to clear the Kerch Peninsula in the Crimea and bring about the fall of Sevastopol."

An essential problem of this wide-ranging offensive was the long flank on the Don. In order to avert the resulting danger Hitler made a fateful decision which precipitated the catastrophe of Stalingrad. He ordered: "Primarily allied units will be used to occupy the Don front as it lengthens in the course of this operation .. . (They) are largely to be used in their own sectors so that the Hungarians are employed farthest north, then the Italians and farthest to the southeast the Romanians."

This decision was based on political considerations, because both the Romanian head of state Marshall Antonescu and Italy's Duce Mussolini had requested that their forces be employed cohesively for reasons of national prestige.

Execution of the great plan began with Operation *Trappenjagd* (Bussard Hunt) in the Crimea. The Soviet war historian Colonel P.A. Shilin described the situation in the Crimea in early 1942 in his book *The Most Important Operations of the Great Patriotic War*: "The stubborn struggle of the Soviet forces and the Black Sea Fleet brought us great strategic gains and frustrated the enemy's calculations. The Eleventh German Army which was tied down here could not be used in the attack toward the Volga and the Caucasus."

This is completely true. And because it was so important for the Soviets to keep Manstein's Eleventh Army penned up in the Crimea, Stalin had mustered a mighty force for this task:

Three Soviet armies with seventeen rifle divisions, two cavalry divisions, three rifle brigades and four tank brigades barricaded the narrow, eighteen-kilometer Parpach Isthmus, the access road from the Crimea to the Kerch Peninsula. Kerch on the other hand was a springboard across to the eastern Black Sea coast and thus to the approaches to the Caucasus.

Each kilometer of this vital bridge was defended by about 10,000 Soviet soldiers, ten men to every meter.

The Red Army troops sat behind a ten-meter-wide and five-meter-deep anti-tank ditch which ran across the entire isthmus. Behind it the defenders had put down wide barriers of barbed wire and laid thousands of mines. Spanish Horsemen, huge iron hedgehogs of welded-together railway track, protected machine-gun posts, strongpoints and gun positions. There was no way to outflank the position, because there was water at either end of the eighteen-kilometer front was water.

"And we're supposed to get through there, *Herr Generaloberst?*", asked Manstein's driver and aide Fritz Nagel. He had just had a look through the scissors telescope at the 114th Artillery Regiment's observation post, which offered a good view of the Soviet positions.

"We have to get through there, Nagel," nodded Manstein. He pushed his cap back on his head and stepped up to the scissors telescope again, having just let the *Oberfeldwebel* have a look.

Fritz Nagel was a welcome sight at any headquarters. The native of Karlsruhe had been driving Manstein's car since 1938. He was at the wheel on every trip to the front, was always as calm as could be and many times had mastered dangerous situations. He was wounded several times, however nothing ever happened to Manstein: Nagel was a sort of talisman.

Manstein had driven to the forward observation post of the 114th Artillery Regiment in the northern part of the front before the Parpach Isthmus, to have another look at the Soviet system of positions.

"Anything new?" he asked the commander of the 46th Infantry Division. "Nothing special, *Herr Generaloberst*," answered *Generalmajor* Haccius.

"Then good luck the day after tomorrow," nodded Manstein. "Let's go, Nagel, home."

The day after tomorrow. That was May 8. The day of "Bussard Hunt," as the breakthrough to Kerch had been code-named.

When one is facing an enemy three times as strong in a clever defensive position, one can only prevail with courage and cunning. And Manstein based his plan on a cunning strategy.

The Soviet front in the isthmus ran in a curious way: in the southern part it was straight as a candle, but in the northern part there was a bulge projecting far to the west. It had come into being after the Soviets had driven back the Romanian 18th Division during the winter. German battalions just managed to seal off the Russian penetration, but the bulge remained.

What opportunities did this situation present? Naturally an assault against the flank of the projection in the front. But just because this was offered – and because the Russians counted on it and had therefore massed two armies and almost all their reserves in this sector of the front – Manstein refused to be lured into this obvious attack operation. The outstanding strategist of the Second World War once again proceeded very differently.

The *Generaloberst* did everything possible to convince enemy reconnaissance that he was going to attack in the north. Fake artillery positions were built, troop movements were staged in the northern and central areas of the front, radio messages meant for the enemy's listening service were sent and feint reconnaissance attacks were started.

In the meantime Manstein was preparing to attack at the other end of the front, in the southern sector. Three infantry divisions of XXX Army Corps under *Generalleutnant* Fretter-Pico were to smash a hole in the southern part of the front. Then the 22nd Panzer Division and a motorized brigade were to race through and drive deep into the Red rear, before turning north in an enveloping move and breaking through further to the east.

A daring plan: five infantry divisions and a panzer division against three armies. Stuka units of VIII *Fliegerkorps* under *Generaloberst Freiherr* von Richthofen and elements of the 9th Flak Division were standing by to support the infantry. Heavy artillery had been moved in from Sevastopol for a massed bombardment.

For the assault on the main fortification, the anti-tank ditch, Manstein had come up with something very cunning indeed.

There was strange activity on the beach east of Feodosia during the night of May 7/8. Assault boats were pushed into the water. Combat engineers and infantry of the Bavarian 132nd Infantry Division climbed in. But the motors remained silent. Boat after boat pushed off from the shore without a sound, propelled only by paddle strokes. Soon the secret fleet had been swallowed up by the night: four assault companies bobbed on the Black Sea. At about 0200 they were drifting along the coast toward the east.

0315: The German artillery opened fire with a noise like a primeval thunderclap. Heavy howitzers thundered. Rockets howled. Anti-aircraft guns hammered. Fire, dust and morning fog seethed over the southern sector of the Parpach isthmus. Stukas came howling in. They dove and their bombs shattered bunkers and wire entanglements.

0325: Pairs of white flares went up everywhere. Infantry attack. Combat engineers led the way. They had the worst business to take care of: clearing mines, cutting wire, all under enemy fire.

The Russians laid down barrage fire. Soviet machine-gunners in the embrasures of the bunkers opened fire. They didn't need to aim. The guns were positioned to lay down flanking fire, meaning that the bursts from the various guns overlapped. All they had to do was shoot, just shoot.

Soviet naval guns roared. Mortars coughed. Always firing to the front, from where the Germans must come. And they had to come over the narrow isthmus. Or did they?

When the German artillery opened up, the assault boats off the coast started their engines. No one among the Russians could hear the noise now.

The boats shot toward the coast as swift as arrows. They headed precisely toward the spot where the broad Soviet anti-tank ditch, open like a barn door and filled with water, ended at the sea.

The assault boats simply cruised into the anti-tank ditch. The troops leapt ashore and immediately began firing their machine-guns from the hip. The Soviets in the rifle positions in the wall of the trench were cut down before they knew what was happening.

But then an emplaced Russian flamethrower hissed to life. The first wave of Germans pressed themselves against the ground. They were pinned down.

A Messerschmitt fighter turned and approached low over the sea. It raced along the trench, firing into it with its cannon and machine-guns, and forced the Russians to take cover.

The men of the German assault boat detachment jumped up and broke into the trench. The first Russians raised their hands. There was unholy confusion.

On the left, meanwhile, on both sides of the Feodosia-Kerch road, the Silesian 49th Light Infantry Division was working its way through the minefields. *Hauptmann* Greve led the advance guard of I Battalion south of the road. He bounded through the hail of iron and raced through the narrow lane which had been cleared through the minefields.

A number of assault guns had been assigned to the division. *Oberleutnant* Buff led three of these armored fortresses and gave Greve's men covering fire.

By 0430 the light infantry had reached the anti-tank ditch. The *Hauptmann* lay gasping at the rim of the ditch. *Unteroffizier* Scheidt fired his machine-gun to the left and right. Combat engineers came with an assault ladder. Greve was the first to slide into the ditch.

The commander of II Battalion, *Major* Kutzner lay severely wounded on "Tartar Hill," under fire from Soviet 76.2mm multi-purpose guns, known to the Germans as the "Ratsch-Bumm." The Russians had set up an anti-tank front with the guns of an entire anti-tank regiment. *Leutnant* Fürnschuss and his assault guns saved the day. His long-barrelled 75mm guns blasted the Russian anti-tank front.

Oberleutnant Reissner bounded forward at the head of his 7th Company. He ran under heavy enemy artillery fire and threw himself to the ground. Then he was on his feet again. The rim of the ditch had been torn up by shell fire. Reissner let himself roll in. A burst of submachine-gun fire from the side knocked the *Oberleutnant* off his feet. Although wounded, he continued to direct his light infantry against the Soviet rifle positions.

The infantry on the left side of the breakthrough area worked their way through the minefields and barbed wire entanglements. Well-camouflaged machine-gun bunkers which had survived the artillery bombardment laid down overlapping and flanking barrage fire.

An assault at right angles to the front eliminated the Soviet machine-gun nests and as evening was approaching the anti-tank ditch was reached here as well.

Leutnant Reimann and his 9th Company rolled up the trench from the right wing as far as Parpach Lake, put out of action all the emplaced rifle positions and bunkers in bitter close-quarters fighting and blasted the walls of the ditch for the construction of tank crossings. The key element of the Soviet defense had been taken on the entire width of the attack front.

Late in the morning of the first day a motorized brigade made up of Romanian and German units drove over hastily-erected crossings directly to the seashore, where early in the day the assault boats had taken the anti-tank ditch, and drove into the rear of the Soviet front.

Meanwhile the attack groups of the 22nd Panzer Division waited for the order to move out. But it was not until late morning on May 9 that the bridgeheads across the anti-tank ditch had been expanded sufficiently to allow the battalions to be moved up.

The tank companies and armored personnel carriers deployed and rolled into the second and third Soviet defensive positions. They crushed all resistance and drove on to the bend in the road leading to Arma Eli, where they surprised a Soviet tank brigade.

As if it had been rehearsed, at the same moment six vehicles from the assault gun battalion arrived. Before the Soviet tanks could deploy they were smashed by the German tanks and assault guns.

As planned, the 22nd Panzer Division now veered north behind the front held by the two Soviet armies, which were far to the front dealing with a containing attack by the 46th Infantry Division from Franconia-Sudetenland and the Romanian brigades. Everything was going according to Manstein's plan. But then things changed abruptly. Late on the afternoon of May 9 a heavy spring rain set in. In a matter of a few hours the roads and loamy soil had been transformed into a bottomless morass. Soon all car and truck traffic had been halted. Only the tractors with their caterpillar tracks could get through. Now Manstein's will was fighting against the contrariety of nature.

The tanks struggled forward until well into the night. Then they assumed an all-round defensive position. When the weather cleared the next morning, May 10, the panzers found themselves in the deep flank and rear of the Soviet Fifty-first Army.

A relief attack by the Russians, carried out with powerful armored forces, was beaten off. A wind came up and dried the ground. The division rolled northward. On May 11 it reached the sea near Ak-Monai and was now in the rear of the Soviet Forty-seventh Army as well. Ten Red divisions were in the bag. The rest fled to the east.

Meanwhile *Oberst* von Groddeck and his mobile brigade made a daring advance toward the east and prevented the Russians from turning and fighting somewhere in the rear positions. Wherever Soviet regiments tried to establish themselves von Groddeck struck and then raced onward.

By the time the brigade had advanced fifty kilometers into the enemy rear and appeared totally unexpectedly at the "Tartar trench" – far in the rear of the headquarters of Lieutenant General D.T. Koslov, the Commander-in-Chief of Army Group Crimean Front – the Soviet command had begun to break down. Units and headquarters disintegrated. On the roads huge columns of fleeing units tramped in the direction of Kerch on the eastern end of the peninsula. From there they hoped to save themselves by crossing the narrow strait to the mainland.

Soviet reserves tried desperately to stop the German spearheads in order to allow as many as possible of the units massed on the beaches of the Kerch Peninsula to be ferried to the mainland by motorboats and cutters, just as the English, almost exactly two years ago to the day, had done with their expeditionary corps on the French mainland.

But Manstein had no intention of allowing a Soviet Dunkirk to diminish his victory. He sent his panzer and motorized units with two infantry regiments in pursuit. Kerch was reached on May 16. There was no Dunkirk for the Soviet high command. Self-propelled guns and assault guns quickly brought the improvised evacuation by sea to an end.

170,000 prisoners: three Soviet armies had been smashed in eight days by a half-dozen German divisions.

Early on May 17 Manstein stood on a small rise near Kerch with *Generaloberst Freiherr* von Richthofen. Before them lay the sea, the Straits of Kerch, and beyond, not twenty kilometers away, in the bright sunshine, the shore of the Taman Peninsula, the approach to Asia, the entrance to the Caucasus. Manstein's victory had kicked open the back door to Stalin's oil paradise.

At the same hour, as Manstein was looking across at the great objective, 650 kilometers farther north, in the Kharkov area, the divisions of Army Group Kleist were moving out to seize the decisive starting position for the summer offensive, for "Case Blue." *Generaloberst* Kleist was launching an offensive which, as far as daring and strategic potential were concerned, had no equal.

In the east the horizon turned red. The sky was cloudless. Quiet. The only sound was breathing and the ticking of the large wristwatch worn by *Leutnant* Teuber, who was resting his hand on the rim of the trench. The ticks were drops of time falling into the sea of eternity.

Then it was time. A roar like thunder filled the air. But while the newcomers on the battlefield heard only an unnerving crashing, the old hands of the Eastern Front could differentiate between the dull thump of the howitzers, the cracking discharges of the cannon and the howling of the infantry guns.

Over in the forest, where the Soviet positions lay, columns of smoke rose up. Fountains of dirt sprayed into the air, branches of trees whirled high above the shellbursts: the backdrop of the massed artillery barrage before an offensive.

As here in the jumping-off position of the Berlin Bear Division, so it was with the regiments of the 101st Light Division, the grenadiers of the 16th Panzer Division and the *Jäger* of the 1st Mountain Infantry Division, the attack spearhead of Mackensen's III Panzer Corps. On the morning of May 17, 1942, everywhere between Slavyansk and Losovaya, south of Kharkov, the companies of Army Group Kleist stood ready to attack beneath the roaring thunderclap of the artillery.

Then the barrage made a visible leap toward the north in front of the waiting German soldiers. At the same moment the Stukas roared over the German lines.

"Move out!" shouted the company commander, *Leutnant* Teuber. At that second a half-thousand other *Leutnante* and *Oberleutnante* shouted the same command: "Move out!"

The questions which had plagued the officers and men in the past days and hours were swept away. The big question was: would they succeed in striking at the roots of the Soviet offensive which had been rolling westward for five days?

What was at stake on this day, May 17, 1942? What was the purpose of the attack by Army Group Kleist? To answer these questions we must look back.

Führer Directive No.41 had ordered the elimination of the Soviet salient on both sides of Izyum, which posed a constant threat to Kharkov, through a pincer operation. The object was to capture the starting positions for the main assault of the great 1942 summer offensive from the Kharkov area toward the Caucasus and Stalingrad. The Commander-in-Chief of Army Group South, *Feldmarschall* von Bock, came up with a simple plan: the Sixth Army would attack from the north, Army Group Kleist with elements of the First Panzer Army and the Seventeenth Army from the south. The operation was to pinch off Timoshenko's packed salient and destroy the massed Soviet armies inside in a battle of encirclement. The plan's code-name was *"Fredericus."*

But the Russians had been making plans too. Marshall Timoshenko wanted to repeat his failed January offensive, and this time he assembled even stronger forces. It was hoped that the outcome would have a decisive effect on the course of the war. With five armies and an armada of tank units at his disposal, Timoshenko planned to strike from the hard-won salient with two spearheads and burst open the German front. The metropolis of Kharkov, the administrative center of the Ukraine's heavy industry, was then to be recaptured in an enveloping operation. For the Germans this would mean the loss of their huge supply center for the southern front and the tremendous stocks of supplies stored there.

At the same time Timoshenko wanted to repeat his January attempt to take Dniepropetrovsk away from the Germans, as well as Zaporozhye, 100 kilometers away. The great dam there had been seen as something of a world wonder in the 1940s.

The realization of this plan would have been even more fateful than the loss of the administrative center of Kharkov. Because through Dniepropetrovsk and Zaporozhye led the roads and rail lines to the broad, lake-like lower course of the Dniepr. Farther south to the Black Sea there were no permanent crossings. All supplies for the armies of the German southern wing, which was standing east of the Dniepr in the Donets region and in the Crimea, rolled through these two transportation centers. Their loss would have unleashed a catastrophe.

So in early 1942 the thoughts of both sides were on the great Izyum salient, which for Bock as for Timoshenko was to be a fateful background for future decisive battles. The only question was who would strike first, who would win the race with time: Timoshenko or Bock?

The German timetable designated May 18 as the day of the attack. But Timoshenko was quicker.

On May 12 he launched his pincer operation against the Sixth Army with surprisingly powerful forces. The Soviet Twenty-eighth Army with sixteen rifle and cavalry divisions, three tank brigades and two motorized brigades formed the northern arm of the pincer. This was an overpowering force against two German corps with a total of six divisions.

The southern arm of Timoshenko's pincer came out of the salient with even more concentrated strength. Two Soviet armies, with twenty-six rifle and eighteen cavalry divisions as well as fourteen tank brigades, surged against the positions of the German VIII Corps and the Romanian VI Corps. A half-dozen German and Romanian infantry divisions, without a single tank at first, found themselves facing a vastly superior enemy with overpowering tank forces.

There was no chance whatsoever of halting the Russian thrust at its points of main effort. The German lines were overrun. Nevertheless, just as in the winter battle, numerous German strongpoints held out in the advancing enemy's rear.

General Paulus threw every available unit of his Sixth Army against the torrent of the Russian breakthrough. Flanking attacks managed to halt Timoshenko's northern arm twenty kilometers from Kharkov, at the last minute really. But the tremendously strong southern wing was not to be stopped. A catastrophe loomed. The Russians broke through far to the west. On May 16 Soviet cavalry units neared the city of Poltava, the headquarters of *Feldmarschall* von Bock. The situation became dramatic. Bock faced a weighty decision. The German attack was to start in two days. But the situation had been changed from the ground up by the Russian offensive. The Sixth Army was pinned down and had to defend itself desperately. It was therefore lost as the northern attack group. The pincer operation had become untenable.

Should he give up the entire plan? Or should he carry out the operation with only one arm? Bock's Chief of Staff, *General* von Sodenstern, repeatedly urged the hesitant *Feldmarschall* to choose the "one-armed" solution. It was risky in view of the powerful enemy. Acting in favor of this daring operation, however, was the fact that with every kilometer he advanced toward the west, Timoshenko lengthened his flank dangerously.

This was Bock's chance and in the end the *Feldmarschall* seized it. He decided to conduct Operation "*Fredericus*" with only one arm. He even began the attack a day earlier than planned so as to give the Russians no chance to screen their long flank.

Thus Army Group Kleist went to the attack o the morning of May 17. Kleist's striking force consisted of eight infantry divisions, two panzer divisions and a motorized infantry division. Romanian divisions guarded the attack's left wing.

At 0315 *Leutnant* Teuber jumped out of the trench at the head of his company

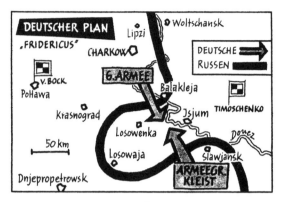

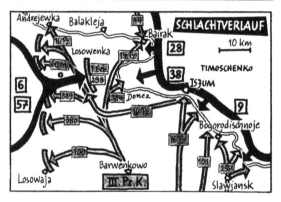

Map 2. The great battle south of Kharkov in early summer 1942, prelude to Operation "Blue."
Top: The German "Fredericus" Plan. Center: The Soviet plan to encircle the Sixth Army. Bottom:
The course of the battle of encirclement south of Kharkov.

and led his men against the Russian positions at the edge of the forest. Stukas howled over their heads, dove and dropped bombs on recognized Russian strongpoints, bunkers and firing positions.

Self-propelled 20mm anti-aircraft guns advanced between Teuber's platoons, taking the place of the missing tanks. The 20mm guns poured shells into nests of Soviet resistance. The infantry thought highly of this weapon and its fearless men, who were always in the leading wave of the attack.

The first well-built Russian positions were smashed by the hail of bombs and shells. Nevertheless the Soviets who survived the artillery barrage mounted resistance. One assault battalion held out to the last man. 450 dead Russians testified to the bitterness of the fighting.

The regiment's progress was halting as it fought its way through dense undergrowth, minefields and barriers of felled trees. *Leutnant* Teuber and his company ran into one especially bitterly defended position, the Majaki collective farm. This honey-producing farm was located just behind the Soviet main line of resistance. The company was unable to advance a single step.

"Request artillery fire," Teuber called to the artillery liaison officer. The latter called in the request to the rear using a backpack radio: "Fire on grid square 14." A few minutes later a great fireworks display began. Russian artillery laid down barrage fire in front of the collective farm.

Teuber and his men dashed forward. There was the Russian trench. The Soviets were still inside, pressed close against the wall of the trench. The onrushing German soldiers jumped inside and ducked under the howling shells which fell in front of, behind and in the trench, likewise pressing themselves against the wall.

They crouched and lay shoulder to shoulder with the Russians. Neither side did anything to the other. They all clawed into the earth. Each was just a man wanting to save himself from the howling, murderous, glowing fragments of iron. It was as if the enmity between them had been blown away in the face of the senseless power which was raining down on Russians and Germans alike.

Not until a half hour later, when the artillery fire suddenly stopped, did Teuber's men get to their feet. Calls of "*Ruki werch! Ruki werch!* – Hands up!" were heard everywhere in the trench. The Russians let their submachine-guns and rifles drop and raised their arms.

Teuber's platoons advanced farther and came upon ten steaming Russian field kitchens which were in the process of making tea and millet gruel. The Russians were stunned when German soldiers suddenly turned up looking for something to eat.

"Come on Ivan, serve it up," they called. The Soviet cooks were fearful at first, but soon they were ladling spoonfuls of millet gruel into the mess kits of the "*Germanskis*" and pouring shimmering green tea into their canteens.

Breakfast ended with a sad spectacle: a Soviet biplane suddenly dove and attacked the resting place with its machine-guns. The soldiers of Teuber's company fired their rifles and machine-guns at the low-flying, old "sewing machine." Numerous hits struck the aircraft's engine and shredded its wings. The machine staggered and went down in a glide, crashing not 200 meters from the resting place.

1st Platoon stormed the aircraft, but the pilot defended himself with the aircraft's flexibly-mounted machine-gun. When he had expended all his ammunition, the pilot and his crewman, both dressed in leather, climbed out of the machine.

"Hands up!" called the Germans. But the two Russians didn't raise their hands. Instead they pulled their pistols.

"Cover," shouted the platoon leader. But there was no need. The two Russian fliers had no intention of defending themselves, only of escaping capture: first the observer, then the pilot, shot themselves in the head. Teuber's men recovered the bodies shaking their heads. Only then did they discover that the second member of the crew was a woman with the rank of Second Lieutenant.

By the evening of May 17 the regiments had reached the Donets in their entire attack lane. On May 18 they took their northernmost objective, Borogodishnoye. At the Donets crossing point a ferry with a full load of thirty horses tried to sail away from the chaos of burning small boats. But the ferryman gave up the venture when he spotted the Germans. Burning boats floated down the river, like spinning islands of fire.

By evening of May 18 the neighboring 101st Light Division had also fought its way up to the Donets. The battalions had to cross a huge wooded area in burning, tropically-humid 30 degree heat, fight their way cautiously past well-camouflaged Russian forest positions in squad columns and struggle through broad minefields. On the first day the engineers disarmed 1,750 mines of all types.

For the first time since the summer offensive of the previous year mine-carrying dogs appeared, German Shepherds and Dobermans with live anti-tank mines on their backs. Crouched in well-concealed positions, the dog handlers repeatedly sent the animals against the advancing German units. The dogs were shot down in a terrible slaughter. Again and again whole packs came and, true to their training, tried to run beneath vehicles and limbers. If they succeeded, and the mine's projecting trigger met resistance, then the powerful explosive charge went off, killing the dog and blowing everything within a radius of several meters to pieces.

With the capture of the Donets line the divisions took over the role of providing flanking cover for the deep advance by the armored assault groups. It was this armored advance which was to create the pocket. As the spearhead of the assault the 16th Panzer Division smashed through the Russian positions with three battle groups under Witzleben, Krumpen and Sieckenius. The enemy was driven back and strong counterattacks beaten off. Then the panzers advanced rapidly to the suburbs of Izyum.

General von Mackensen and his III Panzer Corps were to deliver the main blow of Operation "Fredericus." With the 14th Panzer Division from Dresden in the center and the Viennese 100th Light Division and the Bavarian 1st Mountain Infantry Division on the right and left, the surprised Russians were driven back at the muddy Suchoi Torets. A bridge was thrown across the river. Then the attackers veered north. Brewing dust clouds shrouded the tanks. The powdery black earth made the soldiers look like chimney sweeps.

The Bereka River was crossed in cooperation with Eisenach panzer companies under Sieckenius. Soviet armored attacks were repulsed. On May 22 the panzers were at the northern bend in the Donets.

This was the decisive moment, because on the other side of the river was the leading element of the Sixth Army: the *Hoch- und Deutschmeister*. With this linking-up, the German forces had sliced through the Izyum salient and cut off Timoshenko's army which had advanced far to the west. The pocket was closed.

Marshall Timoshenko recognized the danger too late. He had not reckoned with such a response to his offensive. Now there was nothing left for him to do but break off his advance toward the west which had begun so hopefully, turn his divisions around and try to break out of the pocket to the east. Would the thin German wall of the pocket hold?

For *Generaloberst* von Kleist the important thing now was to strengthen his encircling front so that it could withstand the Soviet breakout attempts.

In a brilliant display of command skill *General* von Mackensen grouped all the infantry and motorized divisions under his command like a fan around the axis of the 14th Panzer Division. After being turned west, the 16th Panzer Division was sent north toward Andreyevka on the Donets. The other four divisions fanned out to the west and formed the pocket front against Timoshenko's armies which were flooding back toward the east.

In the center, like a spider in its web, sat the 1st Mountain Infantry Division.

This foresight brought the battle's final decision. Timoshenko's army commanders sent their divisions against the German pocket front with savage determination. They formed points of main effort. Their aim was to punch a hole in the German front, cost what it may, in order to reach the safety of the Donets front only forty kilometers away.

On Whit-Monday the surrounded armies smashed through the blocking front and drove toward Losovenka. It was clear: the Russians intended to take the main road to Izyum.

But now Mackensen's precautionary measure took effect decisively: the Soviets ran into the 1st Mountain Infantry Division which was manning a blocking position. What followed was one of the bloodiest events of the Russian war.

The former commander of the 1st Mountain Infantry Division, *Generalmajor* Lanz, described what took place in his divisional history: "The Russian columns struck the German lines in the light of thousands of white flares. Orders bellowed by officers and commissars fired up the battalions. The Red Army soldiers stormed forward with arms linked. Their hoarse shouts of 'Urray' resounded terribly through the night."

"The first waves fell. Then the earth-brown columns turned away to the north."

"But there too they ran into the barricades manned by the mountain infantry. They now reeled back and charged into the German front without regard to losses. They slew and stabbed everything in their path, advanced another few hundred meters and then collapsed in the flanking German machine-gun fire. Those who were not dead staggered, crawled or stumbled back to the ravines of the Bereka."

"The scene was repeated the next evening. This time there were several T-34s in the midst of the dense throng of onrushing Red Army soldiers. Some of the masses advancing arm in arm were under the influence of vodka. Where else could the poor fellows have found the courage to charge into certain death shouting *Urray*?"

On the third day the strength of the Russians was finally broken. The Commanders-in-Chief of the Sixth and Fifty-seventh Soviet Armies, Lieutenant General Gorodnyanski and Lieutenant General Podlas, as well as their staff officers, lay dead on the battlefield. The great battle was over, Timoshenko was beaten. He had lost the bulk of 27 rifle divisions and 7 cavalry divisions. Fourteen tank and motorized brigades had been totally destroyed. 239,000 members of the Red Army staggered into captivity. 1,250 tanks and 2,026 guns were destroyed or captured. This was the end of the battle south of Kharkov, in which the Soviets had wanted to encircle the Germans and had been encircled themselves. It was an unusual German victory, which had been conjured up from a defeat in a few days.

But the victorious German divisions had no way of knowing that this success, achieved through command skill and bravery, had opened the door to a sad fate: because now they were marching to Stalingrad.

But no one yet saw the shadow of this city. Kerch and Kharkov dominated the minds of the soldiers and the Wehrmacht communiques. It certainly was amazing: two great battles of destruction within three weeks. Six Soviet armies smashed. 409,000 Soviet soldiers taken prisoner. 3,159 guns and 1,508 tanks destroyed or captured. The German eastern army showed itself to be once again at the peak of its superior strength. Luck once again marched with Hitler's banners. Forgotten was the terrible winter and the spectre of defeat.

And while the last shots were being exchanged in the pocket south of Kharkov and groups of half-starved Russians crawled from their hiding places, the wheels of a new battle were beginning to turn: the battle for Sevastopol, the last Soviet stronghold in the southwest corner of the Crimea, the strongest fortress in the world. The code-word was Operation "Störfang."

CHAPTER II

Sevastopol –
Operation "Störfang"

A Grave in Yalta Cemetery – The Giant Howitzers "Karl" and "Dora" – The "Maxim Gorki" Battery is Blown Up – "There Are Twenty-two of us Left . . . Farewell" – Battle for Rose Hill – Members of the Komsomol and Commissars

"We can cast off now, *Herr Generaloberst*." The Italian Naval Lieutenant saluted. Manstein touched the brim of his cap with a finger, nodded with a smile and said to his party: "Very well then gentlemen, let's board our cruiser."

The cruiser was an Italian motor torpedo boat, the only warship Manstein had available. *Kapitän zur See* Joachim von Wedel, harbor commandant of Yalta, had supplied it. It was June 3, 1942, and Manstein wanted to make a trip along the south coast of the Crimea to see for himself whether the coast road could be observed from the sea. XXX Corps, which was positioned on Sevastopol's southern front under *General* Fretter-Pico, depended on this road for its flow of supplies. A threat to this lifeline by Soviet naval forces could upset the entire program of the battle for Sevastopol.

The boat shot along the Black Sea coast in bright sunshine. The gardens of Yalta with their high trees surrounded the white villas and palaces. The boat cruised west as far as the heights of Balaklava. The old fort on the barren rock summit with its two defensive turrets projected into the blue sky.

The bay which cut into the land at the foot of the summit was also a shimmering blue. It was here, in 1854/55 during the Crimean War, that French, English, Turks and Piedmontese, who had landed an expeditionary force at Yevpatoria, fought in an effort to bring Czar Nicholas to reason. The seige of Sevastopol had lasted almost a year, 347 days, before the Russians gave up. The number of casualties, including those among the civilian population, was very high for that time. Estimates range between 100,000 and 500,000.

Generaloberst von Manstein was aware of these facts. He had read all the studies of the Crimean War. He also knew that the Soviets had laid down completely new, modern defensive works among the old forts: huge casemates, concrete gun positions with armored cupolas and a labyrinth of underground supply dumps. There was no doubt that Stalin would defend the sea fortress tooth and claw in 1942, just as Czar Nicholas I had done in 1854/55, because with its excellent natural harbor Sevastopol was the main stronghold, the support base for the Russian fleet in the Black Sea. If it fell the fleet would have no option but to withdraw to its hiding places on the east coast.

Manstein and *Kapitän* von Wedel were absorbed in conversation when suddenly a terrible crashing, flashing, shattering and screaming filled the boat.

"Aircraft!" cried Manstein's aide, *Oberleutnant* Specht. Too late, the Italians raced to the anti-aircraft machine-gun. Two Soviet fighters had approached from Sevastopol from out of the sun and dove on the Italian vessel, raking it with their fixed weapons.

Deck planks splintered. Fire shot up. *Kapitän* von Wedel, who had been sitting beside Manstein, collapsed – dead. On the railing lay the Italian Chief Petty Officer – dead.

Fritz Nagel, Manstein's loyal aide since the first days of the war, was hit in the upper thigh and thrown against the air-shaft on the deck. The artery had been severed. Blood shot in rapid spurts from the wound. The Italian captain pulled off his shirt to tie off the artery.

Oberleutnant Specht stripped, leapt into the water and swam to shore. Completely naked he stopped an astonished truck driver, who took him to Yalta. There the *Oberleutnant* got hold of a motorboat, raced back to the burning torpedo boat and towed it into Yalta harbor.

Manstein brought Fritz Nagel to the hospital himself, but it was too late. The *Oberfeldwebel* was beyond help.

Two days later, as all around Sevastopol the units of VIII *Fliegerkorps* warmed up their engines in preparation for the first act of the great battle, Manstein stood at the grave of his driver in Yalta cemetery. What the *Generaloberst* said at the coffin of his *Feldwebel* deserves to be included in the otherwise so terrible chronicle of this awful war. Manstein: "In our mutual years of daily life and experience we became friends. The treacherous bullet which struck you cannot sever our bond of friendship. My gratitude and my loyalty, all of our thoughts, follow you beyond the grave into eternity. Now rest in peace, farewell my best comrade!"

The volley of rifle fire rolled over the treetops. From the west there resounded a rumbling thunder: Richthofen's units were taking off against Sevastopol. The great twenty-seven-day battle against the strongest fortress in the world had begun.

There was an excellent view of the entire Sevastopol area from the rocky summit above the town. Engineers had built an observation post in the rock wall, which was relatively secure against enemy artillery fire and air attack. From there, using a scissors telescope, it was possible to see the full extent of the city and fortress as if from a look-out tower.

Manstein spent hour after hour in this observation post with his Chief of Staff, *Oberst* Busse, and his executive officer, "Pepo" Specht, observing the effect of the initial bombardments by the artillery and the Luftwaffe. It was June 3, 1942.

Here, where the Greeks of antiquity erected the first trading centers, where the Goths built their stone citadels during the migration of peoples, where later the Genoese and Tartars fought over the harbor and fertile valleys, and finally where English, French and Russian blood flowed during the Crimean War of the Nineteenth Century, a German Field Marshall now sat pressed close to the rock and directed a new battle for the harbors and bays of the paradise-like Black Sea peninsula.

"A great fireworks display," marvelled Specht. Busse nodded in agreement. But he was sceptical: "But nevertheless it's not certain that we'll get enough holes in the outer belt of fortifications for the infantry attack."

Manstein stood at the scissors telescope and looked across at the Belbek Valley with its projecting summit, which the troops had named "oil mountain." Overhead, squadrons of Stukas raced past, dove on Sevastopol and dropped their bombs. Machine-guns rattled. Then they turned away. Close-support aircraft roared over the plateau. Fighters swept through the sky. Bombers droned resolutely toward the target. Within a few hours of the start of the bombardment the Eleventh Army was in control of the airspace over Sevastopol. The weak Soviet air forces of the coastal army, which started the battle with 53 aircraft, had been smashed.

VIII *Fliegerkorps* flew 1,000, 1,500, even 2,000 sorties daily. The German term for this non-stop air battle was "*rollender Einsatz*, or attack in waves. And while the deadly rain of bombs fell from the sky above Sevastopol, German guns of every caliber hammered the enemy's system of positions. The gunners sought out the enemy's emplaced batteries, levelled trenches and barbed wire obstacles and fired round after round at the embrasures and armored cupolas of the concrete gun positions. They kept up the bombardment twenty-four hours a day for five days, because Manstein had devised this as a decisive opening for the attack. This was not the usual massed bombardment by the artillery and air force of one or two hours followed by a land assault. No, Manstein knew that Sevastopol's fortified defensive system, with its hundreds of concrete and armored defensive works, the broad belt of bunkers, the mighty armored batteries, the three defensive zones with a total of 350 kilometers of trenches, the deep wire and mine obstacles and the firing positions for rocket-launchers and mortars hewn out of the rock of the bluffs were not going to be put out of action by the usual artillery preparation.

Thus was born Manstein's plan for five days of tremendous destructive fire combining the effects of artillery, rocket-launchers, anti-aircraft guns and assault guns. 1,300 pieces pounded the Soviet fortified defensive system and field positions. As well the bomber units of VIII *Fliegerkorps* hammered their bombloads into the target.

It was a murderous overture. Never during the Second World War, neither before nor after Sevastopol, was such a concentration of artillery forces employed on the German side.

It has become a well-known historical fact that at El Alamein in North Africa at the end of October 1942, Montgomery opened the offensive against Rommel's positions with 1,000 guns. Manstein employed 300 more than that at Sevastopol.

The *Nebelwerfer* rocket launchers had a special part in the artillery bombardments. For the first time this sinister weapon was used en masse against a single target. Two rocket regiments as well as two rocket battalions were concentrated at the front outside the fortress under *Oberst* Niemann's special headquarters: twenty-one batteries with 576 launching tubes. Among these were the batteries of a heavy rocket regiment with high-explosive and flamethrower fuel rounds of 280 and 320 mm respectively, which were especially effective against fortified defensive installations.

This regiment alone was capable of firing 324 rounds per second at the enemy field fortifications whose ranges had been measured precisely. The effect on Russian morale was just as great as the rockets' deadly destructive power. The effect of a salvo from a single battery of six launchers, thirty-six huge, fiery-tailed rockets smashing into an enemy position with a nerve-shattering howl, was terrible.

The fragmentation effect of an individual rocket was not as great as that of an artillery shell, but the shock wave produced by the detonation of such a salvo within a limited zone of an area target caused blood vessels to burst. Soldiers not in the immediate vicinity of the impact were demoralized by the ear-shattering noise and the paralyzing pressure of the detonation. Terror and fear led to panic. Stukas had a similar effect on the usually so indifferent Russians. Likewise, German troops often reacted with fear and terror to the massed use of the Russian rocket launcher, the so-called "Stalin Organ."

Among the conventional artillery which pounded at the fortress gates in Sevastopol were three special giants which have gone into history: the "Gamma" howitzer, the "Karl" – also called "Thor" – howitzer and the "Dora" railway gun. All three were high points of conventional artillery development and had been constructed for use against fortresses. Before the war the only fortresses besides the bulwarks in Belgium and the French Maginot Line were those at Brest Litovsk, Lomscha, Kronstadt and Sevastopol. Leningrad was not a fortress in the actual sense, nor were the old fortified cities on the French atlantic coast.

The "Gamma" howitzer was a reborn version of the "Big Bertha" of the First World War. The gun fired shells with a caliber of 427mm weighing 923 kilograms and had a maximum range of 14.25 kilometers. Barrel length was 6.72 meters. 235 artillerymen were required to service this unusual giant.

But "Gamma" was a dwarf compared to the 615 mm "Karl," or "Thor," howitzer, one of the heaviest guns of the Second World War and a specially designed for use against concrete fortresses. The 2,200-kilogram concrete shells, which were capable of penetrating the strongest concrete shields, were fired by a monster which bore little resemblance to a conventional howitzer. The stocky, five-meter-long barrel and the tremendous running gear of the chassis more closely resembled a factory building with a weird, stub chimney.

But even "Karl" was not the ultimate in artillery. This stood in Bachtschisarei, in the "Palace of Gardens," the old residence of the Tartar Khans, and was called "Dora," also known to the soldiers as "Big Gustav." It was the heaviest cannon of the Second World War. Caliber: 800mm. Sixty rail cars were needed to transport the components of this monster. The gun, whose barrel was 32.5 meters long, fired high-explosive shells weighing 4,800 kilograms, or almost five metric tons, over a range of 47 kilometers. "Dora" could also fire even heavier armor-piercing rounds (7,000 kg) over a range of 38 kilometers. Projectile and propellent charge were 7.8 meters long. Raised upright this was equivalent to the height of a two-story house.

"Dora" was capable of firing three rounds per hour. The huge gun sat on two double railway tracks. Two flak battalions were always stationed around the gun. 4,120 men were required to serve, protect and service "Dora." The personnel for fire direction and serving alone included a *Generaloberst*, an *Oberst* and 1,500 men.

These few figures show that these guns had become so huge, so over-dimensional, that their efficiency was questionable. Still a single round from "*Dora*" destroyed a munitions dump near Sevastopol, on Severnaya Bay, buried 30 meters beneath the ground.

Manstein had been in his rocky nest for three hours. He studied the impacts and compared them with the precise maps provided by his two artillery commanders, *Generalleutnant* Zuckertort and *Generalleutnant* Martinek. For all his skilled generalship Manstein was a man of detail. Perhaps this was the secret of his success.

"The flak is simply irreplaceable against these fortifications," and the 18th Flak Regiment became famous in the artillery battle before Sevastopol. The high-velocity "eighty-eight" was the best weapon for engaging the fortifications projecting from the earth. Positioned in the front lines like the rocket launchers, the Flak 88, one of the wonder weapons of the Second World War, knocked out bunkers and gun positions with direct fire. The Flak 88 batteries of the 18th Flak Regiment alone fired 181,787 rounds in the course of the Battle of Sevastopol.

From Manstein's observation post he could see the three in-depth defensive systems which protected the central fortress:

The first was two to three kilometers wide, with four trench positions one behind the other. Between the trenches, which were protected by barbed wire, were wooden bunkers and concrete dugouts. Mines detonated by artillery shells in front of and between the trenches showed that the Russians had also laid dense belts of anti-tank mines. It was thus to be expected that there were many of these invisible mine barriers guarding against an infantry assault.

The second defensive belt was about one-and-a-half kilometers wide and included, especially in the northern sector between Belbek Valley and Severnaya Bay, a series of very heavy fortifications to which the German artillery observers had given easily-remembered names: "Stalin," "Molotov," "Volga," "Siberia," "GPU" and – above all – "Maxim Gorki I" with its heavy 305 mm armored batteries. Its opposite number, "Maxim Gorki II," was located in the south part of Sevastopol and was equally heavily armed.

The eastern front of the fortress was especially enhanced by natural features. Difficult terrain with deep rocky valleys and fortified mountain summits offered an ideal defensive field. "Eagle Hill," "Sugarloaf," "North Nose" and "Rose Hill" came to be unforgettable names for those who fought in Sevastopol's eastern sector.

A third defensive belt ran directly around the city. It was a true labyrinth of trenches, machine-gun nests, mortar positions and gun batteries.

According to Soviet sources Sevastopol was defended by seven rifle divisions, a cavalry division on foot, two rifle brigades, three marine brigades and two marine infantry regiments, as well as various tank battalions and independent formations – a total of 101,238 men. In the defensive front were ten artillery regiments, two mortar battalions and an anti-tank regiment, as well as 45 heavy gun units of the coastal defense, a total of 600 guns and 2,000 mortars.

Sevastopol was truly a fire-spitting mountain, and Manstein intended to take it with seven German and two Romanian divisions.

The night of June 6/7 was hot and sultry. Toward morning a light breeze came up from the sea. But it was not sea air, but instead dust from the shell-torn approaches to Sevastopol that it carried over the German lines. Dust and smoke from the burning munitions depots in the south of the city.

When morning came the German artillery fire once again rose to a crescendo. Then the infantry got to its feet. At 0350, beneath the mighty barrage, assault teams of infantry and combat engineers raced toward the enemy main line of resistance along the entire front.

The point of main effort lay on the northern front, where LIV Corps attacked with four infantry divisions and the reinforced 213th Infantry Regiment. XXX Corps attacked from the west and south.

Above, at the Belbek Valley and in the Kamyschly Gorge, engineers cleared lanes through the minefields so the assault guns could be sent in to support the infantry as quickly as possible. Meanwhile the infantry fought to take the first enemy field positions. To be sure the artillery had smashed trenches and earth bunkers, but the surviving Russians defended desperately. The Soviets had to be driven out of their well-camouflaged foxholes with smoke candles and hand grenades.

Again the difficult task of taking the "Stalin" fort fell to the 22nd Infantry Division from Lower Saxony. Once before, during the previous winter, the assault companies of the 16th Infantry Regiment had scaled the outer wall of the fort, but then they had to withdraw and returned to the Belbek Valley.

Now they had to take that bloody road once again. The first attempt on June 9 failed. On June 13 the men of the 16th tackled the fort again. "Stalin" was a field

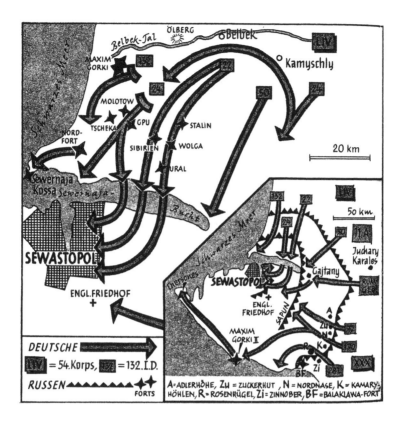

Map 3. The conquest of Sevastopol, Operation "Störfang." On June 7, 1942, following a five-day bombardment by the artillery and the Luftwaffe, the Eleventh Army assaulted the strongest fortress in the world. The last fort fell on July 3, 1942.

of rubble, but the defenders still fired from every corner and hole. In the Andreyev wing the commandant had used only members of Komsomol, young communists, and party members. A combat report stated: "It was probably the toughest enemy we ever saw."

Only one of many examples: thirty dead lay in a bunker which had taken a direct hit in the embrasure. Nevertheless ten survivors fought on. They packed the dead in front of the shattered embrasure as a bullet shield.

Flamethrowers hurled streams of fire against the horrible breastwork. Hand grenades followed. German soldiers were seen vomiting. Not until the afternoon did four completely exhausted Russians stagger from the rubble.

They surrendered, but only after the political officer had shot himself.

The two attacking battalions of the Lower Saxon 16th Infantry Regiment suffered heavily. All of the officers became casualties. A *Leutnant* from the officer reserve took command of the remains of the rifle companies of both battalions.

Bloody fighting raged in the second defensive zone until June 17 in searing heat. An unbearable stench covered the battlefield, on which lay countless dead. Swarms of flies buzzed round the corpses. To the right of the Lower Saxons the Bavarians suffered such heavy losses that they had to be withdrawn from the front for a time.

The situation of the German units was not a rosy one. Casualties climbed ever higher and a serious shortage of ammunition forced a break in the fighting for some time. Some commanders were already advising that the attack be called off until new forces arrived. But Manstein knew that he couldn't count on reinforcements.

On June 17 he ordered a new general attack on the northern front. The two bloodied regiments set out once again, determined to take the main obstacle this time.

Two 355 mm howitzers (Mörser) were moved into position in the Belbek Valley, four kilometers west of "Oil Mountain." Their job was to knock out the armored cupolas of the fire-spitting "Maxim Gorki I." The heavy 305 mm guns of the Soviet fort commanded the Belbek Valley and the road to the coast.

Moving the two giants into firing position was laborious work. After four hours of labor by the construction squad, battery chief *Oberleutnant* von Chadim was finally able to give the order to fire.

The monsters opened fire with a thunderous roar. After the third salvo forward observer *Wachtmeister* Meyer reported that the concrete shells were having no effect on the armored cupolas.

"Special *Röchling* shells," ordered Chadim. The 3.6-meter-long, 1,000-kilogram shells were delivered with the aid of cranes. The "*Röchling*" had proved itself against the fortifications at Lüttich during the French Campaign. This shell exploded after it had penetrated the target rather than on impact.

Unteroffizier Friedel Förster and his fourteen comrades of number one gun held their ears when the *Oberleutnant* raised his hand: "Fire!"

Twenty minutes later the same order was given to both guns at the same time: "Fire!"

Soon afterward a radio message came from *Wachtmeister* Meyer: "Armored cupola blown off its hinges!"

"Maxim Gorki"'s head had been bashed in. The barrel of the 305 mm naval cannon pointed straight into the air. The batteries were silent.

This was the moment for *Oberst* Hitzfeld, the conqueror of the Tartar trench on the Kerch Peninsula. He and the men of his battalion stormed toward the fort and occupied armored turrets and passages.

"Maxim Gorki I" could no longer fire, but the Soviet garrison in the interior of the mighty concrete block, which was 300 meters long and 40 meters wide, did not give up. Squads of Soviets even carried out lightning-quick ambushes through secret passages and drains.

The 24th Pioneer Battalion was given the job of putting an end to this nightmare. The Soviets answered calls for surrender with bursts of submachine-gun fire. The first large explosion was created with a mountain of dynamite, flamethrower fuel and smoke candles. The Soviets started shooting again from embrasures and openings as soon as the gas and smoke had cleared.

The second explosion finally blasted open the concrete structure and created an entrance. A huge belly opened before the engineers. "Maxim Gorki I" was three stories deep. A city. Millions had been spent on its construction. The fort had its own waterworks and power plant, a hospital, messes and an engine room with munitions elevators. Arsenals and fighting tunnels. Every room and every passageway was sealed off by double steel doors, and each had to be blown open individually.

The engineers stood pressed to the walls. As soon as the steel doors burst, they lobbed their hand grenades into the smoke and waited until the gases had cleared before continuing on.

Dead Soviets lay in the passageways. They looked ghostlike as they all wore gas masks. The smoke and stench below had forced them to do so.

Submachine-guns sprayed bullets at the Germans from the next passageway. Hand grenades flew through the air. Pistol shots rang out. Then the steel door crashed shut. The bloody game began all over again. And so it went hour after hour until the battle neared the brain of the fortress, the command center.

The battle in the "Maxim Gorki" fort was also being followed in Sevastopol, in the combat bunker of Vice-Admiral Oktyabrsky, which lay close by the harbor. The radio operator, Second Lieutenant Kuznetsov, sat at his set in the communications center and listened. Every thirty minutes he received a report on the situation in "Maxim Gorki." The admiralty's order to the commanders and commissars read: "Fight to the last man!"

There was the signal. Kuznetsov listened and wrote: "There are forty-six of us left. The Germans are hammering on the armored doors and calling on us to surrender. Twice we have opened the hatch to fire. That is now impossible."

Thirty minutes later came the last message: "There are twenty-two of us left! We are preparing to blow ourselves up. We are signing off now. Farewell!"

And so it happened. The center of the fort blew itself up. The battle was over. Of the one-thousand-man garrison only forty wounded went into captivity. This figure says it all.

On June 17, while the battle for "Maxim Gorki I" raged, the Saxon battalions took the forts "GPU," "Molotov" and "Cheka."

To the Saxons' left the Bremeners of *Generalmajor* Wolff's 22nd Infantry Division worked their way south and on June 17, aided by a battery of assault guns, took the "Siberia" fort. The 16th Infantry Regiment cracked the forts "Volga" and "Ural." On June 19 the Bremeners became the first to reach Severnaya Bay, the last northern barrier before the city to the south.

The 50th Infantry Division and the 4th Romanian Mountain Infantry Division had the most thankless chore. They had to struggle their way from the northeast through the brush-covered rocky terrain to the heights of Gajtany. They succeeded and reached the eastern corner of Severnaya Bay.

As planned, XXX Corps under Fretter-Pico did not attack on the western front until June 11. The divisions advanced along both sides of the large road which led from the coast to the city. Their objective was to capture the commanding Sapun heights. They were the key to the city. Here the two sides fought over hilltops and gorges. Guerilla warfare against well-concealed strongpoints and fortified rocky nests: "North Nose," "Chapel Mountain" and the Kamary heights were hot spots of the battle.

The mountain infantry regiments fought their way across the jagged rocks of the coastal mountains. The fort of Balaklava had been taken by storm in autumn 1941. But the mountain infantry still had plenty to do in June 1942. It was the hour of the assault squad fighters and their gallant officers, men such as *Leutnant* Koslar, *Oberfeldwebel* Keding and *Feldwebel* Hindemith. The battle's bloody stations in this sector had names like "Tadpole Hill," "Cinnabar I, II and III" and "Rose Hill," as well as the notorious vineyard.

The reinforced 170th Infantry Division took the vital Sapun heights. In an hour and a half the 240th Pioneer Battalion under *Leutnant* Mylius fought its way to the top of the heights.

There, having reached its objective, the infantry battalion established a bridgehead, the city and harbor of Sevastopol before its eyes.

On June 18 *Major* Baake and the 72nd Reconnaissance Battalion took "Eagle Hill."

The 420th Infantry Regiment was given a macabre assignment. It had to storm the old English cemetery in which lay the fallen of the Crimean War. The Soviets had turned the cemetery into a heavy battery strongpoint: a gruesome fortress.

On June 20 "Lenin" fort fell.

Finally, after heavy fighting, the north fort and the notorious Konstantinovsky battery on the narrow Severnaya-Kossa tongue of land were taken. German forces now commanded the harbor entrance. Sevastopol was in a stranglehold. All the fortifications around Sevastopol were in Manstein's hands. Nevertheless the Soviet High Command sent another rifle brigade into the city on the night of June 26 using every available vessel. It arrived just in time for the fall of the city.

The death blow was administered by the 22nd and 24th Infantry Divisions.

June 27, shortly after midnight: silently the companies crossed the bay in inflatable rafts. Too late the enemy recognized the maneuver. The first assault squads were already at the power plant. It fell.

The battalions pushed on to the edge of the city. When it got light the Stukas came. The dive-bombers blasted open a path for the infantry. The last large anti-tank ditch was taken.

The Soviet defense collapsed. Only here and there did a commissar, a commander or a member of the Comosomol fight to his last breath.

At the bluffs of the northern bay about a thousand women, children and soldiers sat in a barricaded tunnel. The commanding commissar refused to allow the door to be opened. German engineers prepared to blast it open. Then the commissar blew up the entire tunnel and everyone inside. A dozen German engineers were killed in the blast.

On July 3 it was over. Sevastopol, the strongest fortress in the world, had fallen. Two Soviet armies had been smashed. 90,000 Red Army soldiers went into captivity. On the desolate battlefield lay thousands of dead as well as 467 guns, 758 mortars and 155 anti-tank and anti-aircraft guns.

The fortresses' commanders, Admiral Oktyabrsky and Major General Petrov, did not remain on the battlefield however. They had been taken out of the fortress by a motor torpedo boat on June 30.

Manstein's Eleventh Army was now free for the big plan, for the offensive which was just getting under way against Stalingrad and the Caucasus.

CHAPTER III

The Operational Plan Falls into Russian Hands

An Interrupted Celebration – Major Reichel Has Disappeared – A Fateful Flight – Two Mysterious Graves – The Russians Know the Offensive Plan – The Attack Is Started Nonetheless

The commissar's villa was furnished with surprisingly good taste. The two-story building was located in a small garden at the edge of Kharkov. Even the basement level was finished. The comrade commissar had not lived badly, but nonetheless he had been a responsible man. The heavy industry of the Kharkov region had been under his control. Had been. Because now *General der Panzertruppe* Stumme and his staff resided in the villa.

Stumme was an outstanding officer and a philosopher as well: spirited, small in stature, but great in energy. Never without the monocle he had worn even as a young cavalry officer. His face had a slight reddish tinge due to high blood pressure. With such a physical and spiritual constitution his nickname was an obvious one: "ball lightning" was what the officers and soldiers of his staff secretly called him. Stumme was of course aware of this, but he pretended not to suspect. In this way there was no need for him to react if by chance he heard himself referred to in this way.

Stumme was no scientific general staff officer, rather a man of action with a true feeling for tactical or operational chances. He was among the leading German armor commanders, a clever planner and one quick to seize an opportunity. He was a man of the front, loved by his soldiers whom he looked after with restless energy. But he was also respected by his officers, who admired his energy and flair.

His weakness, a secret weakness, was good food and drink. "War – and then eat poorly? No, gentlemen!" was one of his favorite sayings. Nevertheless he always shared with guests the good things provided by the commandant of the officers quarters.

One such occasion took place on June 19, 1942, when Stumme invited some guests for supper. The commanders of the corps' three divisions and the artillery commander were there: *Generalmajor* von Boineburg-Lengsfeld, *Generalmajor* Breith, *Generalmajor* Fremerey and *Generalmajor* Angelo Müller, the corps artillery commander. Also present were the corps Chief of Staff, *Oberstleutnant* Franz, the Ia, *Oberstleutnant* Hesse and the O1, *Leutnant* Seitz, as well as the corps adjutant, *Oberstleutnant* Harry Momm, the famous show jumping rider.

"We can sleep our fill for a few more days, gentlemen," Stumme greeted his officers. "Hopefully we'll succeed in forcing Stalin to his knees this time."

"Hopefully," murmured the robust *Generalmajor* Breith.

Stumme had verbally informed the three division commanders of the corps' role in the first phase of Operation "Blue" several days earlier. Verbally, because according to the very strict secrecy rules ordered by Hitler, even a division commander was not permitted to learn the plan or corps orders for an offensive before the beginning of the attack.

"Can't we have a few general principles in writing," one of the commanders had asked. This was contrary to the strict secrecy rules, but Stumme agreed.

"One can't lead a Panzer korps on too short a rein," he said to his Chief of Staff, and then dictated a memorandum from a half page of typewriter paper: "For division commanders only!" It concerned only the first phase of Operation "Blue." *Oberstleutnant* Hesse had the super-secret papers sent to the divisions by especially reliable couriers.

This was common practice in many panzer corps. Because how was a division commander, the leader of a mobile unit, supposed to exploit an opportunity presented by a surprise breakthrough if he didn't know whether he should advance north, south or west?

For example, according to the first phase of the operational plan the Stumme corps was to advance across the Oskol within the Sixth Army and then veer north for an encircling operation. Should the divisions get across the river quickly, it was important that the division commanders were aware of the overall plan and acted correctly with no loss of time.

Stumme had always had good results with his method of sending brief written notes to his division commanders. In this way he had never missed an opportunity and nothing had ever happened, at least not until this June 19.

Stumme happily enjoyed the evening's surprise: there was saddle of venison from a roebuck which *Oberstleutnant* Franz had shot while on a reconnaissance trip. A can of caviar was served as an appetizer and there was Crimean champagne as well. Both had been discovered in a Kharkov warehouse by a keen mess officer and the guests helped themselves.

Sweet Crimean champagne has a cheering effect. Table guests of the Czars spoke of this as well as those of the Soviets. Gaiety reigned at Stumme's table, too, on the evening of June 19. The officers, all of whom had lived through the terrible winter, once again saw things in a confident way.

The commanding general in particular was full of energy and optimism. That afternoon he had spoken with army headquarters. There, too, the mood was good. *General* von Mackensen had just smashed a breach for the Sixth Army above Kharkov in the Volchansk area, east of the Donets, capturing excellent jumping-off positions beyond the river at the Burluk for the big offensive.

In a daring encircling operation with his four mobile and four infantry divisions, Mackensen had smashed significantly stronger Soviet forces which were dug in on the commanding high ground at the Donets. The area was taken by the corps and 23,000 more prisoners taken. Now *General* Paulus' Sixth Army would not have to undertake a risky crossing of the Donets under enemy fire in the upcoming offensive.

Using his knife and fork, a desert spoon and a schnapps glass, *Oberstleutnant* Franz gave a demonstration of Mackensen's interesting operation, which had led to a great success with extremely low casualties. This operation was further proof that the German Army had regained its old striking power after the winter catastrophe.

It was five minutes to ten. No fiery message appeared on the wall as at Belshazar's banquet. No bomb struck the happy circle. Instead it was the Ia clerk Odinga who came in. He bent down to *Oberstleutnant* Hesse and whispered something to him. The Ia stood up and said to Stumme in explanation: "I'm wanted urgently on the phone, *Herr General*."

Stumme laughed: "Don't bring us any false rumors!"

Hesse: "I don't think so, *Herr General*, it's the executive officer of the 23rd Panzer Division."

When the two had left the room and were going down the stairs to the map room, *Feldwebel* Odinga observed: "Looks like something's up at the 23rd, *Herr Oberstleutnant*."

"Oh?"

"Yes, apparently the Ia, *Major* Reichel, hasn't been seen since this afternoon."

"What?"

Hesse leapt down the last few steps to the telephone and picked up the receiver: "Yes, what is it, Teichgräber?" He listened. Then he said: "No, he's not here with us!" Hesse looked at his wristwatch: "He took off at 1400 you say? It's now 2200. Man! What did he have with him?" Hesse listened intently. "His map board? What? And the map with the memorandum? For heaven's sake, he went up scouting with something like that?"

Hesse was thunderstruck. He crashed the receiver down onto the cradle and raced up the stairs to the dining room. The cheerful chatter at the table abruptly died down. Everyone could tell by looking at the Ia that something had happened.

Oberstleutnant Hesse reported tersely, turning alternately to face Stumme and von Boineburg-Lengsfeld: the Ia of the 23rd Panzer Division, General Staff *Major* Reichel, an outstanding and reliable officer, had taken off at 1400 in a Fieseler *Storch* piloted by *Oberleutnant* Dechant. His destination was the command post of XVII Army Corps where he intended to have another look at the division's march area as specified in the memorandum to the division commanders. Reichel had obviously flown far beyond the corps command post and over the front lines. So far he had not returned or landed in the division area. He had with him the memorandum as well as his map board with the corps' divisions pencilled in and the entries on the attack objectives of Operation "Blue."

Stumme stood up immediately. Boineburg-Lengsfeld tried to placate him: "He's come down somewhere behind our divisions. The worst might not have happened." He restrained himself from thinking what was in everyone's mind: caught by the Russians. With the order. With the objectives of Operation "Blue."

Now Stumme lived up to his nickname "ball lightning." Every division in the front was contacted by telephone: division and regimental commanders were instructed to check with artillery observers and company commanders at the front to find out if they had seen anything.

The corps headquarters was like a swarm of bees, buzzing and ringing. Forty-five minutes later the 336th Infantry Division reported: a forward artillery observer had seen a Fieseler *Storch* in the brooding, hot, afternoon haze, between 1500 and 1600. It had twisted and turned between the very low clouds and then, just as a heavy summer thunderstorm struck the entire sector, landed near the Russian lines. "Send out a strong combat patrol," ordered Stumme.

Oberstleutnant Hesse issued detailed orders for the patrol: the main concern was of course the two missing men. Should Reichel and his pilot not be found, then search for the briefcase and map board. If the enemy was already present, check for evidence of fire or fighting which would indicate that the papers had been destroyed.

At dawn on June 20 the 336th Infantry Division sent a reinforced company into the very complex terrain. A second company provided flanking cover and laid down fire to distract the Russians.

The aircraft was found in a small valley. But it was empty. No briefcase, no map board. The instruments had been removed as the Russians liked to do whenever they captured a German machine. There were no signs of fire to indicate that the map and the papers had been destroyed. There were also no traces of blood. No indication of fighting. The fuel tank had a single bullet hole. The gasoline had run out.

"Search the area," ordered the *Hauptmann*. The soldiers moved out by squads. Then a call came from an NCO: "Here!" He pointed to two mounds of earth, thirty meters away from the aircraft: two graves. That settled the matter for the company commander. The lookouts were brought in and the company withdrew.

General Stumme shook his head when he received the report of the two graves. "Since when is Ivan so full of piety? Buried the dead? And right beside the aircraft?"

"I also find it hard to believe," observed *Oberleutnant* Franz.

"I want to know for sure, perhaps it's a trick," decided Stumme.

The 336th Infantry Division received orders to carry out the operation again, this time to open the graves and check whether Reichel and *Oberleutnant* Dechant lay inside.

The men of the 685th Infantry Regiment set out again. *Major* Reichel's aide went along to identify the missing men. The graves were located. The young man believed he recognized one of the dead as his *Major*, even though the body was dressed only in underclothes and obtaining a good view was difficult. The second grave also contained no items of uniform.

It is no longer possible to determine with certainty what report was made by XXXX Panzer Corps, in whose headquarters the entire investigation and report to the army came together, concerning the bodies. Some staff officers do not even remember that the bodies were found. The signals officer of XXXX Panzer Corps, who at the time in question was stationed a few kilometers from the accident site as the advance party of Stumme's corps headquarters and who was immediately drawn into the search effort, believes Reichel disappeared without a trace. On the other hand the former *Oberstleutnant* Franz is of the opinion that the bodies were definitely identified. In spite of the absolutely clear statements made by the staff officers of the 336th Infantry Division, one could harbor doubts as to whether the Soviets had not in fact pulled a trick to mislead the Germans. At any rate Frau Reichel received a letter from *Oberst* Voelter, the Ia of the Sixth Army, informing her that her husband had been buried "with full military honors" at the military cemetery in Kharkov. She also received photos of the grave; however, the wedding ring worn by her husband was not sent. So even today there remains a glimmer of doubt over the entire affair.

For the German command in late June 1942 it was naturally of vital importance to know whether Reichel was dead or alive as a prisoner of the Russians. If he was dead the Russians knew only what was on his map board and in his briefcase: the first phase of Operation "Blue." If the *Major* had fallen into their hands alive there was a danger that GPU specialists might force him to tell what he knew. And Reichel naturally knew in rough outlines everything about the big plan. He knew that it was aimed at the Caucasus and Stalingrad. It didn't bear thinking about – if the Soviet secret service had found ways and means to get a live Reichel to talk! There was reason enough to fear that.

It was no secret that the front-line Russian troops had strict orders to handle any officer with red stripes on his trousers, which meant any general staff officer, with kid gloves and to immediately take him to the next highest headquarters. Dead German general staff officers were also to be recovered whenever possible, as this caused the Germans uncertainty and uneasiness as to whether those concerned were still alive. This uncertainty was increased through clever front-line propaganda.

Why should the Soviets suddenly deviate from all that? And even if they had, why the burial?

There is only one logical solution to this mystery: Reichel and his pilot were taken prisoner by a Soviet patrol and then killed. When the patrol leader brought the map and briefcase to his commander, the latter immediately realized that their owner had been a senior German staff officer. In order to dodge trouble and avoid an eventual investigation or questions about the bodies, he sent the patrol back and had the two murdered officers buried.

Naturally Stumme had to report the Reichel case to Sixth Army at once. *Oberstleutnant* Franz had already discussed the matter by phone with the Sixth

Army's Chief of Staff, the former *Oberst* and later *Generalleutnant* Arthur Schmidt, at about 0100 on the night of June 20. There was nothing left for *General der Panzertruppe* Paulus to do. Duty-bound and with a heavy heart he reported the matter to army group who relayed the information to Führer Headquarters in Rastenburg.

Fortunately Hitler was in Berchtesgaden and thus did not learn of the incident right away. *Generalfeldmarschall* Keitel led the initial investigations. He was inclined to recommend to Hitler the strongest measures "against the implicated officers."

Naturally Keitel knew what Hitler's reaction would be. A Führer order had made it very clear that operational plans could only be passed on verbally by senior headquarters. In Directive No.41, Hitler had once again issued strict secrecy measures just for the decisive "Operation Blue." At every opportunity, due to his fear of espionage, Hitler referred to the maxim that no one needed to know any more than was absolutely necessary to carry out his assignment.

Three days before the offensive *General* Stumme, his Chief of Staff *Oberstleutnant* Franz and the commander of the 23rd Panzer Division *General* von Boineburg-Lengsfeld were relieved of their duties. Stumme and Franz were brought before the special panel of the Reich court martial. *Reichsmarschall* Göring presided. The charge comprised two points: too early and too far-reaching issuing of orders.

In a twelve-hour trial Stumme and Franz were able to prove that there could be no question of issuing orders "too early." Five of the short June nights were needed for the panzer corps' move into the Volchansk bridgehead over the single Donets bridge. There remained the accusation of the "too far-reaching issuing of orders." This became the principal item of the charge, as the corps had advised the panzer divisions that after crossing the Oskol and veering north they might encounter Hungarian units wearing earth-brown uniforms similar to those of the Russians. This advisory was important, as there was a danger that the German panzer units might mistakenly take the Hungarians for Russians.

But this excuse was not accepted by the court. The two defendants were sentenced to five and two years in prison respectively. At the conclusion of the trial Göring shook hands with both men and said: "You have argued your case openly, bravely and without tricks. I will report this to the Führer."

Göring apparently kept his word. *Feldmarschall* von Bock also intervened on behalf of the two veteran officers in a personal conversation with Hitler at Führer Headquarters. It is impossible to say who tipped the scales, but four weeks later

Stumme and Franz received identical written notices that the Führer had struck down their sentences in view of their service and outstanding bravery. Stumme went to Africa as Rommel's assistant; Franz followed him as Chief of Staff of the *Afrikakorps*. On October 24 *General* Stumme was killed in the El Alamein offensive. He lies buried there.

Following Stumme's departure command of XXXX Corps was passed on to *General der Panzertruppe* Leo Freiherr Geyr von Schweppenburg. It was to be a bitter inheritance.

One must conclude that the Russian High Command knew of parts of the plan and preparations for the first phase of the great German offensive by June 21 at the latest. The Kremlin therefore knew that the Germans intended to launch a direct west-east thrust from the Kursk area and an enveloping thrust from the Kharkov area with the aim of taking the important center of Voronezh and destroying the Soviet forces before Voronezh in a pocket between the Oskol and Don.

However the Soviets could not learn from the map and papers which the unfortunate Reichel had with him that Army Group Weichs was subsequently to advance south and southeast along the Don and that the long-range operational objectives were Stalingrad and the Caucasus, unless Reichel had fallen into Russian hands alive and had been interrogated, and another body placed in the grave near the aircraft.

The question which confronted Führer Headquarters, therefore, was: should they overturn the plan of operations and the appointed date?

Feldmarschall von Bock as well as *General* Paulus declared themselves against such an idea. The attack date was at hand, therefore there wasn't much more the Soviets could do. As well, on June 22 *General* Mackensen had begun his second "preparatory operation." In combination with elements of the First Panzer Army he won jumping-off positions for the Sixth Army in the Kupyansk area with a small, successful battle of encirclement. The result was 24,000 prisoners and the capture of territory across the Donets as far as the lower Oskol.

The springboards for the launch into the adventure of Operation "Blue" had thus been won. Now they couldn't switch the intermeshed gearing of the great plan without endangering everything. The fired-up machine had to run. Hitler therefore ordered that it was to begin as planned: X-Day for Army Group Weichs on the northern wing was June 28, for the Sixth Army with XXXX Panzer Corps June 30. The die had been cast.

Sixty-eight German divisions and about 30 divisions of her Italian, Romanian, Hungarian and Slovakian allies, as well as Wallonian, Finnish, Croatian and other volunteer units from many European nations set out on the decisive offensive "Case Blue."

What happened now is perhaps connected to the tragic Reichel case and represents the hour of birth of the German tragedy in the Russian war. We see the beginning of a chain of strategic errors which inevitably led to the catastrophe of Stalingrad.

Anyone wishing to comprehend this turning point for the German eastern army must make the effort to follow the rather difficult, but dramatic strategic campaigns of Operation "Blue."

The basis of the first phase was the capture of Voronezh. This two-river city was an important armaments and economic center and commanded the Don with its numerous crossings as well as the Voronezh River. Furthermore it was the switching station of the central Russian north-south road, rail and river links from the "transportation spider" of Moscow to the Black and Caspian Seas. In the German "Plan Blue" Voronezh was the turntable for the movements to the south and the backing for flank security.

On June 28 Weich's Army Group began its advance toward Voronezh. Hoth's Fourth Panzer Army formed the spearhead. In its center, as battering ram, was XXXXVIII Panzer Corps under *General der Panzertruppe* Kempf.

The 24th Panzer Division – which had been created from the East Prussian 1st Division and several Wehrmacht cavalry divisions in the winter of 1941/42 – had the task of taking Voronezh.

The division, which was led by *Generalmajor* Ritter von Hauenschild, struck with great force. Air support was provided by VIII *Fliegerkorps*. The Soviet defensive positions were overrun, the Tim River reached, the Tim bridges stormed and the lit fuses ripped away. Then the division commander roared across the bridge in his half-tracked armored personnel carrier, ahead of the reinforced panzer regiment.

Artillery and columns of the Soviet rifle divisions were smashed. Another bridge was captured undamaged. The German advance became a wild pursuit without regard for unprotected flanks, the division commander and command personnel in the lead true to Guderian's recipe: "Armored units are led from the front and are in the happy situation of always having open flanks."

When it was time to refuel, the armored forces regrouped and hastily-formed battle groups roared onward. On the evening of the first day of the attack motorcycle troops and tanks attacked the village of Yefrosinovka.

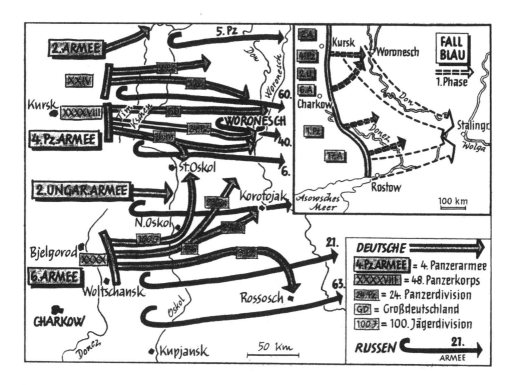

Map 4. The first act of Operation "Blue" (June 28 to July 4, 1942). Voronezh was to be taken and the first pocket formed in the Stary Oskol area in a joint effort between the Fourth Panzer Army and the Sixth Army. However, for the first time the Soviet armies did not stand and fight, instead they withdrew east across the Don.

"What's going on here?" thought *Rittmeister* Eichhorn: there was a forest of signs at the entrance to the village, radio trucks, staff horses, trucks. This could only be a senior headquarters.

The motorcycle troops missed a huge catch only by a hair: the headquarters of the Soviet Fortieth Army, which was stationed in the village, fled at the last minute. The advancing Germans failed to capture it, but the entire army was left leaderless following the loss of its headquarters.

In those hot summer days of 1942 the 24th Panzer Division repeated the classic armored thrusts of the first weeks of the war and in doing so demonstrated what a rested, well-equipped panzer division could accomplish against the Russians. Only a cloudburst-like rain was able to halt the confident units. They moved into an all-round defensive position, waited for the grenadier regiments to catch up and then resumed the advance.

On June 30 the advancing Germans were halfway to Voronezh. They found themselves facing a strongly-built Soviet position which was held by four rifle brigades. Two tank brigades were spotted behind it. The situation became serious.

The Soviets tried with three tank corps to surround the advancing German units and screen Voronezh. Lieutenant General Fedorenko, deputy of the People's Commissar for Defense and commander of armored forces, personally led the operation. It was obvious that the Soviets were aware of the significance of the German thrust to Voronezh.

But Fedorenko had no luck. His large-scale tank attack against the spearhead of Hoth's Fourth Panzer Army misfired. Better German tactics, extensive reconnaissance and flexible command allowed the German panzers to prevail over the more powerful Soviet T-34 and KV tanks.

On June 30, the day the 24th Panzer Division went into its first large tank battle, 150 kilometers farther south the Sixth Army launched its assault toward the northeast: objective Voronezh. The great pincer had been brought out to pull the first of Stalin's teeth.

XXXX Panzer Corps moved out of the Volchansk area, a mighty fist composed of thoroughly battle-tested units.

Freiherr von Geyr's first assignment read: on reaching the Oskol swing north in order to form a pocket around the Soviets in the Stary Oskol area in conjunction with Kempf's XXXXVIII Panzer Corps.

But now something remarkable happened. The troops discovered that enemy rearguards were fighting energetically in well-fortified defensive positions, but that the main body of the Soviets had made an orderly withdrawal to the east. For the first time the Russians did not stand and fight. Instead they pulled out of the threatening pocket. What did it mean? Did they know so precisely what the Germans intended?

Or had the Russians learned from the severe defeats of the previous year and no longer defended strategically unimportant areas so as to avoid being encircled? Or had the Sixth Army launched its attack wrongly, meaning too far north, and missed its opportunity to create a large pocket?

Be that as it may, in any case the decisive order in Hitler's "Case Blue" had not been fulfilled. "Given the now sufficiently demonstrated resistance to strategic encirclements on the part of the Russians, it is of decisive importance to turn individual breakthroughs into tight encirclements."

"The enemy must not be given an opportunity to escape destruction as the result of the encircling units turning inward too late . . . Therefore, with the exception of the overall strategic objective, in each individual case the destruction of the enemy is to be assured through the manner of the attack and the method of command of our units."

CHAPTER IV

The New Russian Tactics

Fateful Voronezh – Hitler Changes the Plan Again – War Council in the Kremlin – The Battle Rolls to the Southern Don – Battle of Rostov – Street Fighting with the NKVD – The Bridge at Bataisk

When the Soviet retreats were reported to XXXX Panzer Corps' commanding general he realized at once that the whole first part of the German operation was in jeopardy. In view of the situation he requested permission to push on to the east to the Don without delay. But the Sixth Army stuck to its encirclement plan and ordered: "You will swing north to link up with the Fourth Panzer Army." Orders were orders. The pocket was closed, but there was nothing inside. The Russians had even withdrawn their heavy weapons. The Germans had swung, but they hit only air.

Now Führer Headquarters, too, realized that things weren't going according to plan. The Russians were withdrawing quickly toward the Don. Would they eventually escape across the river while the Fourth Panzer Army was still concentrating on Voronezh? If so the entire first phase of Operation "Blue" would be a failure. The danger was great. There was no time to lose.

Faced with this situation, on July 3 Hitler came to the entirely correct conclusion that sticking to the plan of taking Voronezh first might threaten all of Operation "Blue." He therefore informed von Bock during a lightning visit to the latter's headquarters: "I no longer insist upon the capture of the city, Bock, I also no longer consider it necessary and I leave it up to you to move south immediately." This was a decisive moment. The fortune of war hung in the balance. Which scale would sink?

Geyr breathed a sigh of relief when late on the evening of July 3 he received the order from Sixth Army to advance due east toward the Don to block the Russian retreat there.

But at noon the next day a new order reached him: he was to move north, rather than east, in the direction of Voronezh, to keep open Fourth Panzer Army's southern flank. What was going on? What had happened near Voronezh? What was behind this back and forth?

It was remarkable. Hitler made all the right decisions of the first half of the war with a strange, otherwise uncharacteristic timidity. In the case of Voronezh he acted differently.

He didn't order *Feldmarschall* von Bock to leave the city alone and follow the timetable to Stalingrad without delay. No, he let Bock know that he no longer insisted on the capture of Voronezh. Responsibility for deciding whether or not to change direction without possession of this important transportation center was left with the Commander-in-Chief of Army Group South. The *Feldmarschall* thus faced the alternative: take the city or leave it alone. The sensible von Bock deliberated: would it not be better to first take the corner post of Voronezh, take it quickly, if it was possible? In any case to attempt it? Bock wavered. He hesitated.

Then came the report that the 24th Panzer Division had captured a bridgehead at a Don ferry crossing with its reinforced 26th Rifle Regiment. The battalions rolled across a Soviet military bridge between retreating Russian columns. By late evening patrols were three kilometers from Voronezh.

To the left the *Großdeutschland* Motorized Infantry Division, which was covering the 24th Panzer Division's northern flank, had also advanced rapidly and likewise reached the Don on the evening of July 4, at about 1800. Farther south the 16th Motorized Infantry Division had reached the river with its reinforced motorcycle battalion.

The Soviets had not blown the Don bridge near Semiluki which led to Voronezh. This fact showed that they still wanted to get the bulk of their armies across the Don. They committed T-34s and launched strong counterattacks in order to keep the Germans away from the bridge and defend a wide bridgehead on the west bank.

At about 2000 on July 4, *Oberleutnant* Blumenthal with men of a company of the *Großdeutschland* Division took the road bridge over the Don to Voronezh and established a bridgehead on the east bank. The Soviets wanted to destroy the bridge quickly, but apparently they hadn't made preparations to set off the charges electrically. They therefore lit normal fuses leading to stacks of dynamite under the bridge piers. The fiery tails of destruction glimmered quickly toward the charges.

Then *Unteroffizier* Hempel jumped into the river. Up to his neck in water, he waded beneath the bridge and ripped away the burning fuses, the last only twenty centimeters from sixty kilos of dynamite.

Meanwhile Russian columns continued to roll across the bridge from the west. They were met on the east bank by Blumenthal's company. They had the bridge. Would they also be able to seize Voronezh quickly?

Squads of the *Großdeutschland* Infantry Regiment riding on assault guns made a reconnaissance in force against the city and got as far as the railway station. They had to be withdrawn when the Soviets counterattacked sharply. Nevertheless they were in the city. This was the news that led *Feldmarschall* von Bock not to follow Hitler's suggestion to leave Voronezh alone and instead to attack the city. He wanted to seize the moment and take the important city in a coup de main. He believed that there would still be time for his fast units to drive from Voronezh and reach the rear of Timoshenko's armies and block their flight across the Don. This was another mistake from which the tragedy of Stalingrad developed step by step.

July 5 had been extremely hot, with temperatures of 40 degrees Celsius. As the day gave way to night the two motorized infantry regiments of the *Großdeutschland* Division as well as tanks and motorcycle troops were east of the Don before Voronezh in wide bridgeheads. Covering to the north were the approaching infantry divisions. But now the false assessment of the enemy situation by the army group showed itself. The city was jammed with Soviet troops. The Russians had quickly reinforced Voronezh in a very special way.

When Hitler learned of the situation he finally put his foot down. Now he strictly forbade the continuation of the attack on the city. "Southwards," he urged, "southwards."

But on July 6 elements of the 24th Panzer Division and the *Großdeutschland* Division were in the city. The Russians appeared to give ground. Hitler allowed himself to be seduced by the spirit of the moment and once again he authorized the capture of Voronezh. But he ordered that at least one panzer corps was to continue the southward advance begun on July 4 and drive to the Don without delay. The Fourth Panzer Army was instructed to free up further panzer units as quickly as possible to send after this panzer corps.

Thus the second phase of Operation "Blue" began with a watering-down.

Although the battle for Voronezh was initially conducted with panzer units, which were quite unsuited to the task, during the battle for the city Bock's most potent divisions were taken from him one by one. Some of these were then stranded for a time south of Voronezh for lack of fuel. So Army Group South was no longer strong enough to force a decision in the battle for the important city of Voronezh, but was also too weak for the thrust to the south as well as the quick blocking of the Don, even though it had been sent additional mobile units.

On July 7 the western part of Voronezh was taken after heavy fighting. But the battalions did not get across the Voronezh River, which flowed through the city from north to south. The Russians made repeated counterattacks and threw infantry and waves of tanks into the battle.

Timoshenko had assembled nine rifle divisions, four rifle brigades, seven tank brigades and two anti-tank brigades – the bulk of the Soviet Fortieth Army – around Voronezh. This massing of forces at Voronezh reinforced the suspicion that Timoshenko had looked into Hitler's hand in the most literal sense and was now making all the right moves: pinning down the main forces of the German northern wing before Voronezh in order to gain time to move the main body of his own army group back from the Oskol and Donets and withdraw across the Don.

To where? To Stalingrad.

The German radio network reported the capture of Voronezh on July 7. But on July 13 fighting was still going on in the university quarter and in the forests north of the city. In the days that followed the Germans failed to take the eastern part of the city and the bridge in the north of the city, nor were they able to cripple the vitally-important north-south railway line on the east bank of the river used to supply the Russian forces. The major supply road down from Moscow also remained in Russian hands.

Instead of striking south along the Don after the rapid fall of Voronezh in order to outrace from the east Timoshenko's divisions withdrawing from the huge area between the Donets and Don and intercept them at the Don as planned, the valuable panzer and motorized divisions were tied down at the cursed city. Marshall Timoshenko directed operations personally. The city was to be held as long as possible to delay the German thrust to the southeast. Each day was a gain for Timoshenko.

In the evening hours of July 6 the spearheads of XXXX Panzer Corps were south of Voronezh, about eighty kilometers from Rossosh. But fuel was running low. Nevertheless, *Major* Wellmann, trusting in the supply echelon, decided to continue the advance with two armored companies and a battery of the 75th Artillery Regiment.

The night was clear and starry as they drove across the steppe. In front was the Busch company, behind the Bremer company. The commander recalled: "If we wanted to capture the bridges over the Kalitva intact we had to reach Rossosh at dawn. All contact with the enemy had to be avoided due to the shortages of ammunition and fuel. So, sticking rigidly to the time distance, we roared unrecognized past advancing Russian artillery and infantry units."

Shortly before three in the morning the Germans reached the first pitiful houses of Rossosh. The battalion interpreter, *Unteroffizier* Krakowka, seized a surprised Russian and interrogated him. The terrified "comrade" informed his captors that there was another bridge across the Kalitva in addition to the two marked on the map. It was a *"Tankimost,"* a tank bridge, which had only recently been completed. Company commanders Busch and Bremer made their attack plan with the battalion commander.

At dawn Wellmann's columns drove through the still-sleeping and unsuspecting Rossosh. Courier aircraft sat on a sports field, here and there a tank. Sentries were drawn up in front of a large, three-story building, but they suspected nothing untoward in the approaching dust cloud.

Close behind 1st Company rolled *Major* Wellmann's armored personnel carrier. The company drove over the bridge. Wellmann reached the Soviet bridge sentry on the north side. The Russian recognized the danger and reached for the rifle slung over his shoulder.

Radio operator Tenning leapt quickly from the vehicle and rammed his submachine-gun into the Russian's stomach. He knocked the rifle from the man's hands and dragged him to the CO, the first, but very important prisoner. The Russian reported that Rossosh was occupied by a senior headquarters and that at least eight tanks were present to guard the town.

Then the first shots were fired on the far side of the river. It was the beginning of a bitter, five-hour battle with the town's surprised but strong garrison.

There was firing from every direction. T-34s rolled through the area. Soviet infantry formed up. Nevertheless Wellmann's men held the bridge. Their salvation was the accompanying howitzer battery. The gun crews were experts and placed their guns where they could command the wide road at the river.

There was wild fighting in Rossosh, but the elan and better nerves of the Germans prevailed. Most of the Soviet tanks were destroyed from close range. *Feldwebel* Naumann made a special catch: he captured the map section of

Timoshenko's army group headquarters and took prisoner twenty-five high-ranking staff officers, most with the rank of colonel. Timoshenko himself was in Rossosh that night. He must have slipped away at the last minute.

Despite the bravery of his troops, the party would probably have ended badly for Wellmann had not the main body of the 3rd Panzer Division finally reached Rossosh. The Soviet resistance was broken. *Generalmajor* Breith's Berlin regiment had reached another decisive point on its journey along the Don.

But the upsetting of the schedule as a result of the battle for Voronezh was making itself felt everywhere. As stronger enemy forces were suspected in the area south of Rossosh around Millerovo, these were first to be destroyed through direct attack. This was another deviation from the plan, another sin committed against the spirit of a fast operation in the direction of Stalingrad.

It was in this rather confused situation that the third phase of Operation "Blue" began, which according to "Directive No. 41" was actually supposed to initiate the decisive phase of the great summer offensive of 1942: the attack by the southern wing with the Seventh Army and the First Panzer Army on July 9. The objective: link up in the area – in the area mind you, not in the city – of Stalingrad so as to encircle the Russians between the Donets and Don.

But just as he had in the north, in the south Timoshenko fought only at certain strongpoints and very quickly decided to fall back toward the east and south with the bulk of his armies.

The attack by the southern wing achieved nothing more than to push the retreating Russians before it into the great Don bend. But there was not yet a German defensive front which could have blocked the path of the retreating Russian units.

When Hitler realized that the encircling operation on the central Don could no longer succeed as a result of the rapid Russian retreat and the delay suffered near Voronezh, he wanted to at least catch and encircle the suspected enemy forces on the lower Don. To achieve this objective, On July 13 he let drop the key element of his great plan: to drive quickly to Stalingrad with all his forces and block the lower Volga.

There is no doubt that Hitler was capable of this operation, indeed in this situation he had to carry it out, because if the enemy refused to allow himself to be encircled and fled, the Germans would have to pursue him. Then they could not allow him any time to establish a defense and had to reach the assigned objective in this way. And the objective was: elimination of the enemy forces in the Stalingrad area.

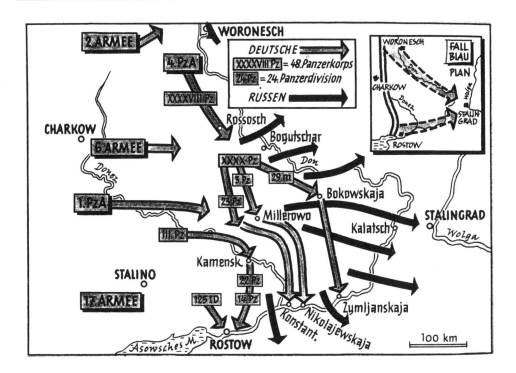

Map 5. Hitler deviated from the original plan of driving as quickly as possible to Stalingrad with all available forces, and instead swung his armies south on July 13, 1942, in the hope of destroying Timoshenko's main forces near Rostov. Timoshenko escaped the encirclement, however.

This objective was attainable. Hitler had two panzer armies at his disposal, important Don crossings had been taken. He could have been in Stalingrad in the shortest space of time. But Hitler had been caught by a great mistake: he believed the Soviets to be at the end of their strength. He saw in the Soviet retreat nothing but flight, dissolution and moral collapse, while in reality it was a planned withdrawal.

The appearances of panic, which were evident in many places, lay in the inability of the lower levels of command on the Russian side. Operationally Timoshenko had the withdrawal well in hand. He had initiated it quickly. His objective was to save the main Soviet forces for a determined resistance deep in the interior of the country.

Hitler failed to see this danger. He believed that he could "force Stalingrad with his left hand" and in the meantime also initiate a great battle of encirclement on the lower Don with Rostov in the center. He therefore interrupted the Fourth Panzer Army's march along the Don toward Stalingrad, halted it before the great bend in the Don and turned it straight south, a complete deviation from phase three of the great plan. Just as he had stopped the march on Moscow in early autumn of 1941 and sent Guderian's mobile units south to the battle of encirclement around Kiev, so now he wanted to surprise the Russians with an improvised operation and smash their forces near Rostov. It was to be the greatest battle of encirclement of the war.

The Sixth Army continued on toward Stalingrad alone without its steel spearpoint, the mobile units of XXXX Panzer Corps, which had also been sent toward Rostov.

On the day of this fateful decision *Generalfeldmarschall* von Bock had to go. He opposed Hitler's intention of two separate operations and wanted to retain the army group as a single force under his command.

Führer Headquarters had already ordered the division of Army Group South. On July 7 *Feldmarschall* von Bock noted in his diary: "Orders have come that Feldmarschall List is to assume command of the Eleventh and Seventeenth Armies and the First Panzer Army. With this the battle will be cut in two pieces."

Hitler could refer to the legendary founder and chief of the Prussian General Staff, Graf Moltke, who correctly taught that no campaign plan could survive beyond the first battle, because the first battle often created an unforeseeable situation.

On the southern front this had happened as a result of Timoshenko's withdrawal. Thus a change in operations plan "Blue." But Hitler forgot another of Moltke's rules, that the basic strategic concept of a plan of operations must not be abandoned as a result of such changes. And that is exactly what happened. Because the correct idea of "Case Blue" was to concentrate its forces against one target at a time and, following a sensible timetable, to make the destruction of the enemy's forces the main objective to which the capture of territory was subordinate. But Hitler not only changed the schedule of his great summer offensive, he also changed the entire structure of the southern front and its objective.

But the Russians were not yet "finished." This phase of the war in the east culminated in an eerie parallel: on the same day that Hitler ordered the fateful shift to the south, split his forces and removed von Bock, a war council met in the Kremlin, presided over by Stalin.

Present were foreign minister Molotov, Marshall Voroshilov, Chief of the General Staff Shaposhnikov as well as an American, British and Chinese liaison officers. The generals had made it clear to Stalin that the Soviet armed forces could not permit another Kiev or Vyazma, and therefore that a policy of "holding at any price" was no longer acceptable. Stalin listened to reason. He approved the decision of the General Staff, which Shaposhnikov outlined at the July 13 meeting: retreat of the Soviet forces to the Volga and into the Caucasus. Defend there so that the German forces would be forced to spend the winter in inhospitable areas. Evacuation of all important industries to the Urals and Siberia.

The German General Staff had already received a report on this meeting from an intelligence agent in mid-July. However, Hitler considered the report a hoax.

Anyone who still harbored doubts that Timoshenko was really withdrawing his army group from the area of operations between the Donets and Don had to be convinced by what happened near Millerovo. After swinging south from Rossosh, the three divisions of XXXX Panzer Corps, the extreme eastern arm of the German pincer, drove into the midst of the Russian withdrawal.

The Soviet masses rolled southeastward on the rail line and highway south of Millerovo. The divisions of the German corps were not strong enough to stop the enemy columns. But because of the resistance around Millerovo they were unable to simply drive through to set up a southern blocking position on the lower Don.

The battle now rolled southwards. Hitler sought the enemy in the south.

Following heavy fighting, on July 20 Geyr's XXXX Panzer Corps reached the lower Don and set up bridgeheads near Konstantinovka and Nikolayevskaya. First Panzer Army had also fought its way through to the south, crossed the Donets and now stormed toward Rostov together with the Seventeenth Army advancing out of the Stalino area. The Soviets viewed Rostov as a large bridgehead and defended it tenaciously.

West of Rostov the Seventeenth Army had broken through the enemy positions on July 19 and advanced toward the Don between Rostov and Bataisk with LVII Panzer Corps on the left and V Corps on the right. *General* Kirchner, once again assisted by the capable General Staff *Oberst* Wenck, prepared for a daring thrust toward Rostov with LVII Panzer Corps. The objective was to take this important city at the mouth of the Don by surprise and capture intact the large Don bridge between Rostov and Bataisk. His corps also included the Slovakian "Fast" Division.

Spearheading the First Panzer Army, *General* von Mackensen's III Panzer Corps advanced on Rostov from the north. Again, as in November 1941, von Mackensen's units were involved in the battle for this city. The northern approaches to the city, which by now resembled a fortress, were strongly fortified and studded with obstacles. The bitter fighting there dragged on throughout the entire day and night.

Since the beginning of the year the Russians had worked to turn Rostov into a fortress. In addition to strong positions in the approaches to the city, it possessed three ring positions with broad minefields, anti-tank ditches and anti-tank obstacles. But the assault groups of LVII Panzer Corps succeeded in taking the city's outer defenses by surprise. They broke through and drove into the northern city. Overcoming numerous nests of resistance and anti-tank ditches, the attackers broke through the outer ring and took Rostov's airfield. A mounted motorcycle battalion dashed into the metropolis on the Don. While the attack spearheads fought their way forward, behind them enemy resistance flared up again from the flanks from side streets, fortified blocks of houses and especially city squares.

Initially the tanks became bogged down in street fighting. Then the Germans were able to get the attack going again. But before the motorcycle troops reached the Don bridge leading to Bataisk, a section of the bridge was blown up and plunged into the water. After much hard work, by the next day the engineers had made the bridge passable for men and light vehicles. By evening the part of the city north of the bridge was taken. Rostov was ablaze in many places.

The battle for the city flared up again early on the morning of July 24. While the German forces succeeded rather quickly in crushing the enemy in the postal quarter, the NKVD building was skillfully defended by an elite unit. Not until about midday, with the aid of tanks, was the enemy resistance broken and the block taken. Meanwhile other units had cleared the center of Rostov and forced the hard-fighting enemy away to the east or west.

In the meantime the fierce street fighting went on in the center of Rostov and didn't end until days later. The nature of the fighting there is illustrated by a combat report by *General* Alfred Reinhardt, who in July 1942 led the 125th Infantry Division's 421st Infantry Regiment as an *Oberst*. The report outlines the bloody street-by-street and house-by-house battle for a large, fortified city. It is unlikely that such a battle was fought with such bitterness again. It was the fight the German troops had expected in Leningrad or Moscow.

July 23, evening: A burning hot day comes to an end. The battalions of the Schwabian 421st Infantry Regiment are in the northern section of Rostov. Panzer companies and infantry of two panzer divisions have already advanced past both sides of the city to the Don. They are already fighting in the city center itself, but have not been able to get through the heavily fortified city core everywhere, as they lack the necessary infantry forces. But they must get through there if they are to set out across the big Don bridge for the push south, against the Caucasus.

NKVD troops and NKVD combat engineers have barricaded Rostov. These guardians of the bolshevik regime, Stalin's SS, backbone of the state police and the secret service, are in their own way an elite: fanatic, very well trained, tough, skilled in all the tricks of the trade and unconditionally obedient. Above all the NKVD troops are masters of street fighting. As guardians of the regime against possible revolutionary uprisings, this is in fact their primary function.

What these street fighting specialists have done to Rostov is unimaginable: the streets have been torn up, the paving stones piled up into meter-thick barricades. The side streets are blocked by deep brick bunkers. Spanish horsemen and mines make a stealthy approach almost impossible. The doors of the houses have been walled up, the windows made into firing positions with sandbags. Balconies have been turned into machine-gun nests. On the roofs are well-camouflaged sniper positions. And lying in the cellars are tens of thousands of Molotov cocktails, those primitive but effective anti-tank weapons consisting of bottles of gasoline combined with phosphorous and air-ignited flammable materials.

Behind every inviting, unblocked door lies a concealed mine, ready to explode when the door handle is depressed, or a fine trip wire, mounted just above the doorstep, connected to an explosive charge.

This arena was no battlefield for panzer units and offered little chance for victory through surprise attack. To be sure the panzer troops had smashed the first, decisive breach in the city's defenses, but the center of Rostov was the battlefield of the assault squad. Here each house, street and bunker had to be taken one by one in a laborious battle and the treacherous booby-traps cleared away.

Reinhardt's Schwabian soldiers tackled this bulwark. The *Oberst* fought his clever enemy with the same methods: with precision and cunning.

I Battalion under *Major* Ortlieb and III Battalion under *Hauptmann* Winzen were each organized into three assault companies. Each company was given a heavy machine-gun, an anti-tank gun and an infantry gun, as well as a light artillery piece for the main streets.

The battalions attacked in a north-south direction. The city map was divided into precise sectors. Each assault company was allowed to advance along its assigned north-south street only as far as a designated blocking line, which was drawn across the city map for all companies from west to east. There were four lines: A, B, C and D.

Then the entire quarter had to be cleared and contact established with neighboring assault groups. When a company reached a given line it was supposed to wait there until its neighbors were at the same line and regiment ordered the continuation of the attack. In this way the six assault companies always fought at the same level. A company which advanced faster than the others could be taken in the flank by the enemy. By adopting this tactic combat operations always remained firmly in the hands of the German command.

After the assault companies of I and III Battalions had cleared their quarter, Reinhardt immediately sent in the six spearheads of II Battalion. It was their job to "pick over" the remains and search the blocks of houses from cellar to roof. All civilians, including women and children, were taken from the combat zone to designated assembly points.

No hand that could toss a hand grenade or operate a submachine-gun remained in the houses behind the assault squads. The rear of the companies fighting up front had to be kept clear.

The plan worked. It was probably only through this plan that Rostov was taken so quickly: it was a tough, fifty-hour struggle.

General Reinhardt said: "The struggle for the city core of Rostov was a struggle without pity. The defenders refused to allow themselves to be captured, fought to the end, fired from concealment when overrun and not discovered or wounded until they were killed. German wounded had to be placed in armored personnel carriers and guarded. If this was not done we found them later murdered or stabbed."

The toughest fighting was in Taganrog Street, which led straight to the approach to the Don bridge. The attack bogged down several times here because it was impossible to spot the well-camouflaged NKVD men at their machine-guns.

"Büsing," called Reinhardt. The *Oberleutnant* and commander of 13th Company crawled over. Reinhardt pointed to a balcony on the second floor of a house: "There, Büsing, the balcony with the orange crates. I just saw sand whirl up there. That's where Ivan is. Get going, the balcony has to go!"

Büsing raced back to his heavy infantry gun.

"Fire!"

The second shot brought down the balcony.

The fighting in the old city and the harbor quarter was equally hard. The streets, which to that point ran relatively regularly, lost themselves in a jumble of crooked alleys. There was no room for the infantry guns, even the machine-guns were useless.

A close-quarters battle! The German soldiers crept up to cellar windows, doors, corners of houses. They sensed the breathing of the enemy, heard them working the bolts of their rifles, listened with racing hearts as they whispered to their neighbors. They grasped their submachine-guns firmly. Up. Loose off a burst. Back into cover.

The wooden houses went up in flames. The biting smoke made the battle more difficult, although the wind was favorable and blew the smoke toward the Don. It was dark when the D-Line was finally reached. Only a few hundred meters still separated the infantry companies from the battle groups of the armored units on the north bank of the Don on either side of the road bridge to Bataisk. Night fell. The men lay among the wooden huts, equipment dumps, sheds and dumps. Machine-gun fire ripped the night. Again and again illumination flares lit up the eerie backdrop as bright as day for a few seconds.

The assault companies of the 125th Infantry Division attacked again before dawn. But all of a sudden it became light. The last enemy groups at the river bank had withdrawn across the Don during the night. By 0530 all of the regiment's assault companies had reached the Don. All of Rostov was now in German hands.

But for the Germans Rostov did not achieve its significance as the gate to the Caucasus until the gateway was also in their hands: the bridge over the Don and the subsequent six-kilometer-long raised roadway across the swampy terrain on the far side of the river which turned into the large bridge to Bataisk. Beyond Bataisk lay the plains, an open road to the south, into the approaches to the Caucasus.

It was the "Brandenburgers," that secrecy-shrouded, unbelievably fearless special formation of daring volunteers, who finally opened this gateway. It was they who captured the bridges before Bataisk, especially the approximately three-kilometer-long viaduct on the south bank of the Don which consisted of numerous small bridges and over which led the single road to the south.

At 0230 *Oberleutnant* Grabert ran toward the bridge with the leading squad. Ghostlike they scurried forward on both sides of the roadway. The other two squads followed at brief intervals. Then the Russians noticed something was up. Machine-guns fired, mortars coughed. The German covering forces likewise opened up with everything they had. Now everything depended on whether or not Grabert got through.

Grabert did get through. He drove away the strong Soviet bridge guard and established a small bridgehead. For twenty-four hours he held out against all enemy counterattacks.

The companies and their commanders sacrificed themselves for the bridge in the truest sense of the word. *Oberleutnant* Grabert and *Leutnant* Hiller of the "Brandenburgers" were killed. NCOs and men fell under the hellish fire of the Soviets.

Stukas came at the last minute. Then the first reinforcements followed over the raised roadway and the bridge. Siegfried Grabert lay beneath the last pillar. 200 meters in front of him, in a muddy hole, *Leutnant* Hiller. Beside him, a packet dressing still in his hand, the first-aid NCO, killed by a bullet through the head. But on July 27 the panzer and armored personnel carrier companies of LVII Panzer Corps rolled across the bridges toward the south, toward the Caucasus.

CHAPTER V

The High Mountain Front

A Blockhouse near Vinnitsa – Führer Directive No.45 – To Asia in an Assault Boat – In the Approaches to the Caucasus – Race through the Kuban – In the Land of the Chechen

In July 1942 Führer Headquarters was located deep inside Russia, near Vinnitsa in the Ukraine. The working staffs of the Commander-in-Chief of the Army with the Chief of the General Staff had moved into quarters at the edge of Vinnitsa. The Todt Organization had built well-camouflaged blockhouses beneath the pines of a broad, wooded area. Hitler moved in on July 16. The days were extremely hot and the shadows of the fragrant coniferous forest brought no coolness. The nights, too, were sultry and oppressive. Hitler couldn't bear this climate and was usually ill-tempered, aggressive and extremely suspicious of everyone. Generals, officers and political liaison men belonging to Hitler's entourage are all unanimous in describing the period in the Ukraine as filled with tension and conflict. Code name for the Führer Headquarters near Vinnitsa was "*Werwolf*," and Hitler resided in his blockhouse like a werewolf.

On July 23 *Generaloberst* Halder was ordered to report on the situation. Hitler was suffering terribly from the heat and reports from the front increased his uneasiness. The German forces were victorious, the Russians fled, but strangely the great destructive blow between the Donets and Don had not come to pass near Stary Oskol or near Millerovo. It also appeared that it was not going to come about at Rostov either. How was that? What was going on?

"The Russians are conducting a planned withdrawal, *mein Führer*," argued Halder.

Hitler cut him short. "Nonsense, they're fleeing, they're finished, they're at the end after the blows we've inflicted on them in the past months."

Halder stayed cool, pointed to the map which lay on the large working table and replied: "We haven't caught Timoshenko's main body, *mein Führer*. Our encircling operations were failures. Timoshenko has directed the bulk of his army group, in some cases even with their heavy weapons, to the east across the Don into the Stalingrad area, other elements to the south into the Caucasus. We don't know what reserves are there."

"Oh, you and your reserves. I tell you we didn't catch Timoshenko's fleeing masses in the Stary Oskol area and then at Millerovo because Bock spent to much time with Voronezh. Then we were unable to catch the southern group, which was fleeing in panic, north of Rostov because we turned south with the mobile units too late and forced the Seventeenth Army to the east too soon. But that's not going to happen to me again. It's imperative that we disentangle the massing of our mobile units in the Rostov area and deploy the Seventeenth Army as well as the First and Fourth Panzer Armies to quickly catch and encircle the Russians south of Rostov, in the approaches to the Caucasus. At the same time the Sixth Army must deliver the death blow to the remaining Russian forces which have fled to the Volga in the Stalingrad area. On neither of these two fronts can we allow the reeling enemy to regain his composure. But the emphasis must lay with Army Group A's attack against the Caucasus."

On July 23, 1942 the Chief of Army General Staff tried in vain to refute Hitler's thesis in the blockhouse of Hitler's Ukrainian Headquarters. He implored him not to split his forces and not to advance into the Caucasus until Stalingrad had been taken and the flank and rear on the Don as well as between the Don and Volga had been adequately secured.

Hitler brushed aside the objections of the Chief of the General Staff. Just how sure he felt of himself and how much he was ruled by the notion that the Red Army had already been finally smashed was demonstrated by several other facts: he transferred the bulk of *Feldmarschall* von Manstein's Eleventh Army, whose five divisions were in the Crimea ready for action against the Caucasus, to Leningrad to finally take this tiresome fortress.

But that was not all: Hitler also withdrew the extremely well equipped "*Leibstandarte*" SS-Panzer-Grenadier Division from the Eastern Front and sent it to France to rest and reequip as a panzer division. A short time later he pulled another of the southern front's elite units, the "*Großdeutschland*" Motorized Infantry Division, out of the battle. He ordered it withdrawn from the front after reaching the Manych dam and transferred it to France at the disposal of the OKW.

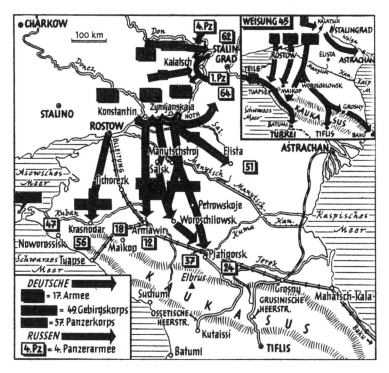

Map 6. Situation on the southern front from July 25 to August 11, 1942, and (inset) the original plan according to "Directive 45." The withdrawal of the Fourth Panzer Army from the Caucasus was supposed to permit the timely seizure of Stalingrad, but only led to a weakening of the Caucasus front.

Hitler based these decisions primarily on false information from the British that an invasion was imminent in the West. It was a fateful mistake, because the forces which were needlessly withdrawn from the southern front – a total of seven divisions – would very probably have been enough to prevent the catastrophe of Stalingrad.

It was an embittered Halder who drove back to his headquarters on the outskirts of Vinnitsa on July 23. He wrote in his diary: "The underestimation of the enemy possibilities which still exists is gradually assuming a grotesque shape and is becoming dangerous."

But Hitler stuck to his incorrect assessment of the enemy situation and concentrated his thoughts in the fundamental "Führer Directive No.45," code-named *Braunschweig.* He dictated it on July 23, the day of his argument with Halder.

The directive reached the army groups on July 25. In the preamble Hitler presupposed, in contradiction to the findings from the battles of the past three weeks, that only relatively weak elements of Timoshenko's army had escaped the German encirclement and reached the south bank of the Don.

He now fixed the further operational objectives – in contrast to "Directive No.41," "Case Blue," according to which it was planned to first reach the Stalingrad area, then the offensive into the Caucasus to capture the Russian oil – as follows:

1. It is the next task of Army Group A to surround and destroy the enemy forces which have escaped across the Don in the area south and southeast of Rostov.

To this end strong mobile units are to be committed from the bridgeheads to be established in the Konstantinovskaya-Tsymlyanskaya area in a generally southwesterly direction, roughly toward Tikoretsk, and infantry, light infantry and mountain infantry divisions in the Rostov area across the Don.

In addition the task remains of cutting the Tikoretsk-Stalingrad railway line with forward elements . . .

2. Following the destruction of the group of enemy forces south of the Don, Army Group A's most important assignment is to take possession of the entire east coast of the Black Sea and thus neutralize the Black Sea ports and the enemy's Black Sea Fleet . . .

A further group of forces, in which are to be concentrated all remaining mountain and light infantry divisions, is to force a crossing of the Kuban and take possession of the high ground of Maikop and Armavir . . .

3. At the same time a group of forces formed from mobile units is to capture the area around Grozny and block the Ossetian and Georgian military roads, if possible at the high mountain passes. This is to be followed by an advance along the Caspian Sea during which the area around Baku is to be occupied . . .

The army group can reckon on the later dispatch of the Italian Alpine Corps.

These operations by Army Group A receive the code name "Edelweiss."

4. In addition to establishing the Don defense, to Army Group B falls the task – as ordered – of advancing on Stalingrad, smashing the group of enemy

forces being formed there, occupying the city itself and barricading the land bridge between the Don and Volga.

Subsequent to this mobile units are to be committed along the Volga with the mission of advancing as far as Astrakhan and there likewise blocking the Volga.

These operations by Army Group B receive the code name "Heron."

Instructions for the Luftwaffe and Kriegsmarine followed, which, among other things, stated:

"Because of the decisive importance of Caucasian oil production to the further conduct of the war, air attacks against the production and storage facilities there as well as against the transshipment ports on the Black Sea are only to be carried out if army operations make it absolutely necessary.

"However in order to block enemy oil shipments out of the Caucasus as soon as possible, the early cutting of the still-usable rail and oil lines as well as interruption of shipping on the Caspian Sea are of special importance."

"Moreover the OKM is making preparations to send light naval forces into action in the Caspian Sea to disrupt enemy shipping (oil transports and links with the Anglo-Saxons in Iran)."

It was a huge assigning of orders for the capture of territories in three different directions: the entire east coast of the Black Sea, the area around the Baku oil region and the occupation of Stalingrad. And all this with corps and divisions with weeks of costly fighting behind them. The plan could only succeed if the enemy really was finished, if in fact "only weaker enemy forces had succeeded in reaching the south bank of the Don" as Hitler supposed in the preface to Directive No.45.

Generalfeldmarschall List, a Bavarian from Oberkirch, a man of the old Bavarian general staff school, who had won his spurs in the Polish and French Campaigns and who now led Army Group A, possessed a sharp and calculating mind. Not one to be impetuous, he was instead a man of solid operational planning and command, ill disposed toward taking risks.

When he received "Directive No.45" on July 25, delivered to Stalino by special courier, he shook his head in disbelief. Later, in captivity, he told the author: Only the conviction that the supreme German command must have extraordinary and reliable information on the enemy situation had allowed the new plan of operations to appear comprehensible to him and his Chief of Staff,

General von Greiffenberg.

The formation of a point of main effort had been the strategic and operational wisdom since Clausewitz. But here this wisdom was renounced. For example, among the units being conveyed behind the Sixth Army, which was striving toward Stalingrad, was the Italian Alpine (*Alpini*) Corps with its outstanding mountain divisions. In contrast List's Army Group A, which faced the first real high mountain assignment of the eastern war – the forcing of the Caucasus – had available only three mountain infantry divisions, two German and one Romanian. The light infantry divisions of Army Group Ruoff were neither trained nor equipped for a battle in the high mountains. Four German mountain divisions with hand-picked men from the German alpine provinces, trained in mountain warfare, were scattered all over the globe. Those in Führer Headquarters remembered this too late when, several weeks later, *General* Konrad's mountain infantry battalions became bogged down among the peaks of the Caucasus with their objective in sight.

Feldmarschall List came up with a passable plan from what was prescribed to him by "Directive No.45" using the forces he had: Army Group Ruoff, the reinforced Seventeenth Army, was to drive frontally out of the area around Rostov southward toward Krasnodar. To the east, the mobile units of the First Panzer Army, followed on the left wing by Hoth's First Panzer Army, were to break out of the Don bridgeheads and drive through toward Maikop as the outer arm of the pincer. In this way the suspected enemy forces south of Rostov were to be surrounded and destroyed in a joint operation between Ruoff's slowly advancing infantry and Kleist's fast mobile units. To *Generaloberst* Hoth's Fourth Panzer Army on the eastern wing fell the job of providing flanking cover for the operation. Its first objective was Voroshilovsk.

The southward advance was continued according to this plan. And it began an operation which was extremely dramatic as it unfolded and which was of decisive significance to the entire outcome of the eastern war.

The Russian command still showed itself to be determined not to allow its units to be encircled any more. The Soviet general staff and the unit commanders held firmly to the new – but basically old – strategy which had been used to defeat Napoleon: lure the enemy into the depths of the country and split his forces, in order to attack on a broad front at the right moment.

The German units encountered completely new conditions south of the Don: 500 kilometers of steppe had to be crossed, after which one of the world's mightiest mountain chains, which lay before the German attack forces between the Black and Caspian Seas, had to be forced.

The steppe region north of the Caucasus offered the enemy outstanding conditions for fighting a delaying action. The countless large and small rivers which flowed from the Caucasian watershed into both the Caspian and Black Seas were obstacles which the defenders could easily hold with relatively weak forces.

As in the desert, here too the available sources of drinking water determined the attackers' route of advance. It was a foreign world into which the fight was carried. And whoever set foot on the far bank of the 700-kilometer-long Manych River had left Europe and entered Asia. The river is the boundary between the two continents.

The first German units to cross this border between continents were the Westphalian 16th Motorized Infantry Division and the 3rd Panzer Division from Berlin-Brandenburg.

Spearheading the advance, the 3rd Panzer Division had pursued the retreating Russians from the Don across the Sal to Proletarskaya, which lay on a tributary of the Manych, the Karytsheplak. Breith's panzer soldiers had thus reached the bank of the broad Manych River. Actually the river consisted of a chain of dammed lakes, in many places kilometers wide, with coffer-dams for the power generating plants in Manychstroy.

There, well dug-in, sat the Soviet rear guard. The Manych was an ideal defensive line for the Soviets, the great barrier on the approaches to the Caucasus.

"How are we going to get across there?" an anxious *General* Breith asked his Chief of Staff, *Major* Pomtow, and the commander of the 3rd Rifle Regiment, *Oberstleutnant* Zimmermann.

"The Russians are thickest where the river is narrowest," answered Pomtow, pointing to the aerial reconnaissance report.

"Prisoners have said that there are NKVD troops over there," added Zimmermann.

"And well dug in, as the aerial photographs show," nodded Breith.

"What if we fooled Ivan and chose the widest spot, near the large coffer-dam, where the river is two to three kilometers wide? The Russians would be expecting an attack there least of all," suggested Pomtow.

The idea was a good one. And so it was done. Luckily the armored combat engineer battalion had brought along twenty-one assault boats. The blazing summer heat had so dried them out that two the boats sank like stones when put into the water. The other nineteen were somewhat leaky, but would stay afloat if enough water was bailed out of them.

Leutnant Moewis and a dozen intrepid "Brandenburgers" scouted out two suitable crossing points, precisely at the widest spot on the river. The two crossings were located above the town of Manychstroy, which lay directly on the far approach to the coffer-dam. The town secured this important dam, which had been mined and made impassable at several points. It was vital that Manychstroy be taken in a surprise attack, making it impossible for the Soviet demolitions squad which was surely in position there to completely destroy the dam.

A battle group was formed for the action. 3rd Panzer-Grenadier Regiment's II Battalion attacked on the left, I Battalion on the right. A strong assault company was formed. *Oberleutnant* Tank, the veteran commander of 6th Company, led the battle group. Its orders read: "A bridgehead is to be established on the far bank of the storage lake under cover of darkness. Once all elements of the battle group have crossed, the enemy blocking position is to be pierced and the town of Manychstroy stormed."

In order to assure effective artillery support from the northeast bank, the battle group included an artillery observer who was to direct the fire of the guns.

The daring attack across the Manych succeeded. The main body of the 3rd Panzer Division feigned an attack from the northwest, while at the same time one battalion forced a crossing of the river. The operation began between 2400 and 0100 with a preparatory bombardment by the divisional artillery.

Tank's men lay on the shore. The combat engineers had put the boats into the water. Shells howled overhead and impacted on the far bank, shrouding it in smoke and dust.

"Go." The soldiers got into the boats and shoved off. They bailed vigorously with cans to keep the assault boats from filling with water. The roar of the motors was drowned out by the artillery fire. Not a shot came from the Russians.

They crossed the river without loss. The keels of the nineteen boats slid over the gravel of the far shore. Tank was the first to jump ashore. He was standing in Asia.

"White signal flare." The company headquarters squad leader raised the flare pistol and fired. The German artillery abruptly shifted its fire farther forward. The engineers immediately turned their boats around to fetch the next wave.

Tank's grenadiers raced over the flat beach. The Soviets in the first trench were completely bewildered and fled. Before they could alert the second trench, Tank's machine-guns mowed down the enemy sentries and lookouts.

But now the Russians to the left and right of the landing site were wide awake. When the assault boats crossed the second time they were caught by machine-gun fire from the Soviets. Two boats sank. The other seventeen arrived with 120 men, including II Battalion headquarters, and supplies of ammunition.

This brought the crossing operation to an end, however the German forces already on the far shore managed to expand the bridgehead there. *Oberleutnant* Tank, the oldest company commander in II Battalion, took charge in the bridgehead. The Soviets blanketed the entire shore with flanking fire. Russian artillery shells of every caliber thundered in. The arrival of dawn ended any further transport of men across the river.

Oberleutnant Tank and his men were still in the flat area along the shore in captured Russian trenches and hastily-dug foxholes. The Russians fired on them with mortars, raked them with machine-gun fire and twice launched counterattacks which got to within a few meters of Tank's position.

But worst of all, ammunition was running low. The machine-gun on the right wing had only two belts of ammunition left. The others were not much better off. The mortar ammunition had already been expended.

"Why doesn't the Luftwaffe attack?" asked Tank's men, looking into the overcast, hazy sky. And as if the commander of the bomber *Geschwader* had heard their deep, heartfelt lament, at about 0600 the German close-support aircraft came roaring in. The sun had broken through, clearing away the fog from the airfields. The bombers silenced the Soviet artillery positions and machine-gun nests. Under cover of the hail of bombs and strafing attacks, the third wave finally succeeded in crossing the river.

Oberleutnant Tank seized the moment. He ran from platoon leader to platoon leader and briefed each man. Then the attack began quickly: against Manychstroy.

The Soviets were completely taken aback. They had not expected an attack on the strongly-defended town from behind and from the side. Their entire attention was directed ahead, toward the dam. Tank's men quickly rolled up the rear Russian positions.

By the time the Soviet commander had finally reorganized his defense and began fighting with his back to the dam, the first tanks and armored personnel carriers were already rolling across the narrow road atop the structure.

Manychstroy fell. The Manych had been forced, the last great blocking position on the road leading south to the Caucasus and the oil had been overcome.

On the morning of August 2 Battle Group von Liebenstein broke through to Iku-Tuktum. XXXX Panzer Corps and III Panzer Corps were fighting in Asia.

The daring crossing of the Manych and the opening of the gateway to the Caucasus were supplemented by an equally audacious and successful operation by the 23rd Panzer Division from Baden-Wurttemberg. The division overcame a powerful Soviet ambush which seriously threatened the German flank, without anyone being aware of the danger.

Timoshenko had positioned an entire motorized corps with many tanks in a well-camouflaged ambush position at the Sal crossing near Martinovka.

Generalmajor Mack's 23rd Motorcycle Battalion advanced toward Martinovka, which aerial reconnaissance had reported as "only weakly occupied."

The attack took place at the moment the Russian corps was moving into position. Mack recognized the danger immediately. He pinned down the enemy through frontal attacks, encircled him in a clever maneuver and early on the morning of July 28 took him in the rear.

In turbulent tank duels, in some cases from very close ranges of twenty to thirty meters, the Soviet T-34s were knocked out and their anti-tank front smashed.

The tank battle at Martinovka was the first operation in some time in which superior tactical command and tank-versus-tank skills enabled the Germans to engage and destroy a large Soviet force. Seventy-seven enemy tanks were destroyed and numerous guns captured.

At the same hour as grenadiers and tanks were setting out into the Kalmuck Steppe in 40 degree temperatures in pursuit of the Soviet forces withdrawing from the Manych, past giant herds of cattle, watched by camels and dromedaries, Hitler was sitting in front of the big map table in the hot, humid wooden house of his Ukrainian headquarters near Vinnitsa. *General* Jodl was addressing those present.

But it was not the success at the Manych, which was mentioned in the OKW communique, that was under discussion, rather the bad situation in which the Sixth Army found itself on the way to Stalingrad in the great bend of the Don. *General* Paulus had reached the Don with his northern and southern attack groups, but the bridgehead around Kalach, which formed the entrance to the narrow land bridge between the Don and Volga, was not only defended by the Soviets, they had also made it the starting base for a counteroffensive.

The Commander-in-Chief of the "Stalingrad Front," Lieutenant General Gordov, had already assembled four Soviet armies as well as two tank armies which were in the process of forming up in front of the German Sixth Army.

The Soviet Fourth Tank Army was preparing to sandwich Paulus' XIV Panzer Corps. *General* von Seydlitz-Kurzbach's LI Army Corps on the southern wing was also in serious trouble. Munitions shortages and lack of fuel were paralyzing the strength of the entire Sixth Army.

As a result of Hitler forcing the attacks on the Caucasus and Stalingrad at the same time, supply also had to be divided. And because the greater distances had to be covered in the south, the Quartermaster General had moved the main fuel distribution point to the Caucasus front. Many motorized, large-capacity supply columns intended for the Sixth Army were diverted to the south.

On July 31 Hitler was finally forced to realize that his optimism regarding the apparent Soviet weakness was unfounded. He could no longer close his mind to the realization that the Sixth Army's strength, which was limited by severe supply shortages, was insufficient to take Stalingrad in the face of the strong Soviet resistance.

On this day he therefore ordered another change of plan: the Fourth Panzer Army – less XXXX Panzer Corps – was withdrawn from the Caucasus front, placed under the command of Army Group B and moved up south of the Don toward the northeast in order to attack from the flank and crush the Soviet Kalach front in front of Stalingrad.

A good idea, but too late. The action by Fourth Panzer Army did nothing to change the complete splitting of forces. What Hitler now took from Army Group A weakened its offensive power against the Caucasus; what he gave to Army Group B was too little and came too late to enable Stalingrad to be taken quickly. Two now equally strong army groups were striving at right angles to each other toward two, widely separated objectives. The most burning problem, that of supply, was completely unsolvable, because the entire operation lacked a point of main effort.

The highest level of German command had maneuvered itself into a hopeless situation where it was subject to the will of the enemy command. In the Stalingrad area the Russians were already determining the time and place of the battle.

The "Führer Directive" of July 31 ordered the beginning of the second phase of Operation "Edelweiss" on the Caucasus Front: the occupation of the Black Sea coast. Army Group A was to commit its mobile forces, which were to be concentrated under the command of the First Panzer Army, in the direction of Armavir-Maikop. Other elements of the army group were to drive along the coast through Novorossisk and Tuapse toward Batumi. On the left wing the German and Romanian mountain divisions were to be sent over the mountain passes of the Caucasus toward Tuapse and Sukhumi in a flanking maneuver.

At first the plan proceeded with breathtaking precision. On the day the new Führer Directive was issued, III and LVII Panzer Corps also made a great leap

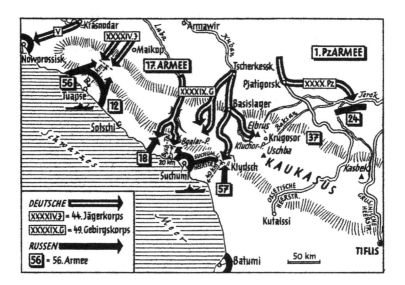

Map 7. End of July to the end of August 1942. The Seventeenth Army's attack from the Kuban toward the Soviet bases on the eastern Black Sea coast and advance through the passes of the Caucasus Mountains.

forward in the direction of the Caucasus. The same evening *General* von Mackensen took Salsk.

On the evening of August 9 the 13th Panzer Division stormed the city of Maikop, the administrative center of a huge oil-producing area. Fifty undamaged aircraft were captured, but unfortunately the oil storage facilities were destroyed and the installations crippled through the removal of vital components.

The advance also went well for XXXXIX Mountain Corps and V Army Corps, which had forced a crossing of the Don east of Rostov. By August 13 the divisions had taken Krasnodar and a crossing site over the Kuban.

Equally successful was the advance by LVII Panzer Corps. After a rapid advance south through the Kuban steppe the armored battle groups found themselves on the north bank of the Kuban. The river was crossed and a bridgehead established, opening the way to the south bank of the Kuban for Army Group Ruoff.

The German forces now swung toward Tuapse. The Scandinavian, Baltic and Danish volunteers of the *"Wiking"* Division advanced into the Maikop oil region.

On the entire steppe front in the first days of August 1942 the mobile units of Army Group A raced across the Kuban and Kalmuck Steppes in an effort to bring to battle the slow-moving Russian divisions, which were conducting a fighting withdrawal, before they reached the Caucasus and prevent them from escaping into the mountains and settling down there again for a determined defense.

Otto Tenning, who at that time was radio operator in the command vehicle of the 3rd Panzer Division's spearhead battalion, reported: "I carried out a motorized patrol with *Feldwebel* Goldberg. As we crept up to a small village, the patrol leader suddenly spotted something suspicious and reported by radio: 'Enemy tanks parked at the outskirts of the village.' But how great was our surprise when we discovered soon afterward that the 'tanks' were in fact camels. There was much laughter. From then on dromedaries and camels were no longer an unusual sight. They proved to be excellent pack animals, especially for our supply train."

On August 3 the leading elements of the 3rd Panzer Division reached the city of Voroshilovsk. The Russian forces were surprised and the city was taken at about 1600 after a brief fight.

The advance continued. "Brandenburgers" accompanied the panzer troops, always ready for special assignments. Romanian mountain troops also marched with the 3rd Panzer Division. The population, old established Caucasians, was friendly and greeted the Germans as liberators.

It should also be mentioned that entire families and villages voluntarily, and actually against the will of the German supreme command, reported for battle against the Red Army. These freedom-loving people believed that the great hour of their independence as a people had begun. Stalin's wrath, which struck them later, was terrible. All of these families were exiled from their magnificent homeland to Siberia.

The faster the progress of the advance into the Caucasus, the clearer it became: the Russians were continuing to withdraw without major losses in men and materiel. The German units captured territory, ever more territory, but were unable to strike hard at the enemy or destroy him. A few overturned panje wagons, a few dead horses, that was all that lined the advance road.

In order to screen the lengthening east flank of the deep thrust into the Caucasus, LII Army Corps was diverted east on a broad front and deployed to secure toward the Caspian Sea. Elista, the only larger city in the Kalmuck Steppe, fell on August 12.

Meanwhile the panzer divisions continued to roll south. The Kalmuck Steppe shimmered in the heat. The thermometer showed 55 degrees. In the brilliant blue sky the men saw in the distance a white, dome-shaped cloud. But the cloud did not move. It was there in the same place the next day and the day after that. It was no cloud. It was the 5,633-meter-high Mount Elbrus with its shimmering glaciers and year-round snow cap: the mighty mountain massif of the central Caucasus.

"How many kilometers was it today?" the commander of the 421st Infantry Regiment, *Oberst* Reinhardt, asked his adjutant. *Oberleutnant* Boll looked at the map on which the march route had been pencilled in. He measured the distance with dividers. "Sixty kilometers, *Herr Oberst*."

Sixty kilometers. Sixty times a thousand meters the infantry had marched that day. In the burning heat. Through the treeless Kuban Steppe.

The march columns were shrouded in dense, grey-brown clouds of dust. Only the heads of the riders were visible. The farther south they went, the looser the contact between regiments. Dust trails were the only indication that there were other columns on the left and right also advancing south.

Reinhardt studied the map in the shadow of a radio truck.

"These distances are enough to frighten one," observed the adjutant.

Reinhardt nodded. His finger traced a path across the map to the Kalmuck Steppe. "Kleist's panzers have it no better there."

No, they had it no better. On August 10 XXXX Panzer Corps – since August 2 attached to the First Panzer Army – had taken Pyatigorsk with the 3rd Panzer Division and Mineralnye Vody with the 23rd Panzer Division. It was now at the foot of the Caucasus. The last great obstacle still before them was the Terek River. Would they be able to make it across and capture the passes on the Ossetian and Georgian army roads?

Oberst Reinhardt tapped Krasnodar with his finger: "That is our objective." Then he pointed to Maikop: "And Kleist has to get there. Then we'll see what's inside the pocket which our Seventeenth Army and Kleist's First Panzer Army will create with these two corner-points."

The adjutant nodded: "Well planned, *Herr Oberst*, but I have a feeling that Ivan won't do us the favor of waiting until the sack is closed."

Reinhardt handed the map back to Boll. "We'll see," he grumbled. "Do you have a sip of water left?"

"Not a drop left, *Herr Oberst*. For the past hour my tongue's been stuck to my palate like fly-paper."

They climbed into their vehicle. "Move out, we have to make another ten kilometers today."

It was the same everywhere for the infantry, light infantry and mountain infantry units of Army Group Ruoff in the first days of August 1942. For a while the war on the southern front assumed the character of the desert conflict. The pursuit of the Soviets across the Kuban Steppe became a race from one watering hole to the next. Ration stops were rare. Large water trucks carried drinking water for the soldiers in the event of an emergency, but not enough could be carried to meet the needs of the horses. This forced the lower levels of command to take possession of new watering holes daily.

The Russians carried out a fighting withdrawal on the right wing of Army Group A, just as they had successfully done on the middle Don. The Soviets dug in at the few villages and numerous rivers and defended fiercely at first, but then withdrew in time to avoid suffering major losses in prisoners. They were following Timoshenko's new directive: delay the enemy's advance, but pull back at the decisive moment to avoid encirclements at all costs.

This was the Russians' new, elastic strategy. The Red general staff had divested itself of Stalin's old fighting style of defending every foot of ground, which always led to encirclements and huge losses.

The lower levels of Russian command quickly learned the tactic of the "delaying battle," a style of fighting that had been stricken from the German training plan since 1936. By cleverly using the many streams running across the path of the German attack, the Russians repeatedly slowed down the German advance and meanwhile withdrew their infantry.

In these conditions the German divisions were unable to fulfill the key point of "Directive No.45:" To encircle and destroy in the area south and southeast of Rostov the enemy forces which had escaped over the Don." Hitler's plan had failed again.

They pursued, drove, marched. Ever farther, ever farther. From river to river: the Kagalnik was crossed, then the Jeja. But eight rivers still crossed the advance route to the Kuban.

Near Tikoretsk the oil line from Baku to Rostov crossed the road and railway. The Russians defended this junction determinedly with powerful artillery and anti-tank gun forces and three armored trains.

The crews of the 88mm anti-aircraft guns had their hands full, but finally the advance detachments linked up. Tikoretsk fell. The Russians retreated, but they longer fled in panic.

The Russians frequently ambushed the German troops from the huge fields of sunflowers, which grew as tall as a man. When the Germans tried to come to grips with the enemy they found he had disappeared. By night lone vehicles were ambushed, and it was no longer safe for dispatch riders.

By August 10, 1942, V Corps had reached the area around Krasnodar. In just sixteen days of marching and fighting the infantry had covered the approximately

300 kilometers between Rostov and the capital city of the Kuban cossacks, advancing over the scorched earth of the Kuban Steppe and through the wonderfully fruitful river valleys.

Endless fields of sunflowers stretched into the distance, mighty areas with wheat, millet, hemp and tobacco. Huge herds of cattle wandered over the endless steppe. The gardens of the cossack villages were true oases. Apricots, plums, apples, pears, melons, grapes and tomatoes grew in luxurious abundance. There were eggs like sand at the seashore, pigs in huge herds. These were good days for the field kitchens and rations officers.

Krasnodar, the capital city of the Kuban district, situated on the north side of the Kuban River, had about 200,000 inhabitants at that time. It was a major oil refining center.

General Wetzel deployed his V Corps for a concentric attack on the city: the troops came from Franconia, Hesse and Württemberg.

The Russians wanted to hold the city center with its bridge over the Kuban as long as possible, so as to get as many men and in particular as much materiel across to the far side as they could. What couldn't be taken away was set ablaze, including the huge oil tank farm.

By about midday on August 11 the Württembergers had worked their way to within assault range of the bridge. Fifty meters to go. Pressed tightly together, Russian columns moved across the river.

2nd Company received orders to break through. *Hauptmann* Sätzler got to his feet, his pistol in his raised fist. He took only three steps then fell, shot through the head.

The company stormed onward. The leading soldiers were only twenty meters from the approach to the bridge. At that moment the alert Soviet bridge officer lit the demolition charges.

With a thunderous roar the bridge blew up at half a dozen places, taking the Russian columns with it. Amid the dust and smoke one could see men and horses, wagon wheels and weapons whirling through the air. Bolting teams raced over the shattered bridge railings and plunged into the water.

The destruction of the bridge cost the Germans two days. Not until the night of August 13/14 was the 125th Infantry Division able to cross the river in assault boats and inflatable rafts.

Throughout the day *Major* Ortlieb had calmly scouted the crossing points under the watchful eye of the Russians, dressed as a farmer's wife with a hoe over his shoulder and a basket on his arm. The jump to the far bank of the Kuban and the construction of a pontoon bridge took place under covering fire from the German artillery and a 37mm flak battery. V Corps marched into the "land of the Chechen." The Moslem population had placed flags on their houses bearing the Turkish half moon and they greeted the Germans as liberators from the atheist-communist yoke.

CHAPTER VI

Between Novorossisk and the Klukor Pass

"Thalatta, Thalatta" (the Sea, the Sea) – In the High Passes of the Caucasus – Battle for the Old Military Roads – Expedition to the Top of Elbrus – Twenty Kilometers to the Black Sea Coast – Missing the Last Battalion

With the crossing of the Kuban the last major river barrier in front of Army Group Ruoff had been overcome. The divisions could now tackle their actual operational objective: the ports of Novorossisk, Tuapse, Sochi, Sukhumi and Batumi.

This operational objective was extraordinarily significant. The loss of these ports would have deprived the Soviet Black Sea Fleet of its last support bases and enabled the German Caucasus front to be supplied by sea, but there was another major reason behind it. Following the capture of the last strip of Russian territory on the Black Sea coast, Turkey would very probably have gone over to the German camp. This would have had incalculable consequences for the allied conduct of the war. The English-Russian positions in northern Persia would have collapsed and thus cut off the southern delivery route for American arms aid for Stalin from the Persian Gulf to the Caspian Sea and then up the Volga.

The plan to direct Rommel and his *Afrikakorps* through Egypt into Mesopotamia would also have been moved into the realm of possibility. Following their splendid defensive battle in the summer of 1942, the soldiers of the German-Italian panzer army were outside El Alamein, at the gates of Cairo. The engineers were already calculating how many bridging columns were necessary over the Nile and the troops cockily answered the question "where are you going" with: "to Ibn Saud."

This fantastic objective was no less popular in Army Group Ruoff. When the units of XXXXIX Mountain Corps learned that they were going into the Caucasus they came up with their own catch phrases. In his book *Gebirgsjäger an allen Fronten* Alex Buchner described the response of one soldier to a comrade's question as to the sense and objective of the march through the steppe: "Down into the Caucasus and around behind, and after that we take the British from the rear and say to Rommel 'greetings, here we are.'"

At the end of August 1942 the divisions of V Corps began the attack on Novorossisk, the first great sea fortress on the eastern Black sea coast. Novorossisk, which then numbered 95,000 inhabitants, was a significant port and industrial city with large cold-storage plants and shipyards, a fish processing industry and cement works.

The infantry fought its way through the foothills of the Caucasus in the hilly approaches to the city. Suddenly the sea lay before them, the Black Sea! When Oberst Friebe, commander of the 419th Infantry Regiment, caught sight of the sea from atop a rise, he spontaneously radioed an old Greek word to his neighbor, *Oberst* Reinhardt: "*Thalatta, Thalatta* – the sea, the sea!" 2,400 years earlier, according to the historian Xenophon, Greek advance guards had greeted the sea with this shout when they reached the coast near Trapezunt, directly across from Novorossisk, after a laborious retreat through the arid deserts and mountains of Asia Minor.

But it more hard and costly fighting would be required before Novorossisk was in the regiment's hands.

On September 6, 1942, the 186th Infantry Regiment's I Battalion under *Oberleutnant* Ziegler launched the German attack on the port city.

On September 10 the city and surrounding area were in German hands. Army Group Ruoff had reached its first objective. The next was Tuapse. It was the key point on the narrow coastal plain. However, this place was to become the fateful point for Army Group List.

In addition to an infantry corps, a light infantry corps and a panzer corps, the Seventeenth Army also included a mountain infantry corps consisting of the 1st and 4th Mountain Infantry Divisions and a Romanian mountain infantry division. There was a special reason for this combination of infantry, light infantry and mountain troops. While the infantry was taking Novorossisk frontally across the wooded foothills of the Caucasus, the middle mountain specialists of the 97th and 101st Light Infantry Divisions were already advancing through the wooded areas of the Caucasus mountains toward the port city of Tuapse. The mountain infantry were to push through the high passes of the central Caucasus, with elevations of 3,000 to 4,000 meters, to the Black Sea coast, through the back door as it were. Their objective was Sukhumi, the palm city on the subtropical coast and the capital city of the Soviet Abkhaz Republic. From there it was only about 160 kilometers to the Turkish border and Batumi.

Advancing behind motorized battle groups, on August 13 *General* Konrad's mountain infantry set out from the steppe for the assault on the high passes of the Caucasus: the 4th Mountain Division on the right to capture the passes in the source area of the great Laba, the 1st Mountain Division on the left to storm through the high passes at the Elbrus glacier from which springs the Kuban. The most important crossing was the 2,815-meter-high Klukor Pass, which was also the starting point of the old Sukhum military road.

Major von Hirschfeld of the 1st Mountain Division moved rapidly to the barricaded pass entrance which was defended by strong Russian forces. The position could not be taken frontally. However, von Hirschfeld showed the nature of German mountain battle tactics. While feigning an attack at the front and tying down the enemy, he outflanked the pass across the steep mountain ridge and raised the Soviet position from its hinges from the rear. Thus the highest point on the Sukhum military road was already in German hands on the evening of August 17.

Von Hirschfeld advanced rapidly into the Klydsch valley and took the village of Klydsch at the foot of the mountain, which placed him in the midst of the lush forests of the Black Sea coast. One more leap and the coastal plain would be reached.

But the surprise thrust into the plain failed with the weak forces available. The Russians defended the exit from the mountains furiously and bitterly. The great objective, Sukhumi, lay before Hirschfeld's eyes, only forty kilometers away. Having advanced deep into enemy territory and all alone, the *Major* and his handful of people were in a dangerous position. There were no friendly forces on his left, as Kleist's panzer army was still in the steppe, north of the Elbrus.

In this situation *General* Konrad decided on a daring operation in order to screen the corps' left flank. *Hauptmann* Groth was given the job of climbing into the more than 4,000-meter-high Elbrus passes with a high mountain company of mountain guides and mountaineers and blocking the valley of the Baksan, from which the Russians were threatening the German flank.

Before the German mountain troops unfolded the most adventurous battlefield of the war: the fissured, rust-red, porphyritic flanks of the Elbrus massif fell away for more than 1,000 meters. Far and wide the ice fields of the great Asau glacier sparkled in the sun: ice walls, fissured rocks, wild debris slopes.

Looking down solemnly over the deep furrows of the Baksan valley onto the bloody mountain battle for the old, czarist Krugosor hunting lodge, which sat at the 3,000 meter level – or as high as the Zugspitze in Germany – was the 4,697-meter-high Ushba, one of the most beautiful mountains in the world. Even higher were the Kazbek, far to the east on the Georgian military road, and the double peaks of Mount Elbrus.

It is understandable that the men of the 1st Mountain Division, in whose path lay Elbrus, were ambitious to conquer the giant. The operation had no military value, but the world would of course sit up and take notice if it was reported that German troops had raised the Reich war flag on the highest mountain of the Caucasus.

General Konrad thus gave his consent to the proposal to scale Elbrus. He did however make it a condition that the attempt was to be carried out as a joint effort by men of the 1st and 4th Mountain Divisions. The 4th Division was not to be made to feel slighted.

Hauptmann Groth led the expedition. The participants of the 4th Mountain Division were under the command of *Hauptmann* Gämmerler. The operation began with a curious surprise. *Oberleutnant* Schneider and the men of his signals squad left the base camp ahead of the main body because with their signals equipment they had a greater load to carry than the others.

In the distance before them, on the far side of the great glacier, they saw the fantastic *Intourist* house which the Soviets had erected at the 4,200-meter level. It was a huge, oval-shaped concrete structure, without any kind of sill or ledge, completely covered with sheet aluminum. It looked like a gigantic zeppelin gondola. The fantastic glacier hotel had forty rooms with a hundred beds. Above it was a meteorological station and below the main structure there was a cook-house.

Schneider and his squad advanced quickly across the snow of the glacier, which had not yet been melted by the sun. Peering through his binoculars, he suddenly realized that there was a Russian soldier standing in front of the house. Schneider warned his men to be cautious and then had them veer off and go around the hotel. He positioned his men in the rocks above the hotel, ready for battle.

At that very moment *Hauptmann* Groth came marching up to the house all alone. Before they could warn him the Russians had seized him. The Soviet garrison consisted of only three officers and eight men. They had come up that same morning.

Groth immediately assessed the situation and kept his nerve. A Russian officer who spoke German explained the hopelessness of his situation. The *Hauptmann* pointed to the approaching German roped parties and to the signals squad in the rocks above.

He finally convinced the Soviets to withdraw voluntarily. Four Red Army soldiers even preferred to wait with Groth for the German main body and later signed on as bearers.

The next day, August 18, was declared a rest day. The mountain infantry were to get used to the altitude gradually. The assault on the peak was to begin on August 19. But the ascent failed due to the sudden appearance of a snowstorm. Again on August 20 bad weather with sleet kept the men in the Elbrus house.

Not until August 21 did early morning sunshine promise a fine day. The troops moved out at 0300: *Hauptmann* Groth with sixteen men and *Hauptmann* Gämmerler with five.

By 0600 the fine weather was already over. A west wind blew up from the Black Sea. Fog and soon afterward a snowstorm defended the peak of Mount Elbrus. Groth and Gämmerler and their men took refuge in a tiny hut. Should they go back? No! The mountain infantry wanted to get on with it!

On they went. The march in the thin air and biting cold became a ghastly foot race. The climbers' eyes were stuck together by snow. The hurricane howled over the ice flank of the ridge. Visibility was no more than ten meters.

By 1100 the ice wall had been conquered. *Hauptmann* Gämmerler stood on the highest point of the wall of boulders they had reached. Before him the ridge fell away gently, therefore he must be at the summit.

Oberfeldwebel Kümmerle rammed the shaft of the Reich war flag deep into the snow. Then the standards of the 1st and 4th Mountain Divisions, with the edelweiss and the gentian, were thrust into the ground. A handshake and the party scrambled back into the east slope where the western storm was broken somewhat. An astonished world learned that the German flag now flew on the highest mountain of the Caucasus.

The storming of the summit of Elbrus by the German mountain infantry, who had conquered a completely foreign mountain in such hellish weather on the first attempt, was an outstanding alpine achievement. It was not diminished by the fact that several days later when the weather cleared, the corps' special correspondent, Dr. Rümmler, discovered that the ensigns had obviously not been placed at the trigonometric point of the highest peak, but at a point some 800 meters lower at the wall of boulders, which the mountain infantry had taken to be the highest point in the fog and ice-storm of August 21.

Let us now return to the battles in the high mountain passes. While the mountain infantry struggled through the Klukor Pass and over the old, dilapidated Sukhum military road in view of the 5,633-meter-high summit of Mount Elbrus, on the right flank *Generalmajor* Eglseer and his Austrian-Bavarian 4th Mountain Division were going over the high passes of the main mountain ridge.

Oberst von Stettner captured the Ssantscharo and Alustrachu passes, at elevations of between 2,600 and 3,000 meters, with two battalions of the 91st Mountain Infantry Regiment. He had thus crossed the crest of the mountain range. The German mountain infantry now moved down to the passes of the foothills into the sub-tropical forests of the Sukhum hills.

Major Schulze and his battalion of mountain infantry stormed through the Bgalar pass, which placed them directly above the wooded slopes which fell away steeply to the coastal plain. It was twenty kilometers to the coast. Twenty kilometers to their objective.

The mountain troops had covered 200 kilometers of mountainous terrain and high mountains. With limited forces they had fought at altitudes of over 3,000 meters, driven back the enemy in all situations, advanced across dizzying rocky ridges, storm-swept icy slopes and dangerous glaciers to take enemy positions which had been considered impregnable. Now they were close to their objective.

The battle group under the command of von Stettner had two guns each with twenty-five rounds of ammunition in its decisive position at the threshold of the coast. "Send ammunition" he radioed. "Are there no aircraft? Aren't the Alpinis coming with their pack animals?"

No. There were no aircraft. And the Alpinis were marching in the direction of the Don, to Stalingrad.

Oberst von Stettner, the commander of the courageous 91st Mountain Infantry Regiment, was in the Bysb Valley, twenty kilometers from Sukhumi.

Major von Hirschfeld was in the Klydsch Valley, forty kilometers from the coast. *Generalmajor* Rupp's 97th Light Infantry Division had battered its way to within fifty kilometers of Tuapse. Within his unit fought the Walloons of the *"Wallonie"* volunteer brigade under *Oberstleutnant* Lucien Lippert.

As the attack spearhead, the 421st Grenadier Regiment had fought its way to within thirty kilometers of Tuapse as the crow flies.

Yes, that is how it was at the end of 1942. The German armed forces had achieved unbelievable success and were close to the long-range goals set for them by Hitler in "Case Blue." They were fighting in the sub-tropical valleys beyond the Caucasian passes, were in sight of the Black Sea coast and the Caspian Sea and had captured the first oil fields in the oil paradise of the Soviet Union. They were fighting at the 43rd and 44th degrees of latitude, the southernmost position reached by the German Army, had their hand on the door handle of Astrakhan, which marked the southern end of the Astrakhan-Arkhangelsk line, the objective laid down in the Barbarossa plan and were already at the banks of the Volga near Stalingrad. With them as they moved over the battlefields between the Black Sea coast and the Baltic against Stalin's Red Army and the Soviet Union were not just the forces of Germany's European allies and volunteer units, but Cossacks, Turkmenes and Kalmucks as well.

Would the last dash across the few kilometers to Tuapse succeed? And to Maikop and Batumi on the Turkish border? And the 120 kilometers to Astrakhan in the Volga delta on the Caspian Sea, war objective and end point of Operation "Barbarossa." Would it succeed as had all the operations of the recent weeks?

The troops were optimistic, but there was worry at headquarters. The attack forces of Army Group A had been weakened by the weeks of heavy fighting and its supply lines had been overextended beyond the limits of improvisation. The forces of the Luftwaffe had been split by actions between the Don and the Caucasus. The Red air force suddenly controlled the air. Soviet artillery enjoyed numerical superiority. The German side was short a few dozen fighters, half a dozen battalions and a few hundred pack animals. Now, when the decision appeared close enough to grasp, they weren't there.

It was the same on every front: everywhere resources were missing. Everywhere, where the war stood at its zenith and the decisive objectives had almost been reached: before El Alamein, one hundred kilometers from the Nile, Rommel called for a few dozen aircraft against British air power and for a hundred tanks with a few thousand tons of fuel.

In the ravines west of Stalingrad the assault companies of the Sixth Army begged for a few assault guns, for two or three fresh regiments with a few anti-tank guns, combat engineers and tanks.

Before the first houses of Leningrad and in the approaches to Murmansk, everywhere the troops were missing the famous "last battalion," which always decided a battle at its climax.

But Hitler could give none of them this last battalion. The war had become too big, the Wehrmacht blanket too short. The troops were overtaxed everywhere.

CHAPTER VII

Long-range Patrol
to Astrakhan

Across 150 Kilometers of Enemy Territory in a Scout Car – The Unknown Oil Rail Line – Leutnant Schliep Speaks by Telephone with the Astrakhan Station Master – Captain Zagorodny's Cossacks

Guarding the deep, open flank of Army Group A's eastern group of forces, the First Panzer Army, was a chain of powerful strongpoints manned by the 16th Motorized Infantry Division.

It was September 13, 1942, east of Elista in the Kalmuck Steppe.

"Hey, Georg, get ready, we leave in an hour!"

"*Sluschaju, gospodin Oberleutnant* – yes Sir!" shouted back Georg the Cossack, then he roared off.

Georg came from Krasnodar, where he had learned German in the pedagogic seminary. The previous autumn he had run straight into the arms of the division while serving as a runner with the Soviet army. Since then he had served 2nd Company, first as a helper in the field kitchen, then, after volunteering, as an interpreter. Georg hated Stalin's bolshevism for many reasons and he was trusted by everyone in the company. Georg had even filled in as a machine-gunner in several critical situations.

Oberleutnant Gottlieb came directly from a briefing held by the commander of the motorcycle battalion, where they had discussed the final details of a patrol operation through the Kalmuck Steppe to the Caspian Sea. The commander of the Sixteenth, which had relieved LII Corps near Elista, wanted to know what was up in the broad expanse of wilderness on the flank of the Caucasus front. A huge gap nearly 300 kilometers across gaped between the area south of Stalingrad and the

Terek River, which the 3rd Panzer Division had reached near Mosdok on August 30. This unknown land between the Volga and the Terek appeared like a huge funnel. Its base was the coast of the Caspian Sea. All sorts of surprises could come from there. Therefore the area had to be kept under surveillance.

At the end of August the guarding of this huge no-man's-land was entrusted to a single division. Its base was Elista in the Kalmuck Steppe. No reinforcements were to be expected before the end of September, therefore at first the tasks of surveillance and reconnaissance across to the Caspian Sea and the Volga delta had to be taken care of by long-range patrols, which took the form of daring expedition-type operations.

It was at this time that the 16th Motorized Infantry Division earned itself the name of the "Greyhound Division."

Except for a few indispensable specialists, only volunteers were involved in these operations. The first large-scale expedition operation along both sides of the Elista-Astrakhan road began in mid-September. Four patrols were sent out. Their assignment was as follows:

1. Discover if and where the enemy is feeding forces into the gap between the Terek and the Volga, whether he is making attempts to cross the Volga, where enemy strongpoints are located, and if any troop movements can be located on the Stalingrad-Astrakhan shore road.

2. Carefully reconnoiter road conditions, the condition of the Caspian coast and the west bank of the Volga as well as the previously unknown Kizlyar-Astrakhan rail line.

The patrols set out at 0430 on September 13, a Sunday. A sharp wind blew out of the steppe. The sun was not yet up and it was still very cold.

The patrols were well-equipped for their adventurous drive 150 kilometers deep into enemy territory. Each troop had two eight-wheeled armored cars armed with 20mm cannon, a motorcycle platoon with twenty-four men, two or three 50mm anti-tank guns – motorized or mounted on armored personnel carriers – and a squad of engineers with equipment. Five trucks – two each with fuel and water and one with rations – as well as a repair squad completed the equipment. As well there was an ambulance with a doctor, a radio operator, a motorcycle messenger and an interpreter.

Disaster struck the Schroeder patrol straight away. Soon after departure it ran into an enemy patrol on the other side of Utta. *Leutnant* Schroeder was killed, interpreter Maresch and *Feldwebel* Weissmeier were wounded. The patrol turned back and set out again the next day under the command of *Leutnant* Euler.

Meanwhile the patrols led by *Oberleutnant* Gottlieb, *Leutnant* Schliep and *Leutnant* Hilger were advancing north and south of and directly along the major road from Elista to Astrakhan. On September 14 *Oberleutnant* Gottlieb, who had initially the road before veering north into the steppe toward Sadovska, was forty kilometers from Astrakhan. On September 15 he was only twenty-five kilometers from the Volga. From the high sand dunes he had a good view across to the river. Sand and salt marshes made the terrain almost inaccessible, but the armored patrols always found a way.

The maps which Gottlieb had brought with him were not very good. At every well they came to the Cossack Georg made inquiries of the nomadic Kalmucks, who appeared to be very well-disposed toward the Germans. In the course of their long palavers he was able to gather information about the way ahead and other matters of interest.

"The big train? Yes, it runs several times each day between Kizlyar and Astrakhan."

"And Soviets?"

"Yes, they ride around here. Just yesterday a large party spent the night at the well over there, an hour's journey away. They came from Sadovska, there must be many of them there."

"Aha." Georg nodded and gave the friendly nomads a few cigarettes.

The laughter was suddenly interrupted by a shout. One of the men pointed toward the north. Two riders were approaching: Soviets.

The Kalmucks disappeared. The two armored cars were behind a dune and could not be seen by the Russians. *Oberleutnant* Gottlieb called to Georg: "Come here." But the Cossack didn't answer. He stuck his forage cap under his broad motorcycle coat, sat down on the well and lit a cigarette.

The two Russians, an officer and his horseman, trotted cautiously up to the well. Georg called something to them. The officer got down and came toward him.

Oberleutnant Gottlieb and his men watched as the two talked and laughed. They stood side by side. "The dog," said the radio operator. But then they saw Georg whip out his pistol. Grinning, he said to the Soviet officer: "*Ruki werch!*"

The Soviet officer put his hands up and was so surprised that he called to his horseman to surrender as well. The Gottlieb patrol returned to Chalchuta with two valuable prisoners.

Meanwhile *Leutnant* Euler had been given the special assignment of learning precisely how the defensive installations in Sadovska were constituted and whether troops were being sent across the Volga in this area north of Astrakhan.

From Utta to Sadovska was about 150 kilometers in a straight line. Euler immediately veered off from the main road toward the north. They had driven about ten kilometers, when suddenly the *Leutnant*'s heart skipped a beat: a huge dust cloud was approaching rapidly. "Disperse the vehicles!" he ordered. Euler raised his field glasses. The cloud was coming closer, fast. But then the *Leutnant* burst out laughing: it wasn't Soviets coming towards them, but antelopes, a huge herd of Saiga antelopes, which live in the steppes of southern Russia. When they finally caught the scent of the humans they turned away and galloped off to the east. Their hoofs raced over the dry steppe grass and whipped up a dust cloud so big it looked as if an entire panzer regiment was driving across the endless plain.

Next *Leutnant* Euler reconnoitered to the north, found the villages of Justa and Chasyk strongly manned, drove around them and turned toward Sadovska, the main objective.

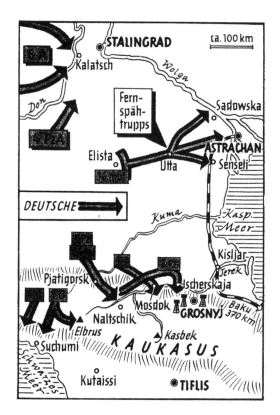

Map 8. The great gap between the Caucasus front and Stalingrad was 300 kilometers wide. Patrols of the 16th Motorized Infantry Division probed right up to the gates of Astrakhan.

On September 16 Euler and his two armored cars were just five kilometers from Sadovska and thus seven kilometers from the lower Volga. It was only thirty-five kilometers to Astrakhan. In all probability the Euler patrol was at the most easterly point reached by any unit of the German Army during the course of "Operation Barbarossa" and had thus come closest to this campaign objective.

What the patrol found was of great significance: the Russians had dug an anti-tank ditch around Sadovska and built an deep bunker line. This suggested a prepared bridgehead position, designed to protect an obviously planned crossing of the lower Volga by the Soviets.

When the Russian sentries recognized the German armored cars a panic-like excitement broke out in the positions: the defenders, who until now had obviously been quite unconcerned, raced into their bunkers and rifle pits and opened up a furious defensive fire with anti-tank rifles and heavy machine-guns. Euler cut off two Russians who were running through the terrain in the general excitement.

Scared to death, the two Red Army soldiers, a staff officer of the 36th Machine-gun Battalion and his runner, gave themselves up. It was a great catch, but now it was time to be off!

Leutnant Jürgen Schliep, the commander of the armored car company, had likewise set out with his patrol on September 13. His route ran south of the large road. His main task was to find out if – as prisoners had stated – there was in fact a usable rail line from Kizlyar to Astrakhan which was not indicated on any maps. It was most important that they find out about this oil rail line, which could also have been used for transporting troops.

Schliep found the rail line. He related: "From a distance we saw a group of fifty to sixty civilians who were working on the railway embankment. The line consisted of a single track and was framed on both sides by a sand wall. Though the guard bolted when we appeared, we were greeted joyfully by the remaining civilian workers. The group consisted of Ukrainian families, old men, women and children, who had been forcibly evacuated. They had been working here for months. Many of the Ukrainians spoke German and we were welcomed as liberators."

The soldiers were still talking with the Ukrainians when a smoke cloud suddenly appeared in the south. "A train," shouted the workers.

Schliep brought his armored cars into position behind a sandy knoll. Then an endlessly-long freight train with oil and gasoline cars came wheezing toward the station. Two locomotives were pulling the train. Six shots from the 20mm cannon and the locomotives blew apart. Steam sprayed from the boilers and glowing coals whirled through the air. The train stopped. Car after car went up in flames.

"Damn, that lovely gas," grumbled the gunners.

The engineers were about to blow up the station building when the telephone rang. Startled, they stood up. "Man, that scared the hell out of me," sighed *Unteroffizier* Engh of the repair squad. But then he thought quickly and called to Schliep: "*Herr Leutnant*, telephone!"

Schliep immediately grasped the situation and ran into the hut with his interpreter. Grinning, the interpreter took the phone: "*Stanzia senseli, natshalnik.*" "*Da, da, tovarich,*" he said reassuringly.

On the other end of the line was the Astrakhan freight depot. Astrakhan! The southern end of the A-A Line (Astrakhan-Arkhangelsk), the objective of the war against Russia. The spearhead of the German Wehrmacht had Astrakhan on the telephone. The supervisor in Astrakhan wanted to know if the oil train from Baku had passed yet. The opposite train had been waiting in a siding near Bassy for an hour already.

An opposite train! The interpreter tried to convince the comrade in Astrakhan that he should send the other train. But this piece of advice made the man in Astrakhan suspicious. He asked a few questions and the inexpert answers he received seemed to justify his suspicion.

He berated the imposter and cursed furiously. Finally the interpreter gave up the game and said: "Just wait, little father, we'll be in Astrakhan soon."

At this the comrade in Astrakhan shouted the worst Russian curse he knew into the receiver and hung up. Thus he couldn't hear how, two minutes later, the wooden station at Senseli blew up with the aid of two explosive charges.

The Schliep long-range patrol returned to Utta on September 17 safe and sound and without loss. Schlief had to make his report that same day to the division and to the Commander-in-Chief of Army Group B, *Generaloberst* von Weichs, who by chance was at the command post.

The senior officers breathed easier. There was still no threat from the steppe and the lower Volga, meaning from the Caucasus flank. This was a decisive discovery, because since the end of August Army Group A had been trying to get its stalled Caucasus offensive going again on its left wing. Panzer Army von Kleist was to smash open the door to Baku in order to capture the Soviet oil paradise and thus reach one of the decisive objectives of the summer campaign.

The last obstacle standing in the way of this objective was the Terek River, in front of which were stalled the armored spearheads of Kleist's army. Kleist tried his luck and in fact the fortunes of war once again seemed to offer the German

Wehrmacht a chance of victory.

In a clever cross-maneuver Kleist withdrew the 3rd Panzer Division from the fiercely-defended Baksan Valley and sent it east along the Terek. On August 25 the division took Mosdok. Afterward it deployed another battle group for a surprise crossing of the river near Isherskaya. The 394th Panzer Regiment from Hamburg made the decisive leap across the river.

August 30, 1942: The minute hand moved to three o'clock. The assault boats, the combat engineers and the panzer-grenadiers were ready. They waited for the artillery barrage which was to cover their leap across the river.

The Terek, about 250 meters wide at the crossing site, with powerful currents and gurgling whirlpools, was a treacherous mountain stream. White columns of spray shot up beside the boats: enemy mortar fire.

The small assault boats danced among the bursting shells. Their bows towered above the water. Behind, in the sterns, crouched low, squatted the grenadiers. In this way the boats flitted through the inferno.

As the attack was beginning, the commander of I Battalion, *Hauptmann* Freiherr von der Heyden-Rynsch, and his adjutant, *Leutnant* Ziegler, were killed while still on the near shore. *Leutnant* Wurm was also fatally hit. *Oberleutnant* Dürrholz, commander of 2nd Company, was wounded during the crossing and fell out of the boat into the river. He was never found.

The infantry fought its way forward step by step under the cover of the German artillery fire. The first stage in the formation of the bridgehead had been completed. It was just a first stage, no more, because the enemy soon proved stronger than first assumed. He defended fiercely from good cover at the edge of the village of Mundar-Jurt. The Soviets were manning extended field positions as well as an anti-tank ditch. From there they straddled the German grenadiers, who were in open terrain, with their fire.

In the afternoon the young regimental commander, *Major* Günther Pape, crossed the Terek with his operations staff to evaluate the situation on the spot. Pape laid down the main line of resistance and positioned his troops in such a way that it was possible to defend the bridgehead with the limited forces available.

The men of the 394th Panzer-Grenadier Regiment held out on the far side of the Terek for five days. They were fighting south of the 44th degree of latitude. Only the leading elements of the 1st Mountain Division in the Klydsch Valley were farther south. They were close to the 43rd parallel, precisely at 43 degrees, 20 minutes, the southernmost point on Soviet territory reached by the German Army in the course of Operation "Barbarossa."

Pape's men battled a numerically stronger and determined enemy in unfavorable terrain and without heavy weapons. The regiment tied down three Soviet divisions. As a result the Soviets were forced to withdraw forces from other areas. In this way the bridgehead created the conditions necessary for the attack by the recently arrived LII Corps. On September 1 and 2 the corps succeeded in crossing the Terek near Mosdok, where it established another bridgehead. The 111th Infantry Division forced a crossing of the raging, five-meter-deep mountain stream. The point forces were led by *Hauptmann* Lyme. He established the first small bridgehead on the far bank and held it until the engineers brought heavy infantry weapons across the river.

But near Mosdok, too, the German forces were insufficient for a resumption of the offensive. The Russians were too strong and the Germans too weak and exhausted. The last chance to capture the Baku oil region could not be exploited.

As in the western foothills of the Caucasus leading down to the Black Sea, here too at the Terek the battle came to a standstill. The front froze. The offensive strength of Operation "Barbarossa" fizzled out just short of the campaign's objective. The Terek marked the end of the German advance.

Fighting beside the German grenadiers in the defensive lines at the Terek was a remarkable unit: Cossacks. The story of how Captain Zagorodny's cossack squadron ended up on the German side was a typical one from this war.

When *General* Freiherr von Geyr's XXXX Panzer Corps took 18,000 prisoners at Millerovo in the summer, the number one question was: who was going to escort the Soviets to the rear? The depleted units of the German divisions couldn't release any troops for the job. Then *Hauptmann* Kandutsch, the corps Ic, came up with the idea of separating the Kuban and Don Cossacks, who were very well disposed toward the Germans, from the prisoners, mounting them on the many horses wandering about and thus using them as an escort detachment for the captured Red Army soldiers. The Cossacks, anything but friends of bolshevism, were enthusiastic. In no time Zagorodny had assembled a squadron and set out with the 18,000 Soviet prisoners. No one in the corps headquarters thought they would ever see Zagorodny and his Cossacks again.

Then, one day in the first week of September, in the headquarters of the panzer corps in Ruski on the Terek, the door to the Ic's quarters suddenly opened. A colorfully-dressed Cossack officer stepped in and declared in broken German: "Captain Zagorodny with squadron reporting." Kandutsch was thunderstruck. Years after the war he related with a smile: "We thus had them back again."

What was he to do with the Cossacks? Kandutsch called the Chief of Staff. A lengthy discussion ensued. Finally it was decided that Zagorodny's unit would be reformed as Cossack Squadron 1/82, trained for four weeks and then deployed at the front.

And that is how it happened. In the Isherskaya position Zagorodny insisted on discipline and order. There was not a single deserter from among his men.

The Captain's dependable right arm was the first platoon leader, Lieutenant Koban, a broad-shouldered Cossack who, like Zagorodny, remained loyal to his squadron until the end. Once, when Koban fell ill, his wife assembled the platoon. This smart, attractive woman had ridden in the cavalry platoon with her husband from the beginning. She went out on patrol like any other Cossack, and she died with her squadron as well, thousands of kilometers from her homeland, which she had believed she could help liberate in 1942.

Hauptmann Kandutsch related: "At the end of 1944, when XXXX Panzer Corps crossed the Romanian border to the west, the squadron was ordered transferred to France. The corps adjutant, *Major* Dr. Patow, bade the Cossacks farewell. Captain Zagorodny received the Iron Cross, First Class he had so longed for. He had earned it. Then he formed up the Cossacks once again – probably for the last time – for a march-past at a gallop. It was an unforgettable sight."

Six weeks later, during the invasion battle, the squadron was caught in a heavy fighter-bomber attack near St. Ló and wiped out.

Only a few men were able to save themselves. They brought news of the Cossacks' fate to Germany. Among those killed were all the officers and the wife of Lieutenant Koban. The men of XXXX Panzer Corps never forgot their Cossack comrades-in-arms with whom they had taken part in many hard battles.

CHAPTER VIII

The Terek

Hitler's Collision with General Jodl – The Chief of Staff and Feldmarschall List Must Go – The Magic of the Oil – Panzer-Grenadiers on the Ossetian Military Road – The Caucasus Front Freezes

On September 7, 1942 late summer heat brooded over the Ukrainian forests. In the gloomy blockhouses of Hitler's "*Werwolf*" headquarters the thermometer climbed to the 90 degree mark. Hitler suffered particularly badly from the climate. It made his gnawing anger over the situation between the Kuban and the Terek even worse. All the reports from the "oil front" suggested that the troops were at the end of their strength.

Army Group A was stalled at the Caucasus and at the Terek. The valleys to the Black Sea coast, especially to Tuapse, had been blocked by the Soviets, and the Terek was proving to be a heavily-fortified obstacle, the last before the old military road to Tiflis, Kutaissi and Baku.

It's not working, reported the divisions. "It's not working, it's not working, that's all I hear," thundered Hitler. He didn't want to admit that he could advance no farther at the Terek and on the mountain front because of a shortage of forces. He sought the blame for this in his senior commanders and what he saw as poor planning of their operations.

On the morning of September 7, therefore, Hitler sent the chief of his Wehrmacht operations staff, *General der Artillerie* Jodl, to *Feldmarschall* List in Stalino to look after things, and in particular to find out why the advance to Tuapse was stalled. Jodl was to lend emphasis to Hitler's orders.

Jodl returned late in the evening and made his report. What he told Hitler in

"Werewolf's" blockhouse quarters resulted in the most severe crisis in the German armed forces command since the beginning of the war. Jodl defended *Feldmarschall* List and defended his view that the forces were too weak for the assigned objectives. Like List, he demanded a comprehensive regrouping at the front.

Hitler refused and accused Jodl of allowing himself to be bamboozled by List. The *Generaloberst*, likewise overexcited by the climate and the exertions of the day, flared up and quoted furiously and in a loud voice the Führer's own orders and directives of the past weeks, which *Feldmarschall* List had followed exactly and which had led to the difficulties in which Army Group A now found itself.

Hitler was speechless at Jodl's reproaches. His most trusted General was not only rebelling, but was questioning straight out his ability as a field commander and blaming him for the crisis in the Caucasus and the impending defeat on the southern front.

"You're lying!" screamed Hitler. "Never have I given such orders, never!" Then he left Jodl standing and stormed out of the blockhouse into the darkness of the Ukrainian forest. It was not until hours later that he returned, pale and exhausted.

Just how hurt Hitler felt is indicated by the fact that from then on he no longer took his meals with his Generals. Filled with bitterness, from that day until his death he ate alone in the spartan rooms of his field quarters, with only his Alsatian bitch "Blondi" at his side.

But this was not the only reaction to Jodl's reproaches. There was an even more drastic one: the Chief of the General Staff, *Generaloberst* Halder, and *Feldmarschall* List were dismissed. Hitler even decided to relieve his devoted Generals Keitel and Jodl and had it in his mind to replace them with Field Marshalls Kesselring and Paulus, a plan which unfortunately was not realized. Perhaps as a result of such sweeping changes, which would have brought Field Marshalls Paulus and Kesselring, with their experience at the front, to the leading positions in the OKW, the catastrophe of Stalingrad would have at least been avoided.

But Hitler didn't divest himself of Keitel and Jodl, his military advisors of many years. All he did was order that in future every one of his words and every utterance by the generals at military conferences were to be taken down. As well he stuck to his order that the attack on the Caucasus front was to continue. Under no circumstances did he want to dispense with the main objective of his summer offensive. Come what may, the oil of the Caucasus, Grozny, Tiflis and Baku as well as the shipping ports of the Black Sea were to be delivered into German hands. The autumn of 1942 was to see the German armed forces reach the objective of the eastern campaign, at least in the south.

Here was proof once again that Hitler was becoming increasingly stubborn in the military sector. This character trait would have fateful consequences for the front.

In the economic sector, Hitler considered oil the outstanding power of the technical century. He was dominated by the significance of oil. He had read everything written on the subject. He knew the histories of the Arabian and American oil regions and knew all about oil production and technology. Anyone who began to talk about oil could be certain of Hitler's interest.

Typical is the story that Hitler once said of a capable official of the foreign office's trade policy department: "I can't stand the fellow, but he knows something about oil." Hitler's Balkan policy was made primarily with a view toward the Romanian oil. He included a campaign against the Crimea in the "Barbarossa" directive, because he feared for the Ploesti oil fields, which he rightly considered threatened by Russian air attacks from the Crimea.

Because of oil Hitler neglected the most revolutionary scientific development of the twentieth century, namely nuclear science. There was no room in his head for an understanding of the military significance of nuclear fission, which had been discovered in Germany and first developed by German physicists.

The magic of oil determined the eastern campaign from the beginning, and in the summer of 1942 it was probably this magic of oil which seduced Hitler into deciding to demand sacrifices of the southern front, which in the final analysis decided the 1942 campaign and the subsequent course of the war. A final look at the oil front of 1942 supplies arguments enough for this thesis:

Army Group A was stalled at the northern and western boundaries of the Caucasus, but Hitler was loathe to admit the limits of his military strength. He wanted to advance along the old Caucasian military roads to Tiflis and Baku. And he renewed the order to carry the offensive across the Terek.

Orders were orders. In weeks of tough fighting the 1st Panzer Division attempted to expand the Terek bridgehead south and west, step by step. All available forces were bought together and on September 20 a crossing of the Terek was in fact forced southwest of Mosdok. *General* von Mackensen launched an attack on Ordzhonikidze, which lay on the road to Tiflis, with all of III Panzer Corps. The *"Wiking"* SS-Panzer-Grenadier Division broke through toward the

Georgian military road, finally reaching the ancient military route to Tiflis was reached.

The battle groups of the *"Nordland"* SS-Panzer-Grenadier Regiment, which included a battalion of Finnish volunteers, arrived from out of the Caucasian forests, and with it the *"Wiking"* Division was able to force its way into the Grozny oil region and block the Georgian military road in two places. The decisive Hill 711 was stormed by the Finnish volunteer battalion with heavy losses and was subsequently held against all counterattacks. Would the attackers have enough strength left for the final advance, for the last 100 kilometers?

It took four weeks for III Panzer Corps to assemble the reserves of men, fuel and replacements necessary to launch the new – and they hoped, the last – attack.

On October 25 and 26 the corps rolled out of its bridgehead for the breakthrough toward the southeast. The battalions fought bitterly. An enemy group of forces totalling four divisions was smashed and about 7,000 prisoners taken. Romanian mountain troops sealed off the mountain valleys leading south. The two panzer divisions drove southeast and on November 1 took Alagir and the Ossetian military road on either side of the city. On November 5 *Generalmajor* Herr's 13th Panzer Division fought its way to within five kilometers of Ordzhonikidze.

But now the last of the attackers' strength had been spent. Soviet counterattacks from the north cut off the German divisions from their rear communications. The First Panzer Army was unable to help and, in the face of resistance from Führer Headquarters, ordered a breakout. It succeeded.

Then, in mid-November, a sudden drop in temperature brought to an end all attempts to get the operation going again.

On the right wing, held by the Seventeenth Army, the mountain infantry had already abandoned the snow-covered passes in the high Caucasus because no more supplies were getting through. The infantry and light infantry regiments had dug in. The attack on the Black Sea ports, on the oil fields and Baku, on Tiflis and Batumi, had failed with the objectives near at hand. The entire front was at a standstill.

Why?

Because the new Soviet tactic of withdrawal had frustrated the boldly-planned encircling operations between the Don and Donets. Because the Soviet commanders had succeeded at the last moment in regaining control of their units withdrawing from the lower Don into the Caucasus. And above all, because American supplies had got through from Iran across the Caspian Sea to the battered Soviet armies. The exhausted German armies were too weak to overcome this last resistance.

The last battalion was missing.

PART II

THE BATTLE

CHAPTER I

Between the Don and the Volga

Kalach, the Fateful Bridge across the Don – Tank Battle on the Sandy Sea of the Steppe – General Hube's Armored Thrust to the Volga – "On the Right the Spires of Stalingrad" – Women Manning the Heavy Anti-aircraft Guns – The First Battle before Stalin's City

Whoever concerns himself with the bitter Battle of Stalingrad soon discovers the truth that the capture of the city was not an objective in the plans for the great summer offensive. "Case Blue" specified that attempts were to be made to reach Stalingrad and bring it under the effects of heavy weapons so that it was eliminated as an armaments and transportation center. This was a job for aircraft and long-range artillery, and not one in which to send an entire army with panzer divisions into a battle of attrition in built-up areas, industrial zones and bunkers.

This aim could certainly have been achieved with bombs and shells, because Stalingrad had no strategic significance. Following the basic concept of the plans, the purpose of the operations by the Sixth Army was to establish flanking cover for the Caucasus front, with its economic objectives. It was a task for which the occupation of Stalingrad would certainly have been useful, but in no way necessary. The fact that the Sixth Army's security assignment eventually became a culmination point of the war and a battle which took on a decisive significance to the campaign, is one of the sadder facts of the Stalingrad tragedy. On examining the circumstances surrounding this battle, one can grasp how much the outcome of a war is determined by chance and mistakes.

When, in September 1942, the main operation of the summer offensive, the battle in the Caucasus and at the Terek, came to a standstill, encouraging news from the Stalingrad Front arrived at Führer Headquarters. There, where the occupation of the Don bend and the knee of the Volga around Stalingrad was to secure the rear and flank of the battle for the oil, there was suddenly progress after weeks of crisis. On September 13 a report came from the Sixth Army that the 71st Infantry Division had broken through Stalingrad's in-depth fortifications and had stormed the heights before the center of the city.

The next day, September 14, 1942, following costly house-to-house fighting, elements of the 71st Infantry Division from Lower Saxony broke through north of the two railway stations and reached the Volga. To be sure *General* Hartmann's assault groups formed only a narrow spearhead, but they were through the city. The Reich battle flag waved over the center of Stalingrad. This was an encouraging success; it gave hope that at least the Don-Volga operation could be brought to a successful conclusion before the onset of winter and then, with this well-protected flank, the offensive could be continued in the Caucasus.

What had brought about this encouraging success of September 14, 1942? For the answer it is necessary to flash back to the summer, in the days of the operation between the Donets and Don when, in the second half of July, the Sixth Army advanced alone along the Don toward Stalingrad, after the main forces of Army Group South had been diverted south for the battle of encirclement at Rostov.

Spearheading the Sixth Army was *General* von Wietersheim's XIV Panzer Corps. It was the lone panzer corps attached to the army and consisted of the 16th Panzer Division and the 3rd and 60th Motorized Infantry Divisions. The Russians fell back before this "armored fist," north across the Don and in particular east in the direction of Stalingrad.

In the case of many Soviet divisions this retreat, which was undoubtedly ordered by the Soviet command and thought of as a strategic withdrawal, nevertheless disintegrated into wild flight, because the orders to retreat came unexpectedly and were vaguely formulated. The withdrawal was badly organized. The officers and troops of the Soviets had no experience in this new tactic. The result was that the middle and lower levels of command lost control of their units. Panic set in in many places. This detail is important in understanding why on the German side this retreat was seen as collapse.

Undoubtedly there were signs of collapse in many places, but the Soviet high command was unaffected by this. It had a clear program: Stalingrad, the city with Stalin's name on the knee of the Volga, the old Tsaritsyn, was to become the final defensive center at the will of the Red general staff. Stalin had allowed his generals to wrest from him the retreat from the Donets and the Don, but it was to end at the Volga.

On July 12, 1942 Stalin had said to Marshall Timoshenko: "I order the formation of Army Group Stalingrad, and the city itself will be defended to the last man by the Sixty-second Army."

Stalin wanted to bring about a turn in Soviet fortunes in a strategically-favorable area, a tactic which had succeeded in the past – against the White Cossack General Deniken in 1920 during the revolutionary war. All they needed was time: time to bring in reserves, time for the construction of defensive positions in the northern approaches to the city on the land bridge between the Don and the Volga as well as on the favorable ranges of hills which extended south of Stalingrad into the Kalmuck Steppe.

But would the Germans give the Red Army time to mobilize its forces and regroup in the Stalingrad area?

At that time Major General Kolpakchi was still in command of the Sixty-second Army. His staff officers stood at the Don crossings in the Kalach area armed with submachine-guns, in order to bring some semblance of order to the retreating Soviet regiments.

But the Germans did not come. "No contact with the enemy," reported the Russian rear guards. Kolpakchi shook his head. He reported to the army group: "The Germans are not pursuing."

There was no news of such changes from the outstanding Soviet espionage organization. Neither Richard Sorge from the German embassy in Tokyo nor *Oberleutnant* Schulze-Boysen from the Air Ministry in Berlin had reported changes in the offensive plans of the Germans. There were no hints of anything of the like from chief agents Alexander Rado in Switzerland and Gilbert in Paris, and one of them would definitely have had this information. Reports from Swiss agent Rössler, which he sent under the name "Werther," showed that the sources of information were functioning well in those days. But there was not a single clue relating to a new German plan with regard to Stalingrad.

Rössler's "Werther" had nothing to say, because his source was not the German High Command – as was believed until long after the war – rather he received his information from the British from the deciphered directives from the Führer Headquarters to the army groups. The British invented the legend of "the man in the OKW" to hide the source of their information from the Russians.

But there were no directives at all from Führer Headquarters on the conduct of the Sixth Army. The feared armored spearheads of Paulus' XIV Panzer Corps were stalled in the Millerovo area, not as part of any operational plan, but simply because they were out of fuel.

The Russians immediately used the time they had gained. "If the Germans are not going to follow up, the defense can be formed west of the Don," decided Timoshenko. Major General Kolpakchi assembled the Sixty-second Army in the great bend of the Don and established a bridgehead around Kalach. In this way he barricaded the decisive Don crossing, sixty kilometers west of Stalingrad. The fortified loop in the Don projected westward like a balcony, flanked by the Don to the north and south.

When the Sixth Army was finally ready to march again, Paulus found himself faced with the task of first having to force open the barrier around Kalach before he could continue the thrust across the Don toward Stalingrad.

Thus began the Battle of Kalach, an interesting and militarily significant operation, the first act of the Battle of Stalingrad. *General* Paulus planned the attack on the Kalach bridgehead as a classic battle of envelopment. He had one

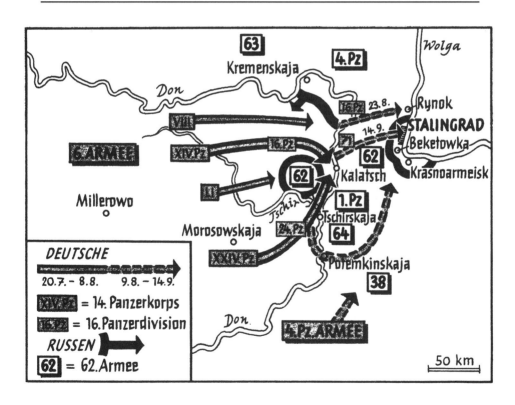

Map 9. In the Don bridgehead. The Battle of Stalingrad was opened near Kalach. General Paulus destroyed the Soviet forces in the pocket west of the Don, and on August 23 the 16th Panzer Division drove from the Don to the Volga. Then began the enveloping attack on Stalingrad.

panzer corps swing left, and sent another, which had been detached by Hoth, wide to the east on the right wing. The objective was for the two panzer corps to link up near Kalach. VIII Infantry Corps guarded the army's deep flank in the north, while the Seydlitz Corps advanced frontally on Kalach between the two panzer corps. (See map on page 119)

The main burden of the heavy fighting in this battle in the great loop of the Don fell to the two panzer divisions. The motorized divisions guarded the flanks.

The East Prussian 24th Panzer Division had the task of forcing the Chir and turning north along the Don toward Kalach. Facing it were strong forces of the Sixty-fourth Soviet Army, which was under the command of Lieutenant General Chuikov at that time.

The first attack failed to clear the mine fields behind which the Soviets had entrenched themselves. But on July 25, at about 0330, the 24th attacked again. The enemy was driven out of his well-built positions and the decisive hills were taken.

Heavy rain fell in the afternoon. The attack became ever more difficult in the softened ground. The weather, as well as three Soviet rifle divisions which defended their positions grimly and doggedly, made a surprise advance to the Don impossible.

Things changed on July 26, however. Panzer-grenadiers smashed the desired gap at the Solenaya Brook. Riding in armored personnel carriers, they drove east. The breakthrough had succeeded.

Tanks raced toward the Chir crossing near Nizhnye-Chirskaya and took the bridge. The large village was occupied in nocturnal street fighting and the ford and the Chir bridge to the east were taken before midnight.

While the panzer-grenadiers established a bridgehead, tanks and armored personnel carriers drove out of the bridge position through the enemy-occupied forest to the Don bridge. They reached the mighty waterway, the fateful river of Operation "Barbarossa," at dawn.

Luckily, attempts by the enemy to destroy the bridge failed. Only a small section was blown, and this was quickly repaired.

However it was too soon to risk the advance on the narrow land bridge between the Don and Volga in the direction of Stalingrad. First the powerful Russian forces west of the river had to be eliminated. As well the Russians had meanwhile assembled two armies east of the Don, against which the weak armored spearheads of the Sixth Army could accomplish little alone.

The last round in the Battle of Kalach began on August 6. An armored assault group under *Oberst* Riebel moved out of the Chir bridgehead and drove northward in the direction of Kalach. The objective was thirty-five kilometers away.

The Russians resisted. They knew what was at stake: if the Germans got through, everything west of the river would be cut off and the barrier before the door to Stalingrad would have been smashed.

But the "armored fist" of the 24th Panzer Division hammered through the Soviet defensive positions and minefields, fought off numerous counterattacks and fetched the unarmored elements of the divisions through the Soviet defenses in convoy.

Then, lined up in numerous columns side by side, the division roared across the steppe in a wild chase. When darkness fell it was astride the commanding Hill 184, just outside Kalach, in the enemy's rear.

Meanwhile, for the left arm of the pincer as well, the operation was running according to plan.

Generalleutnant Hube's Westphalian 16th Panzer Division attacked from the upper Chir on July 23, arrayed in four battle groups. The first serious resistance was offered by a division of the Soviet Sixty-second Army on the heights of Roshka. With its panzer-grenadiers riding in armored personnel carriers, the Hube Battalion drove up close to the bunkers and field positions of the enemy. The grenadiers leapt from their vehicles and smoked the Russians from their hiding places with hand grenades and pistols.

By the afternoon the Germans had smashed open a large gap. The next day, July 24, Battle Group Witzleben reached the Liska Brook, northwest of Kalach.

Twenty kilometers to go.

The Graf Strachwitz panzer battalion, reinforced by artillery, motorcycle troops and mounted grenadiers, raced eastward as part of Battle Group Lattmann and at dawn reached the last blocking position north of Kalach.

The Soviets were driven back. Graf Strachwitz veered south and rolled up the entire Soviet defense.

Ten kilometers to go.

Both German attack groups were now fighting in the rear of the Soviet bridgehead garrison. The pocket behind General Kolpakchi's divisions began to take shape.

The Soviets recognized the danger and threw all available forces against the northern pincer. It was the beginning of a battle which the Soviets fought not only with great determination, but with surprisingly strong armored forces as well.

Mobile armored forces faced each other on both sides of the front. They circled round one another, each seeking to encircle the other. Here there was no front. The tank formations fought on the ocean of sand of the steppe like destroyer and cruiser units at sea. They strove for favorable firing positions, cornered the enemy, held onto villages for a few hours or a few days, broke out, faced about and set out after the enemy again. And while the tanks clashed repeatedly on the grass-covered steppe, the German air fleets fought bitter air battles aove the Don, attacked the enemy in his hiding places in the *balkas* (ravines), blew up his supplies of ammunition and set fuel columns ablaze.

On August 8 the spearheads of the 16th and 24th Panzer Divisions linked up near Kalach. The pocket was now almost closed. The iron ring was formed by two panzer corps and an infantry corps. In the bag were nine rifle divisions and two motorized and seven tank brigades of the Soviet First Tank Army and the Sixty-second Soviet Army. 1,000 tanks and armored vehicles as well as 750 guns were captured or destroyed.

This was the first successful battle of encirclement since the early summer, since the Battle of Kharkov. It was to be the last of Operation "Barbarossa." The battle was fought out sixty kilometers from the Volga, and it deserves attention that here, at the gates of Stalingrad, the commanders and troops of the Sixth Army had once again proved their superiority in mobile warfare against a numerically far-superior enemy. It once again showed in all clarity that if material strength was even somewhat in keeping with the circumstances and the initiative of mobile warfare forced the rules of engagement upon the Soviets, no Soviet resistance was a match for the German formations.

Mopping-up operations in the Kalach area and the capture of bridges and bridgeheads across the Don for the advance on Stalingrad lasted almost fourteen days.

But all the courage of desperation did the Soviets no good: on August 16 the large Kalach bridge was seized by *Leutnant* Kleinjohann with elements of the 16th Pioneer Battalion. Things now moved rapidly.

On August 21 infantry units of the Seydlitz Corps went across the steeply-incised, approximately 100-meter-wide Don. Paulus' plan stood firm: he intended to extend the corridor from the Don to the Volga, seal off Stalingrad in the north and then take the city from the south.

Generalleutnant Hube, originally an infantryman, now an outstanding commander of armored forces, squatted with *Oberstleutnant* Sickenius, the commander of the 2nd Panzer Regiment, at the Wertyatchi pontoon bridge in the garden of a farm cottage. The map lay against a small hay shed.

Hube traced a path across the map with his right hand. The left arm of his uniform jacket was empty and the end of it was stuck in the jacket pocket. Hube had lost the arm in the First World War. The commander of the 16th Panzer Division was the only one-armed tank general in the Wehrmacht.

"Here we have the narrowest part of the land bridge between the Don and Volga, it's sixty kilometers," he said. "Ridge 137, which the army order has assigned us as our attack route, is ideal for tanks. No streams or ravines cross our path. That's the chance for us to smash the corridor through the enemy to the Volga in one go."

Sickenius nodded: "The Russians will defend the land bridge with everything they have, *Herr General*. They've been prepared for a long time. The Tartar trench, which extends from the Don to the Volga, is an old defensive wall against invasions from the north toward the mouth of the Volga."

Hube followed the Tartar trench, which was drawn on the map, with his finger and answered: "The Russians will have developed it as an anti-tank ditch. But we've taken other anti-tank ditches. Everything has to go fast, lightning fast, in the old way."

A motorcycle messenger came roaring up. He brought the final orders from corps for the thrust to the Volga.

Hube read. Then he stood up and said: "It begins tomorrow at 0430, Sickenius."

Tomorrow – that was August 23, 1942.

The 16th Panzer Division was to drive straight east to the Volga, close to the northern edge of Stalingrad, in one go. The flanks of this audacious armored thrust were to be guarded, on the right, by the 60th Motorized Infantry Division from Danzig and on the left by the 3rd Motorized Infantry Division from Brandenburg. It was an adventure quite in the style of the tank thrusts of the first year of the war.

The next day: Stalingrad. The Volga. Hube knew that Stalingrad and the Volga were the last objectives, the most easterly points which were to be reached. Over there ended the offensive war, over there was the final point of Operation "Barbarossa," over there was victory.

"Until tomorrow, Sickenius."

"Until tomorrow, *Herr General.*"

During the night the 16th Panzer Division rolled into the bridgehead near Luchinskoy in a huge column. Russian bombers attacked the important bridge without pause. Like torches, burning vehicles showed the enemy pilots the way to their target. But the Russians had no luck, the bridge remained undamaged. At midnight the units lay just behind the main line of resistance in the open terrain. The grenadiers dug their foxholes, called "Hube holes," and drove the armored vehicles over them for protection. The whole night artillery fire and salvoes from "Stalin Organs" poured down on the bridgehead, which was only five kilometers long and two kilometers wide.

On the morning of August 23, 1942 the leading tanks drove across the Wertyatchi pontoon bridge. On the far side the units deployed in wedge formation. Leading was Battle Group Sickenius, followed by Battle Groups Krumpen and von Arenstorff.

Unconcerned by the enemy forces left and right of the ridge, in the stream beds and ravines, the tanks, armored personnel carriers, tractors and armored elements of three divisions rolled east. Above them the close-support and Stuka units of VIII Fliegerkorps droned toward Stalingrad. On the return flight the machines dropped low over the tanks and let their sirens howl in a display of high spirits.

The Soviets tried to halt the German armored assault at the Tartar trench. In vain. The Russian defense was scattered and the famous, old trench with its walls was overrun. The Soviets had obviously been surprised by the powerful attack and – as was almost always the case in such situations – were confused and unable to improvise an effective defense.

The breakthrough points were often only 150 to 200 meters wide. *General* Hube led from the front, riding in the radio company's command vehicle, and was kept informed of the situation minute by minute. This was the art of leading an armored thrust.

Early in the afternoon the commander in the leading tank called to his men: "To the right the silhouette of Stalingrad." All of the tank commanders stood in their turrets and saw the extended silhouette of the old Tsaritsyn, now a modern industrial city stretching forty kilometers along the Volga. Tall towers, factory chimneys, skyscrapers and to the south, from the old city, onion domes of the cathedrals projected into the sky.

The tracks of the tanks ground up the dry steppe grass. Clouds of dust trailed behind the panzers. The leading tanks of the Strachwitz Battalion drove up to the northern suburbs of Spartakovka, Rynok and Latashinka. Suddenly, as if on a secret command, a barrage opened up from the villages: Russian heavy anti-aircraft guns began the Battle of Stalingrad.

On after another, thirty-seven firing positions were silenced by the Strachwitz Battalion. Direct hit after direct hit smashed into the flak positions and tore them to pieces.

Surprisingly the battalion suffered almost no losses. The mystery was soon solved. When the tank crews reached the shot-up positions they saw to their amazement and horror that the crews of the heavy guns consisted of women, workers from the "Red Barricade" gun factory. They had probably received limited training for the anti-aircraft role but hadn't the slightest idea of how to use their guns in a ground role.

As August 23 came to an end the first German tank drove close past the suburb of Rynok onto the elevated western bank of the Volga. The bank towered almost 100 meters above the two-kilometer-wide stream. The water was dark. A chain of tugs and steamers sailed up and down the river. The Asiatic steppe glistened across from the other side: a melancholy greeting from the infinite space.

The division set up an all-round position for the night near the river, right at the northern edge of the city. In the middle of the position was the division command post. The radio equipment buzzed. Orderlies came and went. Work went on throughout the night: positions were built, mines laid, tanks and equipment repaired, fueled and armed in preparation for the battle for the industrial suburbs of the city.

No one in the victorious and confident 16th Panzer Division could suspect that these suburbs and their factories would never be completely conquered. Or that the last shot in the battle for Stalingrad would also be fired here, where the first had been fired.

Hube's armored thrust to the Volga had covered more than sixty kilometers in one day. The objective, the Volga, had been reached; the river and all lines of communication to the north over the sixty-kilometer-wide land bridge between the Don and Volga had been cut. The Soviets were surprised by this development. Only inaccurate artillery fire fell on the division's hedgehog position during the night. Perhaps the next day Stalingrad would fall before the German assault like ripe fruit into Hube's lap.

And the other side: Stalin, his high command STAVKA, the marshalls, what were their plans for Stalingrad?

Shocked by the German success, Stalin sought a saviour for the city with his name and for the defense of the last great transportation link from the center into the oil region, the Volga. On August 27 he named General Zhukov, his best and toughest man, to the position of acting commander-in-chief of the armed forces and made him responsible for the defense of Stalingrad. He was the only man on the other side who stood up to Stalin and carried out his own strategic measures: no massing of all available forces for the defense of the city of Stalingrad as Stalin demanded, instead the toughest defense of parts of the city by the Sixty-second Army alone, to tie down and wear out German forces, and the planning of a counteroffensive with all reserves in the Stalingrad area with the objective of encircling the Sixth Army. Zhukov's plan was based on a knowledge of German supply difficulties, their neglect in protecting their flank and the reduction in fighting strength likely to be brought about by heavy casualties in a successful battle of attrition in the city. Would Zhukov's calculations prove correct?

CHAPTER II

The Battle in the Approaches

T-34s from the Factory onto the Battlefield – Counterattack by the 35th Soviet Division – The Seydlitz Corps Moves Up – Hoth's Daring Maneuver – Stalingrad's Protective Position Is Torn Open

At 0440 in the morning on August 24, following a dive-bombing attack by Stukas, Battle Group Krumpen launched an attack on Spartakovka, the most northern of Stalingrad's industrial settlements, with tanks, grenadiers, artillery, combat engineers and rocket launchers.

The attackers found an enemy who was neither confused nor irresolute. On the contrary: the panzers and grenadiers were met by a veritable hail of defensive fire. The suburb had been heavily fortified, every house barricaded. A commanding hill, which the soldiers soon dubbed "the big mushroom," was studded with bunkers, machine-gun nests and mortar positions. The Soviet forces included light infantry battalions, workers militias from Stalingrad's factories and elements of the Sixty-second Army. The defenders fought for each meter of ground. An uncompromising order kept them in their positions: "Not one more step back!"

The two Soviet commanders who rigidly enforced this order were Lieutenant General Andrei Ivanovich Yeremenko and his political commissar, member of the Soviet war council Nikita Sergeyevich Krushchev. It was at this time that the officers of the 16th Panzer Division first heard the name Krushchev from captured Soviet soldiers.

The Germans were unable to take Spartakovka with the forces available, as the Soviet positions were virtually impregnable. Soviet forces attacked the northern flank of Hube's hedgehog in an effort to relieve Spartakovka, another indication of how determined they were to defend their position. Battle Groups

Dörnemann and Arenstorff fought off the increasingly strong counterattacks with great difficulty.

Brand-new T-34 tanks, some still unpainted and lacking gunsights, attacked repeatedly. They drove off the production line of the Dzherzhinski Tractor Works through the factory gates and straight onto the battlefield, often crewed by factory workers. Individual T-34s broke through to the command post of the 64th Panzer-Grenadier Regiment and had to be put out of action in close combat.

Only at the Volga, north of Stalingrad, did the attackers meet with success. Engineers, artillerymen and anti-tank units of Battle Group Strehlke were able to seize the landing site of the large rail ferry, thus cutting off communications from Kazakhstan across the Volga to Stalingrad and Moscow.

Strehlke's men dug in among the vineyards on the bank of the Volga. Huge walnut and chestnut trees concealed their guns, which had been moved into position for use against river traffic and landing attempts from the other side.

In spite of its success, the 16th Panzer Division's situation was extremely critical. The Soviets held the approaches to the north city, and at the same time pressured the "hedgehog" with fresh forces brought in from the Voronezh area. Everything depended on the securing of the German corridor across the land bridge and the men of the 16th waited anxiously for the arrival of the 3rd Motorized Infantry Division.

The latter division's advance detachments had moved out of the Don bridgehead wheel to wheel with the 16th Panzer Division and headed east. At noon the paths of the two units separated. While 16th Panzer continued north toward Stalingrad, *Generalmajor* Schlömer's regiments split up and fanned out to the north in order to take up security positions at the Tartar wall in the Kuzmichi area.

The General accompanied the advance detachment. Through his field glasses he saw halted freight trains and feverish unloading activity at the railroad stopping point near Kilometer 564, west of Kuzmichi.

"Attack!"

The motorcycles and tanks of the 103rd Panzer Battalion roared into action. Gunners of the 312th Army Flak Battalion fired a few rounds at the enemy. The Russian columns fled.

The freight cars contained useful goods from America. They had been brought all the way across the Atlantic and Indian Oceans, shipped through the Persian Gulf, then across the Caspian Sea, transported up the Volga and from there sent by rail to the stopping point at the front near Kilometer 564. Now

Schlömer's 3rd Motorized Infantry Division took delivery: lovely new Ford trucks, caterpillar tractors, Jeeps, workshop equipment, mines and equipment for combat engineers.

A new threat emerged as Schlömer's units were racing to join up with the 16th Panzer Division: a Soviet rifle division supported by tanks was hurrying toward the land bridge from the north. As the papers of a captured courier revealed, it was supposed to seal off the German Don bridgeheads and hold open the land bridge for following Soviet forces.

The Soviet division rolled south behind the 3rd Motorized Infantry Division and overran the rear-echelon units of the two most forward divisions of Panzer Corps von Wietersheim. At the same time it slipped between the Don bridgehead of VIII Infantry Corps on the left and the German forces at the Tartar wall and thus initially prevented the German infantry, which had just marched across the Don into the corridor, from linking up with the forward units.

The Soviet thrust severed the lines of communication to the two forward German divisions, which were far ahead of the main force and on their own. Both divisions had to create a twenty-nine-kilometer-wide "hedgehog" position, extending from the Volga to the Tartar wall, in order to fend off Soviet attacks which raged from all sides. At first supplies had to be brought in by air or sent through Soviet lines in strong convoys of armored vehicles.

This unpleasant situation lasted until August 30, when the infantry units of LI Corps under *General* Seydlitz arrived on the right flank with two divisions.

Finally, at the end of August, the land bridge between the Don and the Volga was sealed off to the north. The conditions necessary for a frontal attack on Stalingrad had been created, and the enveloping thrust from the south by Panzer Army Hoth had been safeguarded against surprises from the northern flank.

General von Seydlitz-Kurzbach had won the Oak Leaves in early 1942. It was Seydlitz-Kurzbach, the proven commander of the 12th Infantry Division from Mecklenburg, who had smashed a corridor through to the Demyansk pocket with his Corps Group "Seydlitz" and freed Graf Brockdorff-Ahlefeldt's six divisions from the deadly Soviet encirclement.

In the Battle for Stalingrad Hitler also placed great hopes on the personal bravery and tactical skill of this man, born in Hamburg-Eppendorf with the name of a famous Prussian officer family.

At the end of August Seydlitz launched a frontal attack with two divisions in the center of the Sixth Army across the land bridge toward Stalingrad. His initial objective was Stalingrad's Gumrak airfield.

It was a difficult task for the infantry. The Sixty-second Soviet Army had established a deep and powerful defensive zone at the deeply-eroded Rossoshka. It was part of Stalingrad's inner belt of fortifications which had been laid down at distances of thirty to fifty kilometers around the city to defeat the Sixth Army's attack in the approaches to the city.

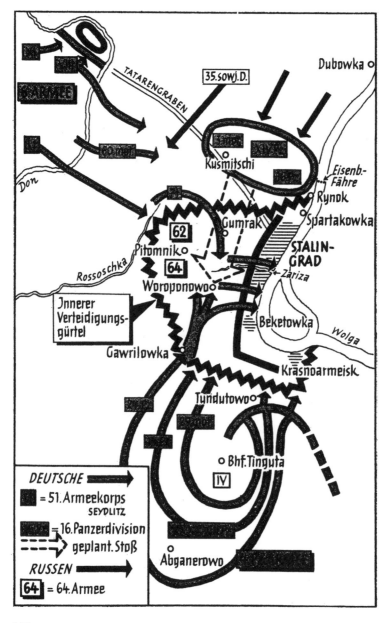

Map 10. On August 30 the Fourth Panzer Army smashed through Stalingrad's inner belt of fortifications. Forces of Paulus' Sixth Army were supposed to drive south to meet them. But XIV Panzer Corps was tied down by enemy attacks. Two days too late Hoth's divisions linked up with the 71st Infantry Division. The Russians withdrew to the edge of the city at the last minute.

Seydlitz was halted by this barrier until September 2. But then, suddenly, there was a break.

The Soviets pulled back. Seydlitz followed, broke through the last Russian positions before the city and on September 7 was already east of Gumrak, eight kilometers from the city limits of Stalingrad.

What had happened? What had led the Russians to suddenly pull back from their inner and final belt of fortifications in front of Stalingrad and surrender the entrance to the city? Had the strength of the troops collapsed? Had the commanders lost control of their units? Exciting questions.

In his memoirs Marshall Chuikov, then still a Lieutenant General and the acting Commander-in-Chief of the Sixty-second Army, cast some light on the mystery of the sudden collapse of the Russian defense in the strong inner belt of fortifications at Rossoshka Brook.

The answer lay in the actions and decisions of the two outstanding antagonists during the battle of movement around Stalingrad: Hoth on the German side and Yeremenko on the Russian.

Yeremenko, the energetic, intrepid and strategically-gifted Commander-in-Chief of the "Stalingrad Front," has provided some interesting details of the great battle in his writings. Chuikov added much in his memoirs and in doing so properly illuminated many aspects of the battle for the first time.

Generaloberst Hoth, the Commander-in-Chief of the Fourth Panzer Army, a Prussian of the best sort, who, like Rommel and Guderian had been with the Goslar light infantry before the war, made available to me, the author, his personal documents on the planning and carrying-out of his offensive which brought the Soviet front to collapse.

At the end of July Hoth's Fourth Panzer Army's direction of advance, toward the Caucasus, was changed and he had been sent from the south through the Kalmuck Steppe toward the knee of the Volga south of Stalingrad. His advance was to relieve the Sixth Army, which at that time was still in the Don bend and in serious trouble.

But the German High Command had only been able to decide upon a half measure, because Hoth was coming with only half his strength: XXXX Panzer Corps, one of two in his army, had to stay behind at the Caucasus Front. His fighting force thus consisted only of Panzer Corps Kempf, with one panzer and one motorized infantry division, and the von Schwedler Corps with three infantry divisions. Later Hoth received the 24th Panzer Division. VI Rumanian Corps under Lieutenant General Dragalina with four infantry divisions was placed under Hoth's command for the purpose of guarding his flanks.

The Soviets immediately recognized the main danger to Stalingrad in Hoth's attack. His panzers were already across the Don, while Paulus' Sixth Army was still pinned down west of the river by Soviet defensive forces.

If Hoth succeeded in driving north from the Kalmuck Steppe and capturing the knee of the Volga with the commanding high ground at Krasnoarmeysk and Betekovka, then Stalingrad's fate was settled and the Volga, the most important shipping artery for American supplies from the Persian Gulf, would be blocked.

On August 19 Hoth approached the southernmost defensive line of the Sixty-fourth Soviet Army and broke through at the first attempt. Panzer Corps Kempf advanced rapidly with the 14th and 24th Panzer Divisions and the 29th Motorized Infantry Division, followed on the left by Schwedler's infantry.

Twenty-four hours later Hoth's tanks and grenadiers were already approaching the heights of Tundutovo, the southern corner post of Stalingrad's inner ring of fortifications.

General Yeremenko had thrown all available forces into this favorable and vital defensive position. Tank units of the First Soviet Tank Army, regiments of the Sixty-fourth Soviet Army, militia units and armed workers defended the in-depth chain of hills, to which had been added barbed wire obstacles and wood and earth fortifications. It was fifteen kilometers to Krasnoarmeysk at the knee of the Volga.

The companies of the 24th Panzer Division attacked repeatedly. But this time the assault failed. *Oberst* Riedel, the commander of the 24th Panzer Regiment, Guderian's longtime adjutant, was killed. The commander of the 21st Panzer-Grenadier Regiment, *Oberst* von Lengerke, was also fatally hit during an advance on the rail line to Krasnoarmeysk. Battalion commanders, company commanders and veteran NCOs fell in the hellish defensive fire of the Soviets.

Hoth ordered a halt. The cool strategist was no risk taker. He realized that here his attack forces were insufficient.

Hoth sat bent over the map at his Plotowitoye command post. His Chief of Staff, General Staff *Oberst* Fangohr, pencilled in the latest situation reports. Two hours earlier Hoth had visited *General* Kempf at his corps headquarters and had driven with him to see *General* Ritter von Hauenschild, where he listened to a report on the 24th Panzer Division's situation. He had also visited *Generalmajor* Heim at the Tinguta railway station. In a *balka*, one of the typical, deeply-eroded ravines of southern Russia, Heim had explained the 14th Panzer Division's difficult situation. Here, too, they could go no farther.

"We have to approach the matter in a different way, Fangohr," reasoned Hoth. "We're bleeding ourselves in front of these damned heights, it's no battlefield for tank units. We must regroup and attack at a completely different spot far from here. Look here . . ."

As the *Generaloberst* developed his plan, Fangohr drew eagerly on the map, compared reconnaissance reports, measured distances. "That will work," he said repeatedly. But he wasn't entirely pleased by Hoth's plan, because they would again lose time by regrouping. As well the shifting of forces would consume a great deal of fuel, and the fuel wasn't there. And finally because those "damned heights" would have to be taken one way or another, because they commanded the entire southern city and its approaches – the same argument raised by *General* Kempf against a regrouping. In the end, however, both Fangohr and Kempf were convinced by their Commander-in-Chief.

Hoth phoned the army group and spoke with Weichs for half an hour. The latter gave his approval and also announced his visit to discuss operational problems, especially the supplying of fuel.

And then it began: orderlies raced off with orders. The telephone wires were never cold. Every man in the headquarters was busy: regroup!

Unnoticed by the enemy, Hoth withdrew his panzer and motorized units from the front by night and replaced them with infantry of the 94th Division from Saxony. In a clever castling maneuver, as if on the sea, he moved his fast units behind and past IV Corps in two nights, assembled them fifty kilometers behind the front in the area around Abganerovo and formed them into a broad attack wedge.

On August 29, to the complete surprise of the enemy, he sent this armada north into the flank of the Sixty-fourth Soviet Army. Instead of fighting his way over the tank and artillery studded heights of Krasnoarmeysk and Betekovka in a frontal attack on the knee of the Volga, he intended to outflank these positions and the masses of enemy troops due west of Stalingrad, then wheel about, attack the entire area of high ground in the south of the city from the flank and at the same time encircle the left wing of the Sixty-fourth Army.

Things began deceptively well. On August 30, together with the hard-fighting infantry of IV Corps, the fast units broke through Stalingrad's inner belt of fortifications near Gavrilovka and overran the rear Soviet artillery positions. By the evening of August 31 Hauenschild and his 24th Panzer Division had reached the Stalingrad-Karpovka rail line. It was an unexpected penetration, twenty kilometers deep.

This changed the entire picture. A great opportunity now presented itself. Not in relation to crossing the heights of Betekovka and Krasnoarmeysk, no, the encirclement of the two Soviet armies west of Stalingrad, the Sixty-second and Sixty-fourth, was suddenly within reach if the Sixth Army drove south toward Hoth with fast forces to close the trap. Hoth's daring operation had created the possibility of destroying the two enemy armies guarding Stalingrad.

The army group command recognized this opportunity at once. An order radioed to *General* Paulus at midday on August 30 said: "After the capture of a bridgehead near Gavrilovka at 1000 today by Fourth Panzer Army, everything depends on Sixth Army concentrating strongest possible forces in spite of the extremely tense defensive situation... attacking in a generally southerly direction ... in order to destroy the enemy forces west of Stalingrad in conjunction with Fourth Panzer Army. Decision requires ruthless stripping of forces from secondary fronts."

On August 31 the army group learned of the 24th Panzer Division's deep breakthrough west of Voroponovo, On September 1 Weichs once again sent Paulus a detailed, and what was probably intended as an admonishing, order. Subparagraph one said: "As a result of the decisive success by Fourth Panzer Army on 31.8. opportunity has arisen to attack and smash the enemy forces south and west of the Stalingrad-Voroponovo-Gumrak rail line. The main point is to establish contact between both armies soon and then break into the city center."

The Fourth Panzer Army reacted quickly: on September 1 *General* Kempf sent the 14th Panzer Division and the 29th Motorized Infantry Division after the 24th Panzer Division, direction Pitomnik, at the same time ruthlessly depleting their former sectors.

But Sixth Army did not come. *General* Paulus initially saw himself unable to release forces for the thrust to the south in the face of heavy Soviet attacks against his northern front. In his view it was impossible to successfully hold the northern barrier with anti-tank guns, a few tanks and assault guns, even with the support of the close-support aircraft of VIII Fliegerkorps, while detaching an armored group consisting of five panzer battalions of XIV Panzer Corps for a drive to the south. He feared the collapse of his northern front.

Perhaps he was right. Perhaps another decision would have been a gamble. In any case the great opportunity was missed. Twenty-four hours later, on the morning of September 2, armed reconnaissance by the 24th Panzer Division ascertained that there was no enemy before the German front. The Russians had withdrawn from their southern defensive position, just as they had abandoned their defensive position in the western sector in front of the Seydlitz Corps the same day. What had caused the Russians to take this surprising action?

General Chuikov, the acting Commander-in-Chief of the Sixty-fourth Army, had recognized the threatening situation at the front resulting from Hoth's advance. He alerted Lieutenant General Yeremenko. The latter not only recognized the danger, but he acted immediately, in complete contrast to the clumsiness of Russian commanders in similar situation in earlier times. Yeremenko made the difficult and dangerous, but correct decision to abandon the well-constructed inner belt of fortifications. He sacrificed bunkers, barbed wire entanglements, anti-tank obstacles and infantry trenches in order to save his divisions from the threat of encirclement, and withdrew his two armies to a new, improvised defensive line near the city limits.

This example shows how thoroughly the Soviet command had declared itself for the new tactic decided on by STAVKA in the early summer: under no circumstances were they to allow large units to be encircled. In the name of this new principle they accepted the danger of the loss of the city of Stalingrad.

When, on the afternoon of September 2, *General* Paulus finally decided to attack southward with the fast forces of XIV Panzer Corps, and when, on September 3, the infantry of the Seydlitz Corps finally linked up with Hoth's armored spearheads, the pocket which the army group had wanted and strived for on August 30 was closed, but by then the enemy was gone. Forty-eight hours too late!

The army group now gave orders to Paulus and Hoth to exploit the situation and enter the city as quickly as possible.

CHAPTER III

The Drive Into the City

General Lopatin Wants to Give Up Stalingrad – General Chuikov Is Sworn In by Krushchev – The Regiments of the 71st Infantry Division Storm Central Stalingrad – Grenadiers of the 24th Panzer Division at the Main Railway Station – Chuikov's Last Brigade – Ten Vital Hours – Rodimzev's Guard

The Tsaritsa flows through the middle of Stalingrad. The river's deep ravine divides the city into northern and southern halves. The Tsaritsa received its name when Tsaritsyn became Stalingrad, and it still has it today even though Stalingrad has again become Volgograd. In 1942 the famous-infamous ravine was the boundary position, the border between the armies of Hoth and Paulus. The inner wings of both armies were supposed to advance quickly along the river, through the city to the Volga. There were indications that there were only Soviet rear guards fighting in the city and that the enemy would give up Stalingrad itself.

In Marshall Chuikov's memoirs one can read how catastrophic was the situation of the two Soviet Stalingrad armies following the surrender of the approaches to the fortress. Even experienced army commanders weren't giving much for Stalingrad's chances. General Lopatin, the Commander-in-Chief of the Sixty-second Army, was of the opinion that the city could not be held and decided to abandon Stalingrad. When he tried to put his decision into action the Chief of Staff, General Krylenko, withheld his permission and alerted Krushchev and Yeremenko. Lopatin was relieved.

Why he made such a decision is understandable when one reads Chuikov's description of the situation in Stalingrad. He wrote: "It was bitter to give up these last kilometers and meters of ground before Stalingrad, and to have to witness the enemy's superiority in forces and military ability and his initiative."

The Marshall experienced and described how the mechanics of the *Sovkhoz*, in which were situated the headquarters of the Sixty-fourth Army, secretly slipped away – over to the Germans. "The roads to Stalingrad and the Volga were clogged. Families of collective farmers and Sovkhoz workers were on the roads with all their livestock. All were striving to reach the Volga crossings, driving their animals before them, carrying their belongings on their backs. Stalingrad was burning. Rumors that the Germans were already in the city spread panic."

That is how it looked. But Stalin was not willing to give up his city, with 445,000 inhabitants, without a bitter struggle. He sent Nikita S. Krushchev, his most trusted follower and an ardent bolshevik, to the front as political advisor to mobilize the armies and the civilian population for the final battle. Nikita Krushchev made sacrificing one's life for Stalin's city a point of honor for every communist.

The three-volume history of the Second World War by Lieutenant General Platanov provides some numbers to back up this fact:

50,000 civilian volunteers were enrolled in the so-called "people's defense."

75,000 inhabitants were assigned to the Sixty-second Army.

3,000 young women were conscripted as nurses and communications assistants.

7,000 thirteen- to sixteen-year-old members of the Communist youth organization "*Komsomol*" were armed and placed in the fighting units.

Everyone became a soldier. Workers were ordered out of the factories onto the battlefield with the weapons they had produced. As quickly as they were built, the cannon of the "Red Brigade" gun factory were taken from the factory buildings, placed in position on the factory grounds and fired. Workers made up the gun crews.

On September 12 Yeremenko and Krushchev appointed General Chuikov to command the Sixty-second Army, which had been led by Chief of Staff Krylenko since Lopatin's removal, and handed over to him the defense of the Volga fortress. Their choice was an excellent one. Chuikov was the best man available: tough, ambitious, strategically gifted, personally brave and exceptionally tenacious. He hadn't been part of the catastrophes suffered by the Red Army in 1941, as he had been in the far east. He was fresh and hadn't been shaken by the terrible failures like so many of his comrades.

At the stroke of ten on September 12 Chuikov reported to Krushchev and Yeremenko in the Jamy army group headquarters, a small nest on the far left bank of the Volga. Interestingly Krushchev led the discussion, not the military

Commander-in-Chief Yeremenko.

According to Chuikov's writings Krushchev said: "The former Commander-in-Chief of the Sixty-second Army, General Lopatin, is of the opinion that his army cannot hold Stalingrad. But there is no more going back. He was therefore relieved of his post. With the approval of the supreme commander the war council calls upon you, comrade Chuikov, to assume command of the Sixty-second Army. How do you see your mission?"

"The question was unexpected," wrote Chuikov, "but there wasn't much time for me to think about it. So I said: 'The surrender of Stalingrad would destroy the morale of our people. I swear not to abandon the city. We will hold Stalingrad or die there.' N.S. Krushchev and A.I. Yeremenko looked at me and said that I understood my mission correctly."

Ten hours later the attack against central Stalingrad by the Seydlitz Corps got under way. Chuikov's army headquarters on High Point 102 were bombed out and the General had to retreat to a shelter in the Tsaritsa gorge with his staff, cook and waitress.

The next day, September 14, the men of *General* von Hartmann's 71st Infantry Division were already in the city. In a surprise move they fought their way to the city center and even seized a narrow corridor to the bank of the Volga.

At the same hour, south of the Tsaritsa gorge the panzer-grenadiers of the 24th Panzer Division stormed through the streets of the old city, the former Tsaritsyn, took the main railway station and on September 16 reached the Volga with the von Heyden Battalion. Elements of the 14th Panzer Division and the 29th Motorized Infantry Division had been between Betekovka and Stalingrad, in the suburb of Kuporosnoye, since September 10 and had sealed off the city and river to the south. Only in the northern part of the city did Chuikov still have a foothold. "We must gain time," he said to his commanders. "Time to bring in reserves, time to wear out the Germans."

Chuikov coldly modified the American maxim "time is money" to "time is blood." Time is blood. From then on this idea dominated the city of Stalingrad.

Chuikov's cook Glinka breathed easier when he had reached his new kitchen in the command post. He now had ten meters of earth over his head. He sighed happily to the General's waitress: "Tazya, my dove, here there won't be any shell fragments falling into the borscht. No shell can pierce this roof." "Well," answered Tazya, "the General said that a 1,000-kilo bomb can." "1,000 kilos, are there many of those?" asked the cook anxiously.

Tazya comforted him: "It would have to be a tremendous fluke, because it would have to fall directly on our bunker – the General said so."

The noise from the front sounded very far away in the quiet keep of the large underground vault. The ceiling and walls had been carefully planked with boards. There were dozens of partitions for the officials of the army headquarters staff. In the middle was a large room for the General and his chief of staff. One exit from this so-called Tsaritsyn dugout, which had been built that summer as headquarters for the army group, led into the Tsaritsa gorge close to the steep bank of the Volga, the other opened into Pushkin Street.

On the planked wall of Chuikov's working room hung a map of the city of Stalingrad, three meters high and two meters wide: the general staff battle map. The map was not of fronts in the hinterland. The scale was no longer the kilometer, rather it was the meter. The battle was for street corners, blocks of houses, individual houses.

The Army's Chief of Staff, General Krylov, pencilled in the latest reports: the German attacks in blue, the Russian defensive positions in red. The blue arrows were moving ever closer to the command post.

"The German battalions are attacking the Mamai Kurgan and the main railway station. They are supported by tanks. A panzer division is fighting in front of the south station," reported Krylov.

The German units he was referring to were battalions of the 71st and 295th Infantry Divisions and panzer regiments of the 22nd and 24th Panzer Divisions.

Chuikov stared at the map of the city. "What has become of our counterattacks?"

"They have been halted. German fliers have been over the city since daybreak. They're nailing everything to the ground."

A runner brought a hand-drawn situation map from the commander of the 42nd Rifle Brigade, Colonel Batrakov. Krylov reached for the pencil and drew a semi-circle around the command post. "The front is 800 meters from us, Comrade General," he reported with studied officialism.

800 meters. It was twelve noon on the 14th of September. Chuikov knew what Krylov was getting at. They had as the last reserve a tank brigade with nineteen T-34s. Should they commit it?

"What's the situation on the south city's left wing?" asked Chuikov.

Krylov extended the blue attack arrow of the German 29th Motorized Infantry Division through Kuporosnoye. The suburb had fallen. General Fremerey's Thuringians pushed on in the direction of the grain silo. The sawmill and the cannery were already within the German lines. The Soviet defensive lines extended only from the southern ferry landing to the tall grain silo.

Chuikov picked up the telephone and called the army group. He described the situation to Yeremenko. The latter implored him: "Use all means to hold onto the central harbor with the landing point. The high command is sending you the 13th Guards Rifle Division. It's 10,000 men strong, an elite unit. Hold the bridgehead open another twenty-four hours and also try to defend the ferry landing in the south city."

There was sweat on Chuikov's brow. The air in the tunnel was sticky. "Get going, Krylov, scrape together everything, make the staff officers battle group commanders. We must keep the crossing open for Rodimzev's guard."

The last brigade with its total of nineteen tanks was thrown into the battle: one battalion in front of the command post, from where it also covered the main station and the central harbor, a second in a line from the grain silo to south of the landing point.

At 1400 Major General Rodimzev appeared, "Hero of the Soviet Union," legendary unit commander, dirty and bloody: German fighter-bombers had harried him. He reported that his division was on the other side of the river and was to cross the Volga during the night. Frowning, he looked at the blue and red lines on the map of the city.

At 1600 Chuikov again spoke with Yeremenko by telephone. It was still five hours until the onset of night. In his memoirs he described his thoughts in those five hours:

"Would our dispersed and battered elements and units in the central sector be able to hold for another ten or twelve hours? That was my greatest worry. If the soldiers and commanders were not equal to this almost superhuman task, the 13th Guards Rifle Division could not cross and would become nothing more than a witness to a bitter tragedy."

Just before dusk Major Chopka, commander of the last reserves which had been committed in the harbor area, appeared. He reported:

"A single T-34 is still able to fire, but can't move. The brigade has only 100 men left."

Chuikov looked at him: "Assemble your people around the tank and hold the entrance to the harbor. If you fail to hold I will have you shot."

Chopka was killed. Half of his people fell. But the rest held.

Night finally came. All the headquarters' officers were at the harbor. As the companies of Rodimzev's guards division came across the Volga they were thrown into the most important defensive positions to halt the assault by the

German 71st Infantry Division and pin down the 295th Infantry Division on the Mamai Kurgan, the commanding Hill 102. These were decisive hours: Rodimzev's guard prevented the Germans from taking central Stalingrad in the first attempt on September 15. Their sacrifice saved Stalingrad.

Twenty-four hours later the 13th Guards Rifle Division had been smashed to pieces, blasted by bombs from the Stukas, wiped out by shells and heavy machine-guns.

A guards division was also fighting in the south city, the 35th under Colonel Dubyanski. Its reserve battalions were brought across by ferry to the south landing point and thrown against the spearheads of the 29th Motorized Infantry Division in an effort to hold the line between the grain silo and the ferry landing.

But Stukas pounded the Soviet battalions, and they were wiped out in the pincers of the 29th and 94th Infantry Divisions.

There was heavy fighting in the grain silo, which was filled with wheat; every floor of this huge, fortress-like cement block was fought over. The assault squads and combat engineers of the 71st Infantry Regiment battled the remnants of the 35th Guards Rifle Division in the smoke and stench of the shouldering wheat.

On the morning of September 16 things again looked bad for Chuikov. The 24th Panzer Division had taken the south station, turned west and smashed the Soviet defenses at the edge of the city and on the barracks hill. There was bloody fighting on the Mamai Kurgan and at the main railway station.

Chuikov telephoned war council member Nikita Sergeyevich Krushchev: "A few more such battles and the army will be wiped out. Once again we have no reserves. I urgently need two to three fresh divisions."

Krushchev mobilized Stalin. He released two fully-equipped elite units from his personal reserve: a marine infantry brigade with tough Arctic Ocean sailors and a tank brigade. The tank brigade was deployed around the main harbor in the city center so as to hold the supply center for the front. The marines were thrown into the south city. The two units prevented the front from collapsing on September 17.

The same day the German High Command transferred command of all German units fighting on the Stalingrad front to Sixth Army. As a result, XXXXVIII Panzer Corps, part of Hoth's Fourth Panzer Army, came under Paulus' orders. Hitler pressed: "You must make an end of it, the city must fall."

One fact explains why this did not happen even though the German tank crews, grenadiers, combat engineers, anti-tank gunners and flak soldiers grimly tackled one house after another: thanks to Krushchev's bitter battle for the last reserves of the Red Army, Chuikov received one division after another in the period from September 15 to October 3, six in total – six fresh and relatively well-equipped infantry divisions, including two guards divisions. These forces were all thrown into the ruins of central Stalingrad and the factory installations and workshop halls of the northern part of the city, which had been transformed into fortresses.

In the first phase the German attack on the city was carried out with seven divisions, units weakened by the weeks-long battles between the Don and the Volga. There were never more than ten German divisions in the battle for the city at any time.

Of course the once so powerful Siberian Sixty-second Army was no longer very strong in the first phase of the battle. Costly battles and retreats had gnawed away at its physical and moral strength. On paper it still had five divisions as well as five tank and five rifle brigades at the beginning of September, or the equivalent of about nine divisions. This sounds like a lot, but the 38th Mechanized Brigade, for example, had a total of only 600 men and the 244th Rifle Division 1,500, which was equivalent to the fighting strength of a regiment.

No wonder that General Lopatin was of the opinion that Stalingrad could not be defended with this army and recommended that it be abandoned and his forces withdrawn behind the Volga. But determination had a great deal of influence, and fortune, which so often favored good commanders, had already decided many battles.

On October 1 Chuikov had eleven divisions and nine brigades, or roughly fifteen and a half divisions. This did not include the armed workers and militia units.

The Germans were superior in the air however: on average *General* Fiebig's VIII Fliegerkorps flew one thousand sorties per day. Chuikov stressed repeatedly the tremendous effect of the German Stukas and fighter-bombers on the defenders. Assembly areas for counterattacks were smashed, barricades torn apart, communications destroyed, command headquarters pounded into the ground.

Later there was a surprising realization: the factory buildings, which were smashed into impenetrable piles of rubble by Stuka bombs and artillery, offered more advantages to the defenders than to the German attackers. The German infantry was too weak to overcome this last stand by the Soviets. And not only were the German forces short on infantry, there were shortages of hand grenades and mortar ammunition as well.

Admittedly the easing of the situation at the Don allowed the Sixth Army to withdraw units such as the 305th Infantry Division, which was then used to relieve one of the exhausted units of LI Army Corps, but *General* Paulus did not receive a single fresh division. Other than five pioneer battalions, which were flown in, he received replacements for his bloodied regiments only from within the army area. In autumn 1942 the German High Command had no reserves on the Eastern Front. Serious crises had arisen in every army group from Leningrad to the Caucasus.

In the north *Feldmarschall* von Manstein had to launch a counterattack with the bulk of his former Crimea divisions against Soviet forces which had penetrated deep into the German front. By October 2, following tough defensive fighting, he had created some breathing space for Army Group North at the Volkhov in the First Battle of Lake Ladoga.

In the Sytshevka-Rzhev area *Generaloberst* Model was able to fend off Russian breakthrough attempts only with great difficulty and by summoning all his forces and was forced to battle three Soviet armies.

In the center and on the southern wing, too, *Feldmarschall* von Kluge needed every hand to prevent a breakthrough toward Smolensk.

Finally, in the passes of the Caucasus and at the Terek the armies of Army Group A were engaged in a desperate race with the onset of winter.

There were divisions enough in France, Belgium and Holland, but they sat idle. Here Hitler, who underestimated the Russians, made the mistake of overestimating the western allies. He already feared an allied invasion in autumn 1942. The secret services of the Americans, British and Soviets promoted this fear by leaking spurious reports of a second front. The specter of invasion, which didn't become a reality until twenty months later, tied down twenty-nine divisions, for example the well-equipped "*Leibstandarte*" and the 6th and 7th Panzer Divisions. A quarter of these would have been enough to turn the tide on the Stalingrad-Caucasus front.

CHAPTER IV

The Last Front at the Riverbank

Chuikov's Flight from the Tsaritsyn Dugout – The Southern City in German Hands – The Riverbank – The Grain Silo – The Bakery – The "Tennis Racket" – Nine-tenths of the City in German Hands

During the night of September 17/18 Chuikov was forced to abandon his bomb-proof Tsaritsyn dugout. In reality it was more of a flight, because at about midday grenadiers of the Lower Saxon 71st Infantry Division, whose tactical symbol was a clover leaf, suddenly appeared at the entrance to Pushkin Street. Chuikov's staff officers had to reach for their submachine-guns. The tunnel quickly filled with wounded and stragglers. Using some pretext or another, drivers, runners and officers smuggled themselves past the guards into the secure bunker "to discuss urgent matters." Since the tunnel installation had no ventilation, the underground rooms were soon filled with stench, smoke and heat. There was only one thing to do: "Out!"

The headquarters guard covered the retreat through the second exit to the Tsaritsa Gorge. But German assault squads of *Major* Fredebold's 191st Infantry Regiment were already roaming about there. Under cover of night Chuikov made his way to the bank of the Volga with the situation map and his most important papers and together with Krylov crossed to the other side by boat.

There he boarded one of the armored cutters and sailed to the northern city's upper landing site. From there he moved into a command post behind the "Red Barricade" gun factory: a few holes blasted out of the 200-meter-high wall of the riverbank, out of reach of the German artillery. The dugouts were linked by well-camouflaged communications trenches dug in the steep bank.

The cook Glinka was installed in the test shaft of the drainage pipe of the "Red Barricade" works. With true acrobatic skill waitress Tazya had to balance the pots and pans and carry them up the shaft's ladder to the daylight and then over a footbridge at the steep bank into the Commander-in-Chief's earth bunker.

The headquarters' rations strength had certainly shrunk significantly. Various senior officers, including Chuikov's representatives for artillery and pioneer troops, for tank and mechanized troops, had slipped away during the change of position and had stayed on the left bank of the Volga. "We cried no tears for them," wrote Chuikov, "the air was purer without them."

The change of scene which the Commander-in-Chief of Stalingrad had to undertake was symbolic, and not only in respect to morale: the focal point of the battle shifted to the north, the southern and central parts of the city could no longer be held.

The last act in the southern city began on September 22. Assault squads of the 29th Motorized Infantry Division, together with grenadiers of the 94th Infantry Division and the 14th Panzer Division, stormed the smoke-blackened grain silo. When engineers blasted open the entrances a handful of Soviet marines, part of a machine-gun platoon under Sergeant Andrei Chosyainov, tumbled out and were taken prisoner. They were the last survivors. Also occupied was the southern landing point of the Volga ferry. The grenadiers of *Generalleutnant* Pfeiffer's 94th Infantry Division from Saxony, whose division emblem featured the Sword of Meissen, secured the bank of the Volga at the southern edge of the city.

Soviet resistance also collapsed in Stalingrad Center, in the heart of the city. Only a few nests of resistance continued to hold out in the rubble of the main station and at the landing site of the large steam-ferry in the central harbor.

On September 27 one could have said that Stalingrad had been taken, based on a standard assessment of a battle for a city. For example, the 71st Infantry Division had reached the Volga along the entire width of the division's sector: the 211th Infantry Regiment south of the Minina Gorge, the 191st Infantry Regiment between the Minina and Tsaritsa Gorges, the 194th Infantry Regiment to the north.

Now the battle was for the northern workers settlements and the city's industrial plants, names that were have become well-known: the "Red Barricade" gun factory, the "Red October" iron works, the "Dzherzhinski" tractor works, the "Lazur" chemical factory with the famous "tennis racket," as the factory's rail installation was called on account of its shape – these were the forts of the industrial city of Stalingrad.

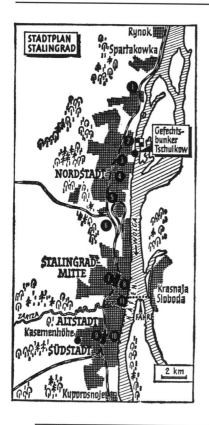

Map 11: 1. Tractor works, 2. "Red Barricade" gun factory, 3. bakery, 4. "Red October" steel or metalurgical works, 5. Lazur chemical factory with "Tennis Racket," 6. "Mamai Kurgan" hill, 7. Main railway station, 8. Department store and "Red Square," 9. South railway station, 10. Grain silo, 11. Chuikov's Tsaritsa dugout.

In terms of determination, concentration of fire and the massing of troops in a small area, the battle for the northern section of Stalingrad can only be compared with the materiel battles of World War I, but especially with the Battle of Verdun, where half a million German and French soldiers were killed in six months in 1916.

The battle in Stalingrad North was a close-quarters struggle. The Russians, especially strong in a defensive role, profited from their superiority at camouflage and their skill in utilizing the terrain. As well the Russian soldier was more practiced and better trained than his German counterpart in fighting from houses and barricades.

In his analysis of the Battle of Stalingrad, Manfred Kehrig declared: "Especially lacking was training in fighting in built-up areas. The high losses were primarily attributable to this last shortcoming."

Another factor was that Chuikov, under the watchful eye of Krushchev, fanaticized Soviet resistance to the boiling point. Three slogans were hammered into every company that crossed the Volga to Stalingrad:

Every soldier a fortress!
There is no land for us behind the Volga!
We must fight or fall!

This was total war. This was the realization of the words: "Time is blood." The chronicler of the 14th Panzer Division, Rolf Grams, at that time a *Major* and commander of the 64th Motorcycle Battalion, cited a combat report which said: "It was an awful, grueling battle on and under the earth, in the rubble, cellars and sewers of the large city and its industrial plants. Man against man. Tanks climbed over mountains of scrap and rubble, crawled screaming through chaotic destroyed workshop halls and fired from close range into blocked-up streets and narrow factory yards... However all this could have been endured. But then there were the deep, weather-beaten loess ravines, which fell away steeply to the Volga and from which the Soviets repeatedly threw fresh forces into the battle. The enemy could not be seen in the dense forests of the lower-lying, east bank of the Volga, neither his batteries nor his infantry, but they were there and they fired, and night after night hundreds of boats brought reinforcements over the mighty river into the ruins of the city."

This supply, this steady flow of replacements for the defenders coming across the river, this fresh blood continually flowing through the lifeline of the Volga, was the problem of the battle. The secret lay in these loess ravines on the bank of the Volga. In this steep bank, which the German artillery could not reach, sat the Soviet headquarters, hospitals and munitions depots. Here were ideal assembly places for the men and materiel transported across the river during the night. Here were the starting positions for counterattacks. Here the run-off drains of the industrial plants, now long, empty tunnels, led into the German rear. Soviet troops crawled through. Cautiously they raised the manhole covers, brought machine-guns into position. Then their bursts of fire sprayed the advancing German units from behind, mowed down the columns bringing up food and supplies. Their ambush completed, the attackers closed the manhole covers and headed back.

The German assault squads sent against these ambushes were helpless. Yes, this steep riverbank was as valuable as an in-depth, bomb-proof system of fortifications. Often the German regiments in their battle sectors were separated from the bank of the Volga by only a few hundred meters.

General Doerr was justified, therefore, when in his study of the Stalingrad battle he declared: "Therefore for both sides, attacker and defender, the decision lay in the last hundred meters before the Volga."

At the end of September *General* Paulus launched a concentrated attack in an attempt to storm the last bulwarks of Stalingrad one after another. The German forces were insufficient for an all-encompassing attack on the entire industrial complex however.

Approaching from the south across the airfield, the East Prussian 24th Panzer Division stormed the "Krasny Oktyabr" and "Barrikady" settlements. The panzer regiment and elements of the 389th Infantry Division also took the workers settlement of the "Dzherzhinski" tractor works and on October 18 were fighting in the brickyard. The East Prussians were thus at the steep bank of the Volga. Having eliminated resistance in this area the division rolled south again into the battle zone of the "Lazur" chemical factory and the "tennis racket."

The men of the 24th had successfully completed their mission, but the division had paid a heavy price: the grenadier regiments were equivalent in strength to battalions, and the remnants of the panzer regiment were no better than a reinforced tank company. Crews without tanks were employed as rifle companies.

On October 14 *General* Jaenecke stormed the "Dzherzhinski" tractor works, one of the largest tank-producing facilities in the Soviet Union, with the Hessians of his 389th Infantry Division and the regiments of the 14th Panzer Division. The tanks and grenadiers struggled through the wreckage of the huge factory complex to the bank of the Volga, then turned south and fought their way into the "Red Barricade" gun factory. They were now not far from the steep riverbank close to Chuikov's command post.

The battalions of the 30th Infantry Division from Baden-Württemburg, the "Bodensee Division," moved into the wreckage of the tractor works' huge production halls, where Soviet resistance flared up repeatedly. The division had been thrown into Stalingrad's tractor factory from the Don front on October 15. The men from Germany's Bodensee area battled companies of the 308th Soviet Rifle Division under Colonel Gurtyev. This state of affairs shows how true was the sentence which General Chuikov wrote in his diary: "The general staff map has been replaced by a city quarter street plan, by a sketch of the maze of ruins of a factory installation."

On October 24 the 14th Panzer Division reached its objective, the first house of the bakery at the south corner of the "Red Brigade." The attack was carried out by the 64th Motorcycle Battalion, which took the so-called first house.

On the 25th the attack on the second house was halted by the defensive fire of the Russians. *Unteroffizier* Esser squatted behind a knocked-out armored car. At the corner of the house lay the company commander – dead. Ten steps behind him the platoon leader – dead. And beside him a squad leader groaned softly in the delirium of a head wound.

Then Esser was seized by fury. He jumped to his feet. "Let's go," he screamed. And the platoon followed. It was sixty meters to the building. Sixty meters across a flat courtyard with no cover. But they made it. Gasping they threw themselves down at the wall of the house, blasted a hole with an explosive charge, crawled through and found themselves inside. The Soviets squatted behind the windows and fired into the courtyard. Before they knew what was happening the submachine-guns roared to life behind them.

Next floor. The Germans climb the stone stairs cautiously. A man before every doorway. "*Ruki werch!*" Shocked, the Russians put up their hands. In this way Esser took the building with twelve men, took eighty prisoners and captured an anti-tank gun and sixteen heavy machine-guns. A hundred dead Soviets lay on the sad battlefield of the bakery's second house.

Meanwhile *Hauptmann* Domaschk and the remnants of the 103rd Rifle Regiment were fighting over at the row of houses belonging to the administration building. All the company commanders had been killed.

The brigade sent *Leutnant* Stempel from its headquarters staff so that at least one officer would be available as company commander. A *Feldwebel* briefed him on the situation.

Then Stempel and his motorcycle troops moved forward between the railroad tracks and the shattered walls to attack. Stukas dropped bombs in front of them. Stempel raced through the bombs and took the ruins of the administration complex. He was now not far from the riverbank.

But only two dozen men were left, and fresh Soviets kept pouring out of the gorges of the steep riverbank. Wounded with bandages, led by staff officers. Train units. Even sailors of the ferry line. They fell, but there were always more.

Stempel sent a runner to the rear with a message: I can't hold without replacements!

Soon afterward seventy men came; they had been sent by the forward personnel directing center straight into the battle. They were led by an *Oberleutnant*. Two days later all seventy had been killed or wounded. Stempel and his men of the 103rd Rifle Regiment had to fall back and abandon the edge of the Volga.

Nevertheless, in those days four-fifths of Stalingrad was in German hands. When, on October 26, the Westphalians of the 16th Panzer Division and the infantry of the 94th Infantry Division, which bore the main burden of the fighting here, took the hotly contested suburb of Spartakovka, having smashed both the Soviet 124th and 149th Rifle Brigades, nine-tenths of Stalingrad had fallen.

The 45th Soviet Rifle Division held only a small section of the shoreline in front of Chuikov's command post in the riverbank, perhaps 200 meters in diameter. To the south, in the "Red October" steel works, only the rubble of the eastern section, the sorting section, the steel casting works and the calibrating station were still in Russian hands. Here elements of the 39th Guards Rifle Division under General Guryev fought for every piece of wall still standing. The German assault squads had to pay a price in blood for every corner, every pile of rubble. Contact with the unit to the north, the 14th Panzer Division, was maintained by the companies of the 100th Light Infantry Division, which had been moved into Stalingrad from the Don bend in late September. It was another example of how the Don front was stripped of German units, which were replaced by Romanian and Italian units, in order to take damned Stalingrad. South of the "Red October" steel works only the chemical factory with the "tennis racket" and a tiny bridgehead around the steam ferry landing in the central harbor were still held by the Soviets.

Taken all together, at the beginning of November Chuikov was still defending a few factory buildings and a few kilometers of the Volga riverbank.

CHAPTER V

Disaster at the Don

Dangerous Signs on Sixth Army's Flank – Unlucky Month of November – Another Assault on the Bank of the Volga – The Romanian Front Collapses – Battle in Sixth Army's Rear – Another Breakthrough South of Stalingrad – The 29th Motorized Infantry Division Hits Back – The Russians Take Kalach – Paulus Flies into the Pocket

Stalingrad lies on the same degree of latitude as Vienna, Paris or Vancouver, Canada. In these latitudes it is still relatively mild at the beginning of November. *General* Strecker, commander of XI Corps in the great Don bend, therefore drove to the command post of the Austrian 44th Infantry Division, the *Hoch und Deutschmeister* Division, wearing his light coat.

In the fields he saw soldiers gathering potatoes and turnips, corn straw and hay: supplies for the winter.

General Stecker's XI Corps was supposed to guard Stalingrad's left flank in the great Don bend. But the loop in the Don was a hundred kilometers long. And one hundred kilometers couldn't be guarded by three divisions. So for better or worse the *General* moved into a position which cut across the loop. He saved fifty kilometers but was forced to leave the Kremenskaya river bend area to the Soviets.

Lieutenant General Batov, the commander of the Sixty-fifth Soviet Army, took advantage of this the opportunity immediately. He crossed the Don and established a fairly deep bridgehead on the south bank. Daily Batov's regiments attacked the positions held by Strecker's divisions in an attempt to bring about the collapse of the German Don flank.

Strecker's divisions were in good positions, however. As a case in point, *Oberst* Boje, who greeted the commanding general at the command post of the

134th Infantry Regiment, had built such an ingenious system of positions that he was able to report with quiet confidence: "The Russians won't get through here, *Herr General.*"

Strecker requested detailed briefings, but he was especially interested in what the division's observation post, which was situated in a small wood southwest of Sirotinskaya, had been observing and reporting to him since the end of October.

There was a good view across the Don from the wooded heights. Using a scissors telescope they could see the positions of the German VIII Corps as far as the Volga. But better than that there was an extremely good view of the enemy hinterland, which lay before their eyes like a relief map. And what they saw was extraordinarily revealing: by day and night the Russians were moving troops and material up to the Don, some in front of Strecker's front, but mostly opposite the neighboring Third Romanian Army on the left.

Each evening the concerned corps headquarters recorded these reports, which were confirmed by the reconnaissance aircraft of *Luftflotte* 4. And every morning Strecker passed them on to the headquarters of *General* Paulus in Golubinskaya.

And Paulus had been forwarding them to the army group since the end of October.

And the army group to Führer Headquarters: the Russians were massing forces in the Sixth Army's deep flank.

Manning this flank on the Don, in addition to Strecker's corps, was the Third Romanian Army, occupying a front of about 150 kilometers. Beyond the Romanians were the Eighth Italian and Second Hungarian Armies.

"Why are there only Romanians in such a wide sector, *Herr General?*" the staff officers asked their commanding general. They had nothing against the Romanians, they were brave soldiers, but everyone them knew that their equipment was miserable, even more miserable than that of the Italians. They carried obsolete weapons from World War I, had insufficient numbers of anti-tank weapons and their supply system was inadequate. Everyone at the front knew it.

But, like Italy's Mussolini, the Romanian head of state Marshall Antonescu had requested that the forces made available for the Eastern Front were only to be used in a body and under their own army command.

Hitler would rather have followed the wishes of his generals and turned to the "corset-stay" method, which meant placing a German unit beside every foreign unit. However this plan failed to come about due to national sensitivity, especially on the part of the Romanians. They formed the largest allied contingent and Marshall Antonescu needed prestige and authority with the military to strengthen his position as head of state.

After a months-long tug of war Hitler gave in, and so the job of guarding the flank of the main German force near Stalingrad was entrusted to allied armies whose fighting qualities were suspect. Not all Romanian soldiers had even a coat or at least a blanket. The Romanian Army possessed no active NCO corps, indispensable in such a campaign. The quality of Romanian officers varied greatly. For many the concept of caring for their troops was a foreign one. In addition to this there was a cumbersome reporting system, a chaotic supply technique and unexplainable command decisions: for example the commander of the 1st Romanian Tank Division was not a tank soldier, rather he was the former police president of Bucharest.

Hitler recognized the danger on the Sixth Army's long flank. He referred to it repeatedly at situation briefings in August and again in September. With great interest he studied an old map from 1920 which *General* Halder had given him. It showed how in that year Stalin had advanced across the Lower Don between Stalingrad and Rostov in a very similar operational situation and destroyed the White Guard General Denikin.

However *General* Gehlen's "Foreign Armies East" Department continued to maintain that all indications suggested that the Russians were going to carry out an offensive against Army Group Center and not at the Don, which calmed Hitler.

In his memoirs Marshall Zhukov boasted that he had caused this error in German intelligence through planned simulated attack operations opposite Army Group Center. "The Soviet High Command wanted to create the impression that a major winter offensive was being prepared there and nowhere else."

But Hitler's hunch about the danger at the Don remained virulent.

On November 4 he even went as far as to order the transfer of the 6th Panzer Division from France to the Eastern Front. And yet he consented to the relieving of German corps by the Third Romanian Army after the Sixth Army had confirmed its battle readiness. Paulus had an interest in this, because he could obtain two German divisions for the battle in Stalingrad as a result: the 100th Light Infantry Division and the 305th Infantry Division.

Hitler was reasonable where Romanian requests for anti-tank and tank support were concerned. But the only large formation which could be freed up for positioning behind the Third Romanian Army, other than a few blocking units consisting of anti-tank guns, tanks, light infantry battalions and army artillery, was XXXXVIII Panzer Corps under *Generalleutnant* Heim with one German and one Romanian panzer division as well as elements of the 14th Panzer Division.

The corps headquarters was withdrawn from the Fourth Panzer Army at short notice and transferred into the area south of Serafimovich.

A German panzer corps was normally a considerable fighting force and strong backing for an infantry army. It would have been enough to secure the Third Romanian Army's threatened front. But Heim's corps was anything but a corps. The corps' key element was the German 22nd Panzer Division. It had partially converted from Czech to German tanks and now possessed 32 Panzer III and Panzer IV tanks. Months earlier the division had detached its 140th Panzer-Grenadier Regiment under the command of *Oberst* Michalik to the Second Army in the Voronezh area. There the 27th Panzer Division was created from the "Michalik Brigade." And finally the division's armored pioneer battalion had been engaged in house-to-house fighting in Stalingrad for some weeks.

On November 10 Headquarters, XXXXVIII Panzer Corps and the 22nd Panzer Division received orders to transfer into the area of the Third Romanian Army. The last elements of the division marched south into the great Don bend on November 16: 250 kilometers in the cold and over icy roads.

But neither the cold nor the snow were the main problem. It was as if this panzer corps was bewitched, and there was one bitter surprise after another.

Because the 22nd Panzer Division had been allotted almost no fuel for training and maintenance testing on account of its stay at a "quiet front," its 204th Panzer Regiment had sat dispersed behind the Italian Don front, camouflaged with reeds and totally immobilized. The tanks remained in their earth blast pens, well camouflaged and covered with straw against the cold. The tankers requested fuel so as to be able to move their vehicles during quiet periods, but in vain. As a result there was no testing of the engines. This was how *Oberst* Oppeln-Bronikowski found the 204th Panzer Regiment shortly before the transfer. When the crews tried to start the tanks for a quick move from their dispersals, half started only with great difficulty or not at all. Another thirty-four broke down during the transfer march: the engines stopped, many turrets would not turn. In short: the electrical equipment refused to work.

What had happened? The answer is breathtakingly grotesque: mice, which had nested in the straw of the dispersals, had gone on raids in the tanks and had gnawed the rubber cables. In this way the electrical equipment was interfered with; the ignitions for the engines, the wires for the batteries, the turret optics and tank cannon were out of service. Several tanks caught fire as a result of short circuits. And as misfortune rarely comes alone, there was a significant drop in temperature on the day of the unit's departure. However the panzer regiment had no track cleats for winter operations. They had been lost somewhere on the long road to the Don.

Without the cleats the tanks slid from one side to the other on the icy roads and forward progress was very slow. Because of a shortage of fuel the 204th Tank Workshop Company could not be taken along, and the regiment was unable to make any major repairs along the way.

Therefore, instead of the 104 tanks listed in the army group strength report, 22nd Panzer Division brought only thirty-one panzers into the XXXXVIII Panzer Corps assembly area. Eleven tanks followed later. On November 19 twenty-four tanks were the entire splendor of the division. The available tanks, armored personnel carriers and motorcycle troops, as well as a motorized battery, were just enough to form the *Panzerkampfgruppe* Oppeln.

On November 19 the corps' second large unit, the 1st Romanian Armored Division, had more than 108 tanks at its disposal. However ninety-eight of these were of the Czechoslovakian Panzer 38 (t) type – good vehicles to be sure, but inferior in armor and firepower to every Russian medium tank. Thus the Third Romanian Army on the middle Don had been fitted with a corset-stay which in reality wasn't one. And the Russians were massing forces before the front.

November 1942 was a catastrophic month: On the 4th Rommel's Africa Army was hit hard by Montgomery near El Alamein and was forced to withdraw from Egypt to Tripoli to save itself. Four days later Eisenhower's invasion army landed in the retreating army's rear, on the west coast of Africa and in Algeria, and marched toward Tunis.

The shock in Africa affected every German front like a distant earthquake: Hitler saw himself forced to secure militarily the previously unoccupied part of southern France. This tied down four very well-equipped mobile units which would otherwise have been available for use on the Eastern Front: the 7th Panzer Division and three Waffen-SS Divisions, 1st *"Leibstandarte,"* 2nd *"Das Reich"* and 3rd *"Totenkopf."* Chuikov and his troops on the bank of the Volga would have been crushed by the strength and firepower of these four divisions within forty-eight hours.

On November 9 Hitler returned to Berchtesgaden. The previous evening in the *Münchner Löwenbräukeller* he had spoken to his old comrades from the putsch of 1923. He said of Stalingrad: "I intended to reach the Volga, and at a specific place at a specific city. By chance it bears the name of Stalin himself. But don't think that I marched there because of that – it could be called anything – instead it's because it's a very important place. Namely we cut off thirty-million tons of traffic there, including almost nine-million tons of oil traffic. All the wheat from these vast areas of the Ukraine, the Kuban region, converges there for transport north. Manganese ore was mined there; it was a gigantic commercial center. I wanted to take it and – you know – we are there, we have it! There are now only a few quite small places there. Now the others say: 'Why don't you fight faster then?' Because I don't want a second Verdun, rather I would prefer to do it with small assault squads. Time plays no role in it. Not a single ship comes up the Volga any more. And that is the decisive thing."

Jodl presented the latest reports to Hitler on November 10 and 11: included were the contents of a signals intelligence report on the radio traffic of high-level Soviet command centers. It revealed how many army and air force units the Soviet High Command had sent to the Don and into the Kalmuck Steppe. The result: the Russians were not just massing forces northwest of Stalingrad, on the middle Don, in front of the Third Romanian Army. No, reports of a Soviet build-up south of the hotly contested city on the Volga, where two corps of the Fourth Romanian Army were guarding the flank of Hoth's Fourth Panzer Army, indicated that an attack was imminent there as well.

Hitler read the reports grimly and bent over the map. One look was enough for him to realize what was taking place: the Soviet build-up on both wings of the Stalingrad front led him to conclude that they were planning an operation aimed at encircling the Sixth Army.

Even though Hitler still tended to underestimate the Soviet reserve strength, he nevertheless saw the danger which lay in the large Romanian sectors. "If there were German units there, I'd have no sleepless nights," he observed, "but this! The Sixth Army must finally put end to it and quickly take the remaining parts of Stalingrad."

Quickly, quickly! He wanted to end the basically useless tying down of so many units in the city, so as to regain freedom of action. "I am aware of the difficulties of the battle for Stalingrad and the reduced combat strengths," the "Führer" radioed to *General* Paulus on November 16. "But with the drifting ice in the Volga the difficulties are even greater for the Russians. If we take advantage of this space of time we will save ourselves much bloodshed later. I expect, therefore, that the command, with all its repeatedly proven energy, and the troops, with their oft-demonstrated courage, will do everything in their power to break through to the Volga, at least near the gun factory and the metallurgical works, and take these sections of the city."

Hitler's reference to the difficulties of the Russians on account of drifting ice on the Volga was correct, as shown by the writings of Lieutenant General Chuikov from those days. Referring to the situation reports of the Sixty-second Soviet Army and its supply difficulties, Chuikov made the following diary entries:

"November 14. The units lack ammunition and provisions. Drifting ice has severed contact with the left bank.

November 27. Deliveries of ammunition and the evacuation of the wounded had to be halted."

The front command now ordered ammunition and provisions flown across the Volga in Po 2 aircraft. They were unable to accomplish much, however, because they had to drop their loads over a strip of territory which was only about 100 meters wide. The slightest deviation and they fell into the Volga or into the hands of the Germans.

On November 17 Paulus had Hitler's request for a quick in Stalingrad read out to all the commanders in the city. The next day the assault squads of the Stalingrad divisions attacked again. They hoped it would be the final assault.

The exhausted combat engineers of the 50th, 162nd, 294th and 336th Pioneer Battalions stormed forward. The grenadiers of the 305th Infantry Division raced out of their dugouts, crouched low, assault rifles under their arms, belts stuffed with hand grenades. They panted as they dragged their machine-guns and mortars across the rubble field and through the maze of ruins of the factory halls. Gathered round a self-propelled flak or walking behind a tank or assault gun, they assaulted the enemy positions amid the howl of Stukas and the hail of enemy machine-gun fire. Soaked by drizzle and snow showers, filthy and ragged, they attacked nevertheless: at the ferry landing, near the bakery, in the tracks of the "tennis racket." At most they "captured" thirty, forty, even one hundred meters on the first day. But they were advancing; advancing slowly, but they were making progress. They must finish it in another twenty-four, perhaps even forty-eight hours. Then they would be free of this accursed city. Then they could form reserves to guard the army's threatened flanks.

But the next morning, November 19, as the assault squads fought their way step by step across the maze of rubble of the factory halls toward the bank of the Volga, stormed the barricades which the Soviets had fashioned from old gun barrels, lobbed explosive charges into the gullies containing the drainage pipes, 150 kilometers to the northwest, at the Don, the Russians launched an attack against the Third Romanian Army.

Generaloberst von Richthofen, commander of *Luftflotte* 4, wrote in his diary:

"Once again the Russians have masterfully exploited a bad weather situation. Rain, snow and ice fog are preventing any action by the Luftwaffe at the Don."

The Fifth Soviet Tank Army came out of the Serafimovich area with two tank corps, a cavalry corps and six rifle divisions. This was exactly where a strong German panzer corps was supposed to be – in fact there was only the shadow of a panzer corps, namely the Heim Corps. At the same time, left of the Fifth Tank Army the Twenty-first Soviet Army struck out toward the south from the Kletskaya area with a tank corps, a guards cavalry corps and six rifle divisions.

The number of Soviet corps sounded dangerous, but in general a Soviet army was equivalent to a powerful German corps, a Soviet corps was equal to a German division and the Soviet division was roughly the same strength as a German brigade. *Generaloberst* Hoth was right when he said: "We have overestimated the Russians at the front, but completely underestimated their reserves."

The attack began with eighty minutes of concentrated artillery fire. Then the first red waves approached through the dense fog. The Romanian battalions defended bravely. The 1st Cavalry Division and the regiments of the 6th Romanian Infantry Division, which belonged to General Mihail Laszar's group of forces, held their positions.

But the Romanians soon found themselves facing a phenomenon to which they were not equal. They fell prey to "tank fright," as Guderian had christened the state of affairs which sometimes beset troops inexperienced in tank warfare: marauding enemy tanks suddenly came up from behind and attacked the Romanian positions. The cry rang out: "Enemy tanks from behind!" There was panic. The front tottered. Unfortunately the Romanian artillery was hampered somewhat by the fog, which made accurate firing impossible.

The first signs of catastrophe were already evident at midday on November 19. Whole divisions of the Romanian front, especially the 9th, 13th and 14th Infantry Divisions, disintegrated and streamed toward the rear, quite often led by their officers.

The Soviets pushed after the retreating Romanians, to the west at the Chir, to the southwest and to the south. But then their main force turned southeast. It was clear that their destination was the Sixth Army's rear.

XXXXVIII Panzer Corps' hour had come, but *General* Heim's units had no luck at all. The army group ordered the corps to counterattack northeast toward Kletskaya, against the infantry of the Twenty-first Soviet Army, which had a hundred tanks. The corps was scarcely rolling when, at 1130, a counter order arrived from Führer Headquarters: attack northwest, in the opposite direction to the breakthrough by the fast units of the Fifth Soviet Tank Army in the Blinov-Pestchany area, which had been recognized by the army group as the more dangerous threat. The corps had no choice but to turn around. Three divisions of the Romanian II Corps were placed under Heim's command to reinforce his corps, but these were shattered divisions with little fighting strength left.

By the evening of November 19 the Soviet armored spearheads had already advanced through the gap near Blinov to a depth of fifty kilometers.

The German corps, especially the armored group of the 22nd Panzer Division under *Oberst* von Oppeln-Bronikowski, carried out the 180-degree turn in masterful fashion and threw itself against the enemy tank forces near Pestchany.

But now the handicap revealed itself: the forced march through the ice-covered ravines, without cleats to prevent the tanks from slipping and sliding, had led to further losses. The brave but unlucky division met the overpowering enemy on the battlefield of Pestchany with a total of twenty panzers. Luckily the anti-tank battalion was on the spot; in bold actions and bloody duels between tanks and anti-tank guns it severed the Soviet armored spearhead.

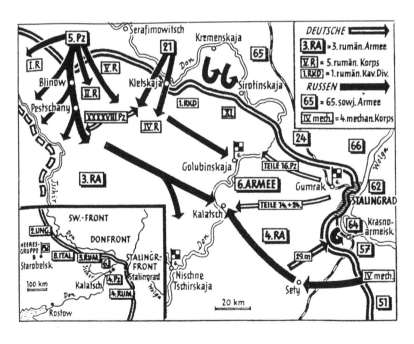

Map 12: On November 19, as the Sixth Army in Stalingrad set out once again to storm the last Soviet positions, four Soviet armies and a tank corps broke through the Romanian-held sectors on the Sixth Army's northern and southern flanks and raced toward Kalach. The small inset map shows Army Group B's front before the breakthrough.

Twenty-six T-34s lay burning before the hastily-erected defensive front. But the Russians were attacking with two armies and more than 500 tanks, and to the left and right there was nothing, nothing at all but fleeing Romanians.

The 22nd Panzer Division, which apart from the armored Oppeln group had only its anti-tank guns, a panzer-grenadier battalion and a few batteries, was threatened with encirclement. It was forced to withdraw.

In this way the 1st Romanian Armored Division, which was fighting bravely under General Radu farther to the east, was separated from the 22nd Panzer Division. The corps was split, its striking power gone. The army group recognized the danger and radioed an order to the 1st Romanian Armored Division to swing southwest in order to reestablish contact with the Oppeln group. But the Heim Corps was plagued by bad luck, and it really seemed as if the devil had a hand in the game: the Romanian division's German radio station was out of commission, the Russians having overrun it in the first attack, and the order did not arrive. Instead of turning southwest, the division continued to fight with its front facing north. The Russians rolled southeast, unmolested.

The Soviet objective was now clear for all to see. They hoped to reach Kalach, and there was nothing standing in their way. The bulk of the Third Romanian Army was in disintegration and panic. In this way it lost 75,000 men, 34,000 horses and all the heavy weapons of five divisions in four days.

The Soviet offensive had been executed after the example of the German battles of encirclement in 1941, and was well planned. While the double-edged northern pincer was cutting through the smashed Third Romanian Army, on November 20 the corps of the southern Soviet pincer on the south flank of the Stalingrad front launched their attack with more than 300 tanks from the Betekovka-Krasnoarmeysk area and from two further points of main effort farther south.

Here too the Soviets had selected the Romanian defensive sectors for their offensive. The sectors chosen were defended by VI and VII Romanian Corps. The Fifty-seventh and Fifty-first Soviet Armies of Army Group Yeremenko struck with two fully motorized corps, so-called mechanized corps, a cavalry corps and six rifle divisions. Lying in wait between the two armies was IV Mechanized Corps with one hundred tanks. Following a successful breakthrough it was to swing wide and sweep toward Kalach.

The bulk of the Fifty-seventh Soviet Army, with its tanks and motorized battalions, met the 20th Romanian Division west of Krasnoarmeysk and smashed it in the initial onslaught.

It was a dangerous situation, because this thrust was aimed directly and by the shortest route into the rear of the Sixth Army.

But now there was a demonstration of what a single battle-tested and well-equipped German division was capable of achieving; it was also shown that the Russian offensive armies were in no way outstanding fighting units.

When the catastrophe began the veteran Thuringian-Hessian 29th Motorized Infantry Division was in the steppe fifty miles south of Stalingrad as the army group's reserve. It had been withdrawn from the Stalingrad front at the end of September and brought up to full strength. Führer Headquarters had earmarked the unit for the assault on Astrakhan. However in view of the difficulties being faced on the Caucasus front, in early November the division received orders from Panzer Army Hoth to stand ready to leave for the Caucasus at the end of November. The 29th was to prepare for the new year's offensive there. This shows how optimistically the German High Command still viewed the situation near Stalingrad at the beginning of November. A special leave train subsequently transported about 1,000 men of the division to Germany.

On November 19 this fully-capable division, now under the command of *Generalmajor* Leyser, was a gift from heaven. Since *Generaloberst* Hoth was unable to reach army group by telephone he acted independently. At 1030 on November 20 he sent Leyser's division, which was in the midst of a field exercise, against the elements of the Soviet Fifty-seventh Army which had broken through south of Stalingrad.

The 29th roared off to meet the enemy. Leading the way was the 129th Panzer Battalion, deployed in wedge formation with fifty-five Panzer III and IV tanks in front. On the flanks were the self-propelled anti-tank guns. Behind in their half-tracked armored personnel carriers came the grenadiers, followed by the artillery. The division drove toward the sound of battle in spite of the fog.

The commanders stood in their open turret hatches. Visibility was less than 100 meters. Then the fog lifted.

At the same moment the tank commanders stood up straight: before them, not 400 meters away, approached the tank armada of the XIII Mechanized Corps. The cupola hatches slammed shut. The familiar commands rang out: "Turret 12 o'clock!" – "Armor-piercing" – "Range 400" – "Many enemy tanks" – "Open fire!"

Lightning flashed. The 75mm guns cracked. Impacts. Fires. The Soviets were bewildered. Such surprises were not their business. They turned in each other's way, retreated, became bogged down, were knocked out.

And then something happened that hadn't been seen before: over on the open rail line sat a long train. Masses of infantry spewed from the freight cars. The Russians had driven onto the battlefield by train.

The 29th's artillery battalion spotted this lucrative target and opened fire. The breakthrough by the Fifty-seventh Soviet Army was smashed.

But scarcely had this hole been plugged when the report came in that thirty kilometers to the south the Fifty-first Soviet Army had broken through the positions of VI Romanian Corps in the center and on the southern wing, and that a fast corps – IV Corps – was driving toward Sety. The battle's decisive moment had arrived. The 29th Motorized Infantry Division was in excellent position. By using it to continue the offensive defense with a thrust to the southwest into the flank of the Soviet mechanized corps, which possessed about 90 tanks, it was very likely that this breakthrough could also have been stopped. *Generaloberst* Hoth envisaged this second thrust into the flank of General Volski's corps.

But then on the 21st came the order from army group: halt attack, occupy defensive position to protect Sixth Army's southern flank. The division was taken away from Hoth's Fourth Panzer Army and, together with *General* Jaenecke's IV Corps, was placed under the command of the Sixth Army. *General* Paulus did not learn of this move until early on the 22nd however.

In this way an outstanding fighting unit with great striking power was tied down and deployed in a defensive role in a line of security like a normal infantry division where there was basically nothing to defend. It was understandable and indeed standard procedure to secure the flank of an army threatened by an enemy breakthrough, but in this case the army group ought to have recognized that the objective of the Soviets' southern pincer was not Stalingrad, but Kalach. It's goal was to meet the northern pincer at the Don and close the great trap behind the Sixth Army.

One could well reproach Army Group Weichs for selecting the obvious strategy of the small solution, the strategy of "charity begins at home." Of course, it is easy to say that afterward, and it is likely that the army group had not yet grasped the full significance of the Soviet attacks at this time. But a functioning reconnaissance apparatus should have soon revealed what was in the offing: General Volski's IV Mechanized Corps had meanwhile reached Sety. But before darkness fell the Russians went into rest positions, halted their advance. Why? The answer is interesting.

The surprising appearance of the 29th Motorized Infantry Division on the battlefield had taken the dash out of the Soviet corps commander, General Volski, who had been informed by radio of the catastrophe which had befallen the Fifty-first Army. He was worried about an attack on his long, unprotected flank. He feared exactly what Hoth had been planning. He therefore halted, even though his army commander insisted furiously that he continue to advance. Not until the 22nd, Germany's veterans day, when no German attack came, did he follow Yeremenko's energetic order and resume the advance. The corps subsequently turned north and twenty-four hours later stood before Kalach on the Don.

Hitler understood and recognized the danger which threatened not only the Sixth Army, but the entire southern front, meaning the army group with a million men. He searched for a saviour. On November 20 he made the Commander-in-Chief of the Eleventh Army, the conqueror of Sevastopol, the strongest fortress in the world, *Feldmarschall* von Manstein, Commander-in-Chief of the new "Army Group Don."

Manstein was to assemble all forces west and south of Stalingrad to defeat the threat. The Fourth Panzer Army, the Sixth Army and the Romanian Third Army were all placed under his command. This was a good choice and an equally good decision in an hour of danger. Manstein had experience with Romanian units. Moreover, he was generally recognized within the Wehrmacht as its most capable commander. His job was to halt the Soviet offensive and retake the lost territory.

Also on November 20, Hitler summoned the Luftwaffe Chief of Staff, Jeschonnek, to Berchtesgaden to discuss the role of the Luftwaffe. There are no clear-cut records of the discussion, but one thing is clear: Jeschonnek told Hitler that the Luftwaffe could supply the Sixth Army from the air for a short time under certain conditions. "Under certain circumstances and conditions," such as holding the airfields close to the front and reasonable flying weather. The latter was especially important given the changeable weather situation in the Stalingrad area.

Hitler heard the fundamental "*Ja*" to supply from the air only too gladly; but on November 20 at Berchtesgaden he hadn't yet made the final decision to keep the Sixth Army where it was and supply it by air.

On November 21 Paulus sent a radio message to the army group and, because of the heavy attacks on the flanks, asked for permission to withdraw the army from Stalingrad and the Volga southwest toward the Don and the Chir. Army Group Weichs forwarded the proposal to Führer Headquarters with its strong endorsement. Hitler replied that same afternoon. "Radio Message No. 1352 – Urgent – To headquarters Sixth Army – Führer Decision: Sixth Army will hold rail line open as long as possible in spite of danger of temporary encirclement. Orders for supply by air will follow."

That sounded reasonable.

On that same November 21 Paulus had moved the army HQ from Golubinskaya on the Don to Gumrak, close to the Stalingrad front. Paulus himself, his Chief of Staff, Arthur Schmidt, and the IIa had flown to Nizhnye Chirskaya, because a prepared army command post had been built there, where the Chir empties into the Don, with direct lines to the army group, the OKW and Führer HQ. Nizhnye Chirskaya had been envisaged as Sixth Army's winter headquarters – for the time after the conquest of Stalingrad.

Paulus and his chief wanted to employ Nizhnye Chirskaya's excellent communications facilities to gather all available information before they went to Gumrak. There was then and there is today not the least glimmer of suspicion that Paulus, separated from his staff, wanted to stay outside the pocket which was forming. But Hitler obviously misunderstood the motives and intentions of the Commander-in-Chief of the Sixth Army. Scarcely had Paulus arrived at Nizhnye Chirskaya, when Hitler ordered the General into the pocket in the harshest manner.

On orders from army group *Generaloberst* Hoth had driven to Nizhnye Chirskaya early on November 22 to discuss the situation with Paulus. He found him nervous and very angry over Hitler's schoolmasterly order. The face of this outstanding military intellectual was overshadowed by a haunted look brought on by the depressing, unclear situation. On the other hand *Generalmajor* Schmidt, the Chief of Staff, was calmness personified. He stalwartly spoke by telephone with the commanders at the front in order to obtain information, get a picture of the enemy's situation and discuss defensive measures. He was the portrait of a reserved, cool, textbook staff officer, who would later prove his firmness of character during twelve years of Soviet captivity.

What Schmidt entered on his pocket map, which he had placed before him by the telephone, was anything but encouraging. Things looked bad in the Sixth Army's rear west of the Don, and not much better on the southwestern flank.

CHAPTER VI

The Sixth Army Encircled

"Mein Führer, I Request Freedom of Action" – Göring and Supply of the Pocket by Air – The OKH Sends a Representative into the Pocket – General von Seydlitz Demands Disobedience – Manstein Comes – Wenck Rescued at the Chir

Low cloud hung in the sky and snow flurries swept out of the steppe, blocking the view of ground and, more importantly, air reconnaissance and making operations by close-support aircraft and Stukas almost impossible. Once again the weather was Stalin's ally. Although it could get only a few aircraft into the air, the Luftwaffe launched desperate sorties against the advancing enemy spearheads. Scraped-together elements of Sixth Army supply units, rear-echelon services, field railway companies, flak artillery and Luftwaffe ground personnel laboriously constructed the first defensive positions at the Chir, in order to at least prevent an expansion of the Russian breakthrough in the empty area to the southwest, in the direction of Rostov.

Especially bad was the news that the forward airfields near Kalach had been overrun and the tactical reconnaissance aircraft of VIII Fliegerkorps smashed. Northwest of Kalach the 44th Infantry Division was still in its good positions at the Don. The division had been cut off from its supply units, but it formed an important crystallization point west of the river. That was hopeful, but unfortunately not for long.

In Stalingrad, *General* Paulus had ceased all attack operations on the evening of the 19th on orders from army group. The offensive was halted before the last 100 meters to the objective. Battle groups were formed from elements of the three panzer divisions, the 14th, 16th and 24th. They were pulled out of the front and sent in the direction of the Don to meet the enemy, who was approaching from the northwest. But given the rapid development of the situation in the breakthrough area these weak forces were able to achieve little.

On November 22, at 1400, Paulus and Schmidt flew over the enemy lines to Gumrak, inside the pocket. The new command post lay two kilometers west of the small rail station.

The northern Soviet spearhead reached the heights overlooking the Don on the evening of the 22nd, as darkness was falling. The 26th Soviet Tank Corps under Lieutenant Colonel Filipov had already seized the bridge over the Don in Kalach in the early morning hours. The southern attack group was likewise outside the city. Kalach fell on November 23, and the trap behind the Sixth Army was closed. Twenty German and two Romanian divisions, about 200,000 men, were surrounded. With them were 20,300 Russians fighting on the German side, as well as forty to fifty-thousand horses.

What to do now?

This question, raised repeatedly in the numerous volumes of literature on Stalingrad, has been answered with contradictory theories. When a battle is lost every sergeant knows how it could have been won; because victory has many fathers, but defeats are orphans. Where military history is concerned, what is interesting is what lies behind mistakes and incorrect decisions, because it is through mistakes and incorrect decisions that most battles are lost. The mistakes and errors which led the Sixth Army into the Stalingrad pocket did not begin in late November. They are not to be charged to Paulus, rather they were made in the directives issued by the highest levels of the German command in late summer.

In any case, the last opportunity to correct these mistakes and errors presented itself in the days between the 19th and 22nd of November. The German High Command should perhaps have recognized the danger on November 19, and it could quickly have restored the situation by ordering the army to withdraw from the Volga and abandon Stalingrad. The Sixth Army couldn't do this on its own. Paulus lacked a clear picture of the overall situation, necessary if he was to independently make a decision which was so far-reaching and dangerous for the entire southern front, namely to take the Sixth Army out of its positions and set out on a precipitous retreat. It was not just his Sixth Army, with its 230,000 men, which was at stake, but the entire Army Group A in the Caucasus with one million men. Furthermore a sober assessment of the situation reveals that on the 19th, 20th and 22nd of November the disaster was in no way a strategic inevitability. A correct evaluation of the facts reveals this.

At the General Staff School in Wehrkreiskommando I, Königsberg (Prussia), the later *General* Osswald had instructed Arthur Schmidt and Wolfgang Pickert in tactics. His students called him "The Southern Cross." One of his favorite exercises was to describe a situation briefly and then to say: "Gentlemen, decision and brief justification in ten minutes." Anyone who ever sat with Osswald in the lecture hall never forgot him.

When *General* Pickert, commander of the 9th Flak Division, greeted his old friend Arthur Schmidt in Nizhnye Chirskaya on the morning of November 22, 1942, the latter blurted out the old Osswaldian school assignment: "Pickert, decision and brief justification."

Pickert's answer was brief: "Nothing to do but get out."

Schmidt nodded: "We want to, but . . ." And then Paulus' Chief of Staff explained the army's point of view: there was no cause for hasty measures. There was still no operational crisis situation which demanded independent decisions without regard to the overall situation. The most important thing was to protect the army's rear. An overly hasty retreat from the secure positions in Stalingrad could only have incalculable consequences. Just how correct these concerns were was to be proved in a few days.

At the time of Schmidt and Pickert's talk in Nizhnye Chirskaya there were in fact only two things to be done: secure the army's threatened rear, which meant establishing a solid front to the west and south, then make preparations for a breakout to the southwest. What was needed most was fuel, which would have to be flown in by the Luftwaffe. Fuel for the panzers. Fuel for the prime movers.

This view corresponded to the position adopted by Army Group Weichs, which on the evening of the 21st had ordered the Stalingrad and Volga Front to hold "at all costs" and to prepare for a breakout. Pickert doubted that the Luftwaffe could supply the army even for a short time, and once again urged that it break out quickly. Schmidt pointed out that the elements of XIV and XI corps still west of the Don and the 10,000 wounded could not be left behind: "That would be Napoleonic."

The events of the next few hours proved that Paulus and Schmidt were also holding firm to the idea of breaking out following the necessary preparations.

On the afternoon of November 22 Paulus received a radio message from the OKH via Army Group Weichs: "Hold on and wait for further orders." This was obviously intended to forestall any precipitous withdrawal movements. Meanwhile the General had obtained an exact picture of the situation on the southwestern flank, where Soviet forces were operating with about 100 tanks, and at 1900 he answered with a radio message to Army Group B which, among other things, said:

"Southern front east of the Don still open. Don frozen over and passable. Fuel soon used up. Tanks and heavy weapons then immobilized. Munitions situation tense. Enough provisions for six days. Army intends to hold remaining area of Stalingrad to both sides of the Don and has initiated all necessary measures. On condition that closure of southern front succeeds and enough supplies are flown in. Request freedom of action in event that formation of hedgehog in south does not succeed. Situation may then force abandoning of Stalingrad and northern front in order to employ total strength to smash enemy on southern front between Don and Volga and link up there with Fourth Romanian Army . . ."

There it was, clear and precise, what Paulus wanted to do on the afternoon of November 22. His plan was well-considered and allowed for any eventuality. He wanted to form a hedgehog, yes, but he requested freedom of action, meaning freedom for a rapid withdrawal if the situation should demand it.

Later, at 2200, a personal message from Hitler arrived. He denied Paulus freedom of action and ordered the army to stay where it was: "The Sixth Army must know," said the message, "that I am doing everything to help it and to relieve it. I will issue my orders in good time."

A breakout from the pocket had been clearly and specifically prohibited. Paulus reacted immediately. At 1145 on the 23rd he radioed to the army group: "Consider breakthrough to the southwest east of the Don with movement of XI and XIV Army Corps across the Don still possible, although with loss of materiel."

Weichs supported this request in a teletype message and emphasized: "Adequate supply from the air is not possible."

On the evening of November 22 Hitler left Berchtesgaden for his "*Wolfsschanze*" Headquarters in East Prussia. He had the train stop every two hours during the eighteen-hour journey. Hitler spoke with Zeitzler by telephone from the train stations and thus kept informed on the situation at the front. He thus received a detailed picture of the dramatic developments in the Sixth Army's situation.

General Jeschonnek accompanied Hitler and conferred with him constantly on the question of supplying the army by air. He also spoke with Göring by telephone, and in the afternoon the *Reichsmarschall* ordered preparations for the setting up of an air bridge to supply Stalingrad. Jeschonnek informed Hitler that Göring was demanding the transport of 500 tons per day from his generals.

In Hitler's telephone conversations with Zeitzler he impressed upon him that any fundamental decisions were to wait until his arrival at the "*Wolfsschanze*," and that he was in no case to authorize the Sixth Army to withdraw or give freedom of action as Paulus had requested in his radio message of November 22. Zeitzler supported this. Obviously Hitler had already made the decision on the train to keep the Sixth Army where it was and supply it from the air.

Paulus didn't know this yet and continued to fight for a breakout.

At 2345 on November 23, following careful consideration and after consulting with the commanding generals of the army, he sent a radio message direct to Hitler, in which he urgently requested authorization for a breakout. Paulus radioed: "*Mein Führer*, the situation has developed rapidly since receipt of your radio message of November 22. The closing of the pocket in the southwest and west has not succeeded. There are signs of imminent enemy breakthroughs there. Ammunition and fuel are running out. Many batteries and anti-tank weapons have expended all their ammunition. Adequate supplies cannot be provided in time. The army is facing imminent destruction unless the enemy, who is attacking from the south and west, can be destroyed by the concentration of all our forces. Therefore all divisions must be withdrawn from Stalingrad immediately, as well as stronger forces from the northern front. This will have to be followed by a breakout to the southwest, since the eastern and northern fronts can no longer be held after being so weakened. We shall have to sacrifice large amounts of materiel but we shall be saving the majority of our valuable fighting men as well as at least some of the materiel. I take full responsibility for this grave message when I inform you that Generals Heitz, von Seydlitz, Strecker, Hube and Jaenecke have arrived at an identical assessment of the situation. In view of this situation I once again request freedom of action."

In closing Paulus added: "All corps commanders share my opinion."

Zeitzler informed Hitler of Paulus' request on his arrival at the "*Wolfsschanze*" on the evening of November 23. Hitler was tired and worn out from the long trip. He didn't refuse Zeitzler outright, rather he gave him the impression that they would talk about it the next day. Zeitzler interpreted that as a positive sign and during the night informed the army group that he hoped to obtain Hitler's authorization for a breakout on the 24th.

This resulted in great euphoria in the Sixth Army. Paulus readied tank forces for the breakout. But a quite different decision came on the 24th. It arrived at 08:38 in the morning in the form of a radio message. It bore the heading: "Führer Decision," the highest and strictest level of order. Hitler gave very precise orders for the formation of the pocket front and the withdrawal of all elements of the army still west of the Don into the pocket front. In closing the order read:

"Existing Volga front and existing northern front to be held at all costs. Air supply."

There they were, those fateful words: air supply. Zeitzler and the High Command still hoped they could talk Hitler out of the decision. There were also the views of responsible generals who doubted that an aerial supply operation could function in the winter: Commander-in-Chief of Luftflotte 4, *General* von Richthofen, the experienced commander of VIII Fliegerkorps, the local Luftwaffe commanders, *Generaloberst* Weichs and naturally Zeitzler, all argued that the air-lifting of at least 350 tons of food and munitions per across enemy territory for an extended period was impracticable.

The problem culminated in a dramatic collision between Zeitzler and Göring in Hitler's presence on the evening of November 24. Zeitzler expressed doubts to Göring about the feasibility of supplying the army by air, even temporarily. He referred to the opinion expressed by the Commander-in-Chief of Luftflotte 4, *Generaloberst* von Richthofen, who in several telephone conversations had pointed out the impracticability of adequately supplying the Sixth Army by air and requested that the army break out.

This was an embarrassing argument for Göring, the Commander-in-Chief of the Luftwaffe, and he declared angrily that the Luftwaffe could very probably fly in an average of 500 tons per day.

Angry and red-faced, Zeitzler shouted back loudly: "The Luftwaffe can't do that, *Herr Reichsmarschall!*" Offended, Göring grumbled back: "The Luftwaffe can do that, *Herr Generalstabschef!*" Turning to Hitler, Göring declared in a clear voice: "They will fly no matter what the weather, *Mein Führer*. Everything will be committed, even the commercial Junkers machines. Demyansk and other instances have proved that they can do it."

According to Wehrmacht Adjutant *Major* Engel, the officers present were dismayed by such optimism. Hitler, however, was thrilled with the *Reichsmarschall*: "He's acting like he did in the early years. There's no faint-heartedness there, as in many places in the army." Hitler informed Zeitzler that he was sticking to the decision he had made that morning.

For Hitler, Göring's assurances were a confirmation of his strategic intentions. A heated exchange motivated by anger, underlined by a conflict of jurisdiction between the army and air force, and probably also dominated by the vanity of the *Reichsmarschall*, had determined a decision that should only have been made through cool deliberation and cold calculation.

There was to be no retreat! Hitler imploringly reminded the generals of the experiences before Moscow in the winter of 1941, where his stand fast order had prevented the destruction of Army Group Center. But what had worked in the winter of 1941 before Moscow was not necessarily correct in the winter of 1942 on the Volga. Rigidly standing fast was no strategic patent recipe. And what was more the holding of Stalingrad while endangering an entire army was not a strategic necessity. It was spelled out clearly in the schedule for "Case Blue": the role of the Sixth Army was to guard the flank and rear of the Caucasus operation. And it was possible to achieve this end without the occupation of Stalingrad, at the Don for example.

Today one repeatedly hears the theory expressed that Paulus should have disregarded Hitler's stand fast order of November 24 and ordered a breakout on his own responsibility to save the Sixth Army. In view of the scale of the disaster at Stalingrad this thesis deserves careful discussion.

On November 24 the quartermaster of the Sixth Army announced a reduction of the daily ration by fifty percent, as ammunition and fuel had priority in the airlift. The daily bread ration was dropped from 750 to 300 grams.

On this day, November 24, *General* Paulus called to a halt all preparations for an independent breakout. In a study by the Research Office of Military History, Manfred Kehrig wrote: "There is no documentary evidence to indicate what caused Paulus and Schmidt to adopt this position. The obvious assumption is that they trusted in the assurances of their superiors and therefore intended initially to wait for the promised relief and the results of an air bridge strengthened by a further 100 Ju 52s. Their attitude therefore appeared logical because they didn't consider possible an independent breakout by the army without authorization and without arrangements, and consequently a breakout prepared and carried out in cooperation with Army Group B and the Luftwaffe remained out of the question. There was thus no room for a rationally justifiable act of disobedience."

In my copy of Kehrig's study *General* Arthur Schmidt added to this statement in writing: "Correct. But after 24. 11. there was also the understanding that a breakout was no longer possible at this time."

Why not?

At the end of November Paulus and his closest advisors in Gumrak could not assess what strategic motives were behind the decision by the supreme commander. And the previous winter had not 100,000 men been encircled in the Demyansk pocket for two and a half months, supplied from the air and finally freed? Had not Model's Ninth Army held out in the Rzhev pocket as ordered? What about Cholm and Sukhinichi?

These experiences had played a role in Hitler's decision, and which were also known to Paulus and Schmidt.

From November 25 there was a witness in the Sixth Army's command center whose observations have generally been paid too little attention in studies of Stalingrad: Coelestin von Zitzewitz, a General Staff Major in the OKH, was sent to Stalingrad with a radio team on November 23 by the Army Chief of Staff, *General* Zeitzler, to act as a personal observer and send daily reports on the Sixth Army's situation directly to the OKH. Zitzewitz was summoned by Zeitzler at eight-thirty in the morning on November 23 and entrusted with his mission.

The manner in which this mission was assigned by the Chief of Staff gives an interesting clue as to the assessment of the situation by the Army High Command. Coelestin von Zitzewitz described it thus:

"General Zeitzler and I went over to the map lying on the table: 'The Sixth Army was encircled this morning. Today you and a radio team from the command signals regiment will fly to Stalingrad. What's important to me is that you report as much as possible directly and quickly. You have no command duties whatsoever. We're not worried, General Paulus has everything under control. Do you have any questions?' – 'No.' – 'Tell General Paulus that everything is being done to reestablish contact. Thank you very much.' With this I was dismissed."

On November 24 *Major* von Zitzewitz and his radio team – an NCO and six men – were flown from Lötzen into the pocket via Kharkov and Morosovskoye. What sort of attitude did he find there?

Zitzewitz told the author: "Naturally General Paulus' first question was what were the views of the OKH on the relief of the Sixth Army. I was unable to give him an answer. He said that the supply problem was his main worry. It was a mission never before attempted, supplying an entire army from the air. He had notified the army group and the OKH of his requirement for 300 tons per day at first, with 500 tons later, if the army was to remain capable of fighting and surviving. This was promised him."

"The Commander-in-Chief had adopted a point of view which to me was completely obvious: The army can hold here if it is provided with the necessary supplies, in particular fuel, munitions and provisions, and if relief from the outside can be reckoned on in the foreseeable future. It was now up to the supreme command to plan the delivery of supplies and the relief effort at the general staff level and then issue the appropriate orders."

"Paulus himself was of the view that a withdrawal by the Sixth Army would be useful within the framework of the overall situation. He stressed repeatedly that in terms of the overall situation the Sixth Army could be employed more profitably at the shattered front between Voronezh and Rostov then there in the Stalingrad area. What was more, the railways, the Luftwaffe and the entire supply organization could then be used for duties in support of the overall situation."

"But he could not make this decision on his own. Neither could he foresee that his demands in respect to relief and supply would not be fulfilled; he lacked the necessary sources for this. The Commander-in Chief informed his generals – who were all in favor of a breakout – of this and subsequently issued his orders for the defense of the pocket."

What else should Paulus, this representative of the best German general staff school, have done, what else could he have done? A Reichenau, a Guderian, a Rommel or a Hoepner might have acted differently. But Paulus was no daredevil and certainly no rebel, he was a general staff officer of the first order.

One General in Stalingrad was of a completely different opinion than Paulus and was opposed to accepting the situation created by the Führer Order: *General der Artillerie* Walther von Seydlitz-Kurzbach, Commanding General of LI Corps. The man who earlier in the year had opened up the Demyansk pocket requested that Paulus disobey the Führer Order and demanded a breakout from the pocket on his own responsibility.

In a memorandum dated November 25 he proposed in writing to the Commander-in-Chief of the Sixth Army what Paulus had already fervently advocated to his superiors on the 23rd but failed to win approval for: there must be an immediate breakout!

The memorandum began with the sentences: "The army faces a clear choice: breakthrough to the southwest in the general direction of Kotelnikovo or annihilation within a few days."

Decisive in Seydlitz's assessment of the situation and decision was the supply situation. In his view it was illusory to place great expectations in the air-lifting of supplies. Consequently: "The order must be revoked or another, independent decision made immediately."

The memorandum's main arguments were no different than the conclusions reached by the Sixth Army's other commanding generals or by Paulus himself. The precise assessment of the situation compiled by LI Corps' outstanding Chief of Staff, *Oberst* Clausius, expressed the views of all the general staff officers in the pocket's headquarters.

Seydlitz proposed freeing up assault forces by denuding the northern and Volga fronts, in order to attack on the southern front and break through in the direction of the weakest resistance, meaning toward Kotelnikovo, while giving up Stalingrad.

Literally it read: "This decision makes necessary the leaving behind of considerable quantities of materiel, but offers the prospect of smashing the southern cheek of the enemy encirclement, thus saving from catastrophe a large part of the army and its equipment and preserving it for the continuation of operations. As a result part of the enemy forces will remain tied down indefinitely, while any tying down of enemy forces will cease after the destruction of the army in the hedgehog position. It is possible to present these events to the outside in such a way as to avoid serious damage to morale: having completely destroyed the Soviet armaments center of Stalingrad, the army has been withdrawn from the Volga after smashing an enemy grouping of forces. The breakthrough's chances of success are all the greater, as previous battles have frequently shown that the enemy infantry's steadfastness is limited in open terrain."

That was enlightening, precise and logical. Every general staff officer could subscribe to it. The problem lay in the memorandum's conclusion. It said:

"If the OKH does not lift the order to hold out in the hedgehog position at once, our own conscience and responsibility to the army and to the German people will make it imperative for us to seize the freedom of action curtailed by the previous order and make use of the opportunity which still exists to avoid total catastrophe by launching our own attack. The complete destruction of 200,000 men and all their equipment and materiel is at stake. There is no other choice."

The ethical argument for independent action and the call to disobedience had no effect on the cool general staff officer Paulus, nor did they move the other corps commanders or the army's Chief of Staff, *General* Arthur Schmidt. What is more, several questionable statements reduced the effect: "The destruction of the army within a few days" was an exaggeration on November 25, and unfortunately where the supply situation was concerned Seydlitz also argued wrongly when he wrote: "Even if 500 machines land per day, no more than 1,000 tons of goods can be brought in, which is insufficient for an army of about 200,000 men engaged in a major battle and without reserves."

Had the army received 1,000 tons per day it would probably have got away!

Paulus nevertheless sent the memorandum to Army Group Manstein. He added that the assessment of the battle situation was in keeping with his own conclusions, and therefore once again requested freedom of action for a breakout, but dismissed the idea of a breakout against the orders of the army group and Führer Headquarters.

Paulus did not receive authorization for a breakout. Was Seydlitz therefore right to demand disobedience of him? If we ignore the order of precedence of orders and obedience for soldiers in warfare, which means ignoring the fact that orders and obedience "are the functioning principle of every army and must be so firmly founded that they endure even in times of deadly danger," as retired *Bundeswehr General Uhl*e-Wetter formulated it in relation to this question, the problem remains: was the requested disobedience at all practicable?

What did Krushchev do when General Lopatin wanted to withdraw his Sixty-second Army from Stalingrad at the beginning of October because, in view of the terrible losses, he foresaw only its destruction? He replaced Lopatin before he could initiate this withdrawal.

Paulus, too, wouldn't have got far with open disobedience to Hitler. It was illusory to believe that in the age of radio, teletype, UHF and courier aircraft an army commander could make decisions against the will of his supreme commander, as did the fortress commanders in the wars of Frederick the Great, without his superior being able to do anything about it.

Paulus wouldn't have retained his command for an hour once his intentions became known. He would have been replaced and his orders cancelled.

Just how efficiently the lines of communication functioned over the thousands of kilometers between Stalingrad and Hitler's *"Wolfsschanze"* is illustrated by a case which affected Seydlitz personally. It was also an incident which provided a warning demonstration of the dangers concealed by a hasty retreat from the secure positions at the Volga.

During the night of November 23/24, or before he submitted his memorandum, Seydlitz withdrew his corps' left wing on the pocket's Volga front in spite of clear orders to the contrary. According to a statement by Seydlitz' Chief of Staff, *Oberst* Claudius, to *General* Schmidt, the action was supposed to become a signal for the breakout, an initial spark for the withdrawal from Stalingrad, and force Paulus to act. Seydlitz denied this strongly in his memoirs. The measure had been a necessary shortening of the front from an exposed corner of the northern front. This is how the affair went:

The 94th Infantry Division, part of Seydlitz' LI Corps, which was manning well-built, although rather over-extended, positions and had not yet lost its supply organization, withdrew from its front on orders. All bulky and hard to carry materiel was burned or destroyed: letters, diaries and summer uniforms were thrown into blazing fires. Ammunition was also blown up. Then the men left their bunkers and foxholes and withdrew in the direction of the northern edge of the city. Holes in the snow and icy ravines replaced their warm quarters. They had only just got the great adventure under way, when suddenly they found themselves under attack by pursuing Soviet regiments. The veteran 94th Infantry Division was overrun and destroyed.

General Chuikov had been alerted to the retreat by the fireworks in the German positions and had immediately ordered an attack into the midst of the withdrawal operation.

The result of this spontaneous withdrawal was disastrous.

But not only is this exemplary, there is something else: Hitler learned of the events on the pocket's left flank before the Sixth Army command did. A Luftwaffe radio team present in the area of the catastrophe sent a report to the Luftwaffe liaison officer at Führer Headquarters. A few hours later Hitler radioed to the army group: "Demand immediate report why front north of Stalingrad was withdrawn."

Furthermore, early on November 24 the army received an order from Hitler to explain how the abandoning of the front at Latchamka had come about, contrary to his special order which forbade the withdrawal of troops in greater than battalion strength without his personal authorization.

Paulus carried out an investigation. He learned the circumstances and – didn't respond to the inquiry from Führer Headquarters. As a result Hitler remained unaware of the role played by Seydlitz, which would certainly have resulted in him facing a court martial.

The army group gave Führer Headquarters an explanation which played down the whole affair. In this way Hitler gained no knowledge of the background and did not learn that Seydlitz was responsible for this disaster. Through his silence Paulus took the responsibility onto himself. How many Commanders-in-Chief would have reacted in this way to such a blatant offense against military discipline? In any case, for Paulus the reaction from the "*Wolfsschanze*" was crushing: Hitler, who had held Seydlitz in great esteem since the battles for the Demyansk pocket and now considered him the toughest man in the pocket, believed that the shortening of the front was Paulus' doing. Therefore, at 2124 on November 24, he radioed orders to Paulus that he wished that the northern part of the Stalingrad fortress area, "be placed under the command of a single military leader," who would be responsible to see to it that the area was held no matter what.

And whom did Hitler name? *General* von Seydlitz-Kurzbach. True to the principle "divide and conquer," he wanted to attach a watch-dog to Paulus to energize him, so to speak. When Paulus personally conveyed the directive from the Führer to Seydlitz and asked him: "What will you do now?" he received the answer: "There's nothing else left but to obey."

General Paulus often referred to this conversation with Seydlitz during his captivity and after his release. *General* Roske, the commandant of Stalingrad Center, even recalled that *General* Paulus had told him in Stalingrad that he had said to Seydlitz: "If I resign command of the Sixth Army, there's no doubt that you will be given command as you are *persona grata* with the Führer. I ask you: will you break out against the Führer's order?" After considering for a moment Seydlitz replied: "No, I will defend the pocket."

Seydlitz' reply sounds suspicious in view of his memorandum, but it is vouched for. Seydlitz confirmed the conversation with Paulus in his memoirs, although with a somewhat modified wording: ". . . To this Paulus added with a trace of irony: 'Now you can act independently and break out!' To that I replied – in the same spirit – that was probably wishful thinking. I had to obey."

"I had to obey." That is exactly what Paulus did.

And he was right, because at that point, on November 25 or 26, on account of his lack of a strategic overview, Paulus had no right to place his assessment of the situation above the orders of Hitler and the High Command. Paulus' attitude was soon confirmed, on November 26, by the army group's newly-appointed Commander-in-Chief, *Feldmarschall* von Manstein, who, in his situation report, talked optimistically of the possibility of a relief attack and a supply corridor.

No, on November 26 the Sixth Army would not have been capable of breaking out to the southwest as suggested by Seydlitz, given the poor supply situation in respect to fuel and munitions.

Kehrig declared in his analysis of the battle: "The numbers presented here allow the conclusion to be drawn that the Sixth Army's munitions and supply situation would not have permitted a breakthrough attempt to the southwest lasting days with any prospect of success."

Like Chuikov on the opposite side, Paulus and his co-workers also lived underground. The army's headquarters were installed in twelve earth bunkers in the steppe six kilometers west of Stalingrad, close to the Gumrak rail station.

The bunker in which *Generaloberst* Paulus lived was four by four meters in size. Covered by two meters of frozen earth, this underground shelter provided adequate protection against medium caliber artillery. The interior was finished with wooden boards and other makeshift materials. Home-made clay stoves warmed the shelter – when sufficient heating materials, which had to be brought from central Stalingrad, were available. Coverings protected the entrances from the wind, which kept the interior from cooling off too quickly. Since the vehicle parks were some distance away, from the air the bunkers blended almost perfectly into the steppe landscape. The only indication of human habitation was a thin banner of smoke emerging here and there from a small hill in the snow.

Shortly after 1900 on that turbulent November 24, the radio officer, *Leutnant* Schätz, entered *General* Schmidt's bunker with a decoded message from army group: "Secret Command Matter, For the Commander Only," meaning the highest level of secrecy. Text: "Am assuming command of Army Group Don on 26.11. We will do everything to get you out. In the meantime it is vital that the army, while holding the Volga and northern fronts as per the Führer's order, ready strong forces as quickly as possible, in order to, if necessary, at least temporarily open a supply road to the southwest." It was signed: "Manstein." Paulus and Schmidt breathed a sigh of relief.

It was no simple task facing the *Feldmarschall*. He brought no fresh forces with him, instead he took over the surrounded Sixth Army, the shattered Third Romanian Army, Army Group Hollidt with scraped-together forces at the Chir and the newly-formed Army Group Hoth.

The headquarters of the new Army Group Don, under whose command Paulus now was, were in Novo Cherkassk. Manstein arrived at his command post late on the morning on November 27 and assumed command.

In spite of the difficulties, Manstein's plan looked hopeful and daring: he intended to attack frontally from the west from the Chir front straight toward Kalach with *General* Hollidt's army group, while Army Group Hoth broke open the Soviet ring from the southwest from the area around Kotelnikovo.

To understand the circumstances it is necessary to take a look back. What was the situation at the Chir and near Kotelnikovo, the two pillars of the starting position of the German relief attack?

Contrary to expectations the situation between the Don and the Chir had stabilized. This was primarily the work of one man: General Staff *Oberst* Wenck. On November 19 he was still the Chief of Staff of LVII Panzer Corps, which was engaged in the heavy battles for Tuapse on the Caucasus Front. On November 21 he received orders from the OKH to immediately fly to Morosovskaya in a special Luftwaffe aircraft in order to take over the position of the German Chief of Staff of the Romanian Third Army.

Wenck reached the severely battered Third Romanian Army that same evening. He later recalled: "I reported to Lieutenant General Dumitrescu. I was briefed on the situation by the interpreter, *Oberleutnant* Iwansen. It was desperate enough. The next morning I flew up to the front in the Chir bend in a Fieseler *Storch*. There wasn't much left there of the Romanian units. Elements of the brave Lascar group were still fighting somewhere west of Kletskaya, on the Don. The rest of our allies were in full flight. We were unable to stop this flood with the limited means at our disposal. Therefore I could depend only upon what was left of XXXXVIII Panzer Corps, the Luftwaffe alert units, the rear-echelon units of the surrounded Sixth Army we had found, which were formed into battle groups by energetic officers, and the men of the Sixth Army and the Fourth Panzer Army already back from or returning from leave. Initially the groups under *Generalleutnant* Spang, *Oberst* Stahel, General Staff *Hauptmann* Sauerbruch and *Oberst* Adam, alert units consisting of rear-echelon and maintenance units of the Sixth Army, tank crews and panzer companies without tanks and several combat engineer and flak units, formed the only military support in the Don-Chir bend, an area several hundred kilometers wide. Later came the main body of XXXXVIII Panzer Corps which fought its way back through to the southwest beginning about November 26. But I was unable to establish contact with the Heim Panzer Corps until *Generalleutnant* Heim had smashed his way through to the south bank of the Chir with the 22nd Panzer Division."

"Initially my primary task was to raise blocking units under energetic officers which, in cooperation with the Luftwaffe units of VIII Fliegerkorps, could at least maintain surveillance over the long front on the Don and the Chir between *Kampfgruppen* Adam, Stahel and Spang, which had already been formed. I literally 'scraped together' my own staff on the road. The same applied to motorcycles, cars and communications equipment, or practically everything needed to operate even the smallest headquarters. The veteran eastern front corporals, who turned up quickly and were capable of filling any role, were invaluable."

"I had no signal communications of my own. Luckily I was able to utilize the signal communications in the Sixth Army's supply area and the Luftwaffe net. Not until after countless conversations on these lines did I gradually get a picture of the situation in our sector of the front, where German blocking units were fighting and where there were still some Romanian units to be found. I myself was under way with a small staff every day, so as to obtain a personal impression and decide on the spot where we could adopt an elastic defense and where we had to hold no matter what."

"The only reserve we could count on in the area of the Soviet penetration was the stream of men returning from leave. Their arms came from army group depots, workshops or simply from 'organized' stocks."

"Drastic measures, sometimes odd but always inventive, were often required to weld together into new formations the units and parts of units of three armies which had been rendered leaderless by the Russian breakthrough."

"I remember how in Morosovskaya we had the head of a Wehrmacht propaganda company put on movie shows at road junctions. The soldiers who were assembled in this way were subsequently formed into new units, reorganized and reequipped. Most of them stood the test."

"Once a *Feldwebel* of the military police reported to me that he had discovered an almost abandoned 'fuel dump without anyone in charge.' We didn't need any fuel, but we desperately needed vehicles with which to transport our newly-formed units. So I had road signs bearing the legend 'to fuel distribution point' put up along all the roads in the rear area of the front. These led fuel-hungry drivers with their trucks, cars and whatever else was driving around behind the front to our dump. Waiting there were detachments under energetic officers. The arriving vehicles received their fuel, but their intended purpose was checked very carefully. And through this 'thinning out' we succeeded in securing so many vehicles and their crews who had been driving around there, intent on getting away to the rear, that we were able to alleviate our worst transport worries."

"Employing such 'stopgaps' new units were created in a short time, which though called 'alert units' in the parlance of those days, in reality formed the basis of the later reformed Sixth Army. Under the command of experienced officers and NCOs, these units proved themselves outstandingly in these critical months. The thrown-together units saved the situation at the Chir with their steadfastness and bravery, stopped the Soviet breakthrough and barred the way to Rostov."

The armored group of the 22nd Panzer Division was a rock in the battle at the Don and the Chir. During the difficult weeks in the Don bend it earned an almost legendary reputation among the infantry as a result of its lightning-quick counterattacks. After a few days the group consisted of only about six tanks, twelve armored personnel carriers and an 88mm Flak. The group's leader, *Oberst* von Oppeln-Bronikowski, rode in a Panzer III/Skoda from which he led his unit in the old cavalry fashion. But the group acted in the truest sense of the word like a "fire-brigade" at the Chir. It was repeatedly thrust into the battle's changing hot spots by Wenck.

When *Generalfeldmarschall* von Manstein took over command of the new Army Group Don on November 27, Wenck reported to him in Novo Cherkassk. Manstein knew the *Oberst*. His laconic order was: "Wenck, you're answerable to me with your head that the Russians don't break through to Rostov in your army's sector. The Don-Chir front must hold. Otherwise not only is the Sixth Army in Stalingrad lost, but the entire Army Group A in the Caucasus as well." And Army Group A was a million men. Was it any surprise then that the front-line commanders often resorted to desperate stopgap measures?

What was missing most of all was a fast, armored, mobile reserve with which to master the enemy tanks which were turning up everywhere and terrifying the army's rear areas. Without a moment's hesitation, Wenck's staff formed an armored unit from damaged tanks, knocked-out assault guns and armored personnel carriers, which was used in action with great success at the critical points of the battle between the Don and the Chir.

Naturally these vehicles had to be supplemented. And so Wenck's officers hit upon the idea of "securing" tanks from the rail transports rolling through the army's area to Army Group A or the Fourth Panzer Army, manning them with experienced tank crews and incorporating them into their panzer companies. Slowly the army put together its "own panzer battalion." Manstein and his staff were taken aback one evening when the Ia, *Oberstleutnant* Hörst, mistakenly reported the successful elimination of a dangerous penetration at the Chir by "our panzer battalion" in the course of the evening situation report. Wenck was ordered to report.

"With what sort of panzer battalion has the army restored the situation? According to our information it has none," asked Manstein. There was no avoiding it, the cat was out of the bag. Wenck described the state of affairs and added: "We had no other choice if we wanted to master the many crises. If necessary I would like to have my conduct examined by a court martial."

Feldmarschall von Manstein only shook his head. Then there was the hint of an amused smile. The Commander-in-Chief excused the desperate stop-gap measure, but forbade any further "tank seizures" in the future. Wenck: "We sent a few of our tanks to the 6th and 23rd Panzer Divisions, but from then on we employed our tanks only in company strength so as not to catch the attention of high places again."

This was how the great hole the Russians had smashed in the German front behind the Sixth Army was closed. It was a terrific feat of command. For weeks a two-hundred-kilometer front was held by units whose personnel included railway employees, men of the labor service and construction crews of the Todt Organization, as well as volunteers from the Caucasian and Ukrainian Cossack populations.

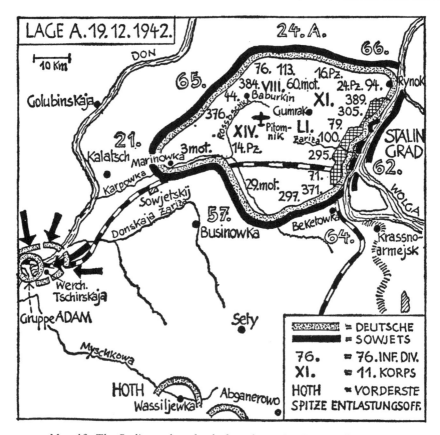

Map 13: The Stalingrad pocket before the major Soviet offensive.

It must be said that numerous shattered Romanian units placed themselves under German command. They stood their ground well under German command, and especially with German equipment, and many stayed in these German units for some time of their own volition.

It was not until the end of November that a regular large formation arrived at the Chir front, when XVII Army Corps under *General der Infanterie* Hollidt fought its way through into the area of the Third Romanian Army. Now at last they could breath easier.

The army group placed the entire Don-Chir sector under Hollidt's command and established "*Armeeabteilung Hollidt.*" Thus the motley, varied collection of units which made up the "Wenck Army," as the troops called it, ceased to exist. It had achieved a feat without parallel in the annals of military history.

The second act of the operation at the Chir was based on this success: the recapture of the hills on the southwest bank of the Chir, which were vital for any counterattack. The 336th Infantry Division and the 11th Panzer Division which followed soon afterward were sent in to accomplish this task, which they successfully carried out in early December.

With this we turn back to the start of this intermediate chapter, because these positions at the Chir were of decisive significance to the relief offensive for Stalingrad planned by Manstein, for which the *Feldmarschall* committed Army Group Hoth east of the Don from the Kotelnikovo area.

The Chir front guarded the flank and rear of this action to save the Sixth Army. What is more, as soon as the situation allowed, XXXXVIII Panzer Corps, consisting of the 11th Panzer Division, the 336th Infantry Division and a Luftwaffe field division, under the command of *General* von Knobelsdorff, was to support Hoth's operation through an attack to the northeast. Springboard for this supporting operation was to be the Sixth Army's last Don bridgehead at Werchne Chirskaya, precisely where the Chir flowed into the Don. Manning a hedgehog position, scraped-together alert units of the Sixth Army under the command of *Oberst* Adam, *General* Paulus' adjutant, held this key point in a truly heroic battle.

All the switches had been thrown, everything humanly possible had been done with skill and bravery at the front to free the Sixth Army.

CHAPTER VII

Hoth Launches the Relief Attack

"Winter Storm" and "Thunderclap" – The 19th of December – Fifty Kilometers To Go – The Conflict over "Thunderclap" – Rokossovski Offers an Honorable Surrender

Hoth attacked on December 12. The experienced and crafty armor commander faced a difficult, but not impossible, task.

As at the Chir, drastic measures had been employed to secure Hoth's right flank. Here it was *Oberst* Doerr, who – like *Oberst* Wenck in the north – had established a thin line of security using alert units and scraped-together elements of German mobile units. *Major* Sauvant's battle group with elements of the 14th Panzer Division and *Oberst* Pannwitz with his Cossacks, flak units and alert formations brought calm to the fleeing Romanian units and the rear-echelon German units, which had been seized by panic. The 16th Motorized Infantry Division withdrew from the Kalmuck Steppe toward a prepared position. Here too on the southern wing the Germans were able to frustrate the attempt by the Russians to drive from the east into the rear of Army Group Caucasus and cut it off.

One should think that Hitler would have now given his energetic support to Hoth's relief attack and placed whatever was needed at his disposal, so that the drive through a hundred kilometers of enemy territory could be carried out with surprise, strength and speed.

But once again Hitler was stingy with units; the Wehrmacht blanket was too short everywhere. All that came from the Caucasus was the 23rd Panzer Division, which hurried overland. The only fully combat-ready unit Hoth received was *General* Raus' 6th Panzer Division with 160 tanks, but it had to be transported by fast train from France. It arrived on December 12 with 136 tanks, the 23rd Panzer Division with 96.

Hoth had one hundred kilometers in front of him, 100 kilometers of strongly-defended enemy territory. Nevertheless things began well. The 6th Panzer Division's 11th Panzer Regiment, under the command of *Oberst* von Hünersdorff, pushed the Soviets back almost effortlessly. The enemy withdrew to the east and evacuated the south bank of the Aksai. *Oberstleutnant* von Heydebeck subsequently secured a bridgehead across the river with elements of the 23rd Panzer Division.

The Soviets were surprised. Worried, Lieutenant General Yeremenko called Stalin and reported: "The danger exists that Hoth might drive into the rear of our Fifty-seventh Army, which is holding the southwest edge of the pocket. If Paulus attacks southwest from the pocket at that moment, it will be difficult to prevent him from breaking out."

Stalin was agitated. "You will hold, we're sending reserves," he ordered menacingly. "I'm giving you the Second Guards Army, the best troops I have left."

But Yeremenko had to help himself before the guards arrived. He pulled the 12th Tank Corps out of the encircling front and sent it against Hoth's 6th Panzer Division. He also ruthlessly stripped his army group of its last reserves and threw the 235th Tank Brigade and the 87th Rifle Division against Hoth's attack spearheads.

For five days the opposing forces fought for possession of the hills north of the Aksai. Fortunately Hitler also released the 17th Panzer Division at this hour. On December 19th the German forces drove the enemy back.

After an eventful night march, early on December 20 the armored group of the 6th Panzer Division reached the Mishkova River near Vasilyevka. Stalin's Second Guards Army was already there. Nevertheless, *General* Raus' units smashed open a three-kilometer-wide bridgehead. As the crow flies, Hoth's spearheads were now only fifty to sixty kilometers from the outposts of Stalingrad.

What was the situation in the pocket in the meantime? The flow of supplies reaching the 230,000 German and allied soldiers was totally inadequate. It was turning out that the Luftwaffe was incapable supply an entire army in winter, deep inside Russia, from provisional airfields, without the necessary workshop installations and in miserable weather conditions. There were not enough dedicated transport aircraft for the job. Bombers had to be employed to haul supplies, but they could carry no more than one-and-a-half tons of freight. As well their absence from bombing operations made itself felt in every sector of the front. Once again the central problem revealed itself: Germany's materiel strength reserves were inadequate for this war.

General Seydlitz had calculated the necessary level of supply at 1,000 tons. That was undoubtedly too high. The Sixth Army considered 600 tons as desirable, 300 tons as the minimum required to keep the army relatively combat-ready. The defenders in the pocket needed forty tons of bread per day alone.

Luftflotte 4 attempted to fly in the required 300 tons per day. *Generalleutnant* Fiebig, the experienced commander of VIII Fliegerkorps, was entrusted with this difficult assignment, and initially it appeared that it might be possible. But cold and bad weather proved the toughest enemies, worse even than the Soviet fighters or the heavy Russian flak. Icing, poor visibility and the resulting flying accidents claimed more victims than enemy action. The crews nevertheless flew with a bravado exceeding anything previously seen.

The handful of fighters of *Jagdgeschwader* 3 "Udet", seven in number, performed amazing feats in safeguarding the airfields and protecting the transport aircraft. As long as there is a history of flying, there will never be another example of such defiance of death, of such an iron determination to fly, as that of the Stalingrad airlift. The operation claimed about 550 aircraft written off as total losses; one-third of the machines committed were lost with their crews, victims of weather, fighters and flak. Every third machine was lost, a terrible loss rate which no air force in the world could endure.

On only two occasions was the minimum requirement of 300 tons reached, and then only barely: according to the diary of the Sixth Army's quartermaster, on December 7 188 aircraft landed at Pitomnik airfield and delivered 282 tons of freight. 291 tons was reached on December 20. According to the outstanding study compiled by *Generalmajor* Herhudt von Rohden, who had access to Luftwaffe documents, the high point of the air bridge came on December 19, when 154 aircraft brought 289 tons of supplies to Pitomnik and flew out 1,000 wounded.

An average of 104.7 tons per day was flown in between November 25 and January 11, and a total of 24,910 wounded were evacuated. At this level of supply the soldiers in the pocket had to go hungry and remained without the necessary supplies of ammunition.

Since early December the army had set the daily ration at half that required by a working man. After a month of supply by air it stood at 200 grams of bread, 200 grams of horse meat (slaughtered or killed by enemy action), 30 grams of cheese, 30 grams of fat and three cigarettes per man per day.

This was less than half what a soldier needed to live and fight; and when the horses had all been slaughtered everything was reduced even further.

Just as inadequate were supplies of ammunition, especially for the light and heavy field howitzers. Deliveries of gasoline were less than ten percent of what was required, so that the mobility of tanks, assault guns and heavy anti-tank guns was limited.

Nevertheless the men held out. To this day the Soviets have never provided any clear figures concerning the number of deserters. Based on available German sources, until mid-January the numbers must have been minuscule. When the news got around from the HQ to the troops that Hoth's divisions had launched the relief attack, a mood of optimism spread. There was scarcely an officer or a soldier who wasn't firmly convinced that: "Manstein will get us out." Even the most decimated battalion felt that it had enough strength to fight its way toward the liberators. Everyone in the pocket knew that such a plan existed. Elements of two motorized divisions and a panzer division stood ready on the southern front to begin a drive toward Hoth's divisions. The code-word for the launching of the operation was "Winter Storm," and it would be issued as soon as the relief force was close enough.

The order of the day for the breakout attack to the southwest by the Sixth Army lay ready in a sealed envelope, and it was only to be opened twenty-four hours before the beginning of the action. In it the soldiers of the Sixth Army were called upon to give their utmost to establish contact with Hoth's relief army and smash the Soviet encircling ring.

The beginning of the breakout attack was planned for the moment when the fighting elements of Hoth's panzer corps had crossed the Mishkova River and were nearing the Businovka area – about twenty kilometers from the rim of the pocket.

The Sixth Army was ready. It was willing, and as the reports show, capable of managing this operation. By December 18 a supply column had been prepared for the Sixth Army with about 2,300 tons of column space; it was to roll through a supply corridor into the pocket. Columns capable of carrying 4,000 tons were standing ready in the pocket itself. Once contact had been established with the Hoth group they were to drive out of the pocket loaded with wounded, then pick up the goods which had been stockpiled and bring them into the pocket.

On the afternoon of December 19 the air was cold but clear. It was excellent flying weather. The transport aircraft roared in over Pitomnik. Quickly they were unloaded and crammed with wounded before taking off again. Fuel containers piled up. Crates were stacked high. Trucks hauled away loads of shells. If only the weather was like this every day!

Twenty-four hours earlier a representative sent by Manstein had arrived in the pocket. His purpose was to inform the army of the Field Marshall's views relating to the breakout. General Staff *Major* Eismann, Army Group Don's 3rd Staff Officer (Ic), had already returned by air. No one yet suspected that this visit was to become one of the irritating episodes of the Stalingrad tragedy, because there is no record of the discussions and a report compiled from memory by the Major ten years later gave rise to conflicting theories.

Had Eismann, as the Field Marshall claimed in his memoirs, transmitted clearly and precisely what Manstein was thinking: that in view of the situation there was only one brutal alternative: to break out quickly or face destruction? Had he clearly reported that Armeeabteilung Hollidt at the Chir was so busy defending against Soviet counterattacks that any support for Hoth was out of the question? Had he told them that increasingly strong Soviet units were being thrown against Hoth? Had he told them plainly that the Field Marshall was absolutely clear about one thing: the breakout would make necessary the step by step abandoning of Stalingrad, and that it would be so portrayed to Hitler so as not to make him mistrustful too soon; because Hitler's order had stated: "Yes, 'Winter Storm,' yes; but the abandoning of Stalingrad no!" Had Eismann made it perfectly clear that in Manstein's opinion the situation at the Chir front and that of the Italians at the Don appeared so strained that every hour was vital in starting the "Winter Storm" breakout to establish a corridor to Hoth's relief attack, even at the risk of having to give up Stalingrad, because there was a danger that forces from Hoth's relief attack would have to be withdrawn in the event of Russian breakthroughs at the Don. According to the version of these events given by *General* Schmidt and *Feldmarschall* Paulus after the war, the dramatic urgency for the "Winter Storm" breakout described by Eismann was not apparent.

But why then would Manstein have sent his Ic into the pocket? Eismann, now deceased, disassociated himself from the matter in a tortuous letter in 1957, but this did not answer the question.

One can call December 19 the day of decision, the day that the Stalingrad drama reached its culmination point.

Paulus and his Chief of Staff, *Generalmajor* Schmidt, stood at a teletype machine in the bunker of the Army Ia. The teletype was coupled to a UHF device, a wireless long-range communications system whose impulses the Soviets could not intercept. In this way the Sixth Army had a valuable, even if a technically somewhat cumbersome, direct link to Army Group Don in Novo Cherkassk.

Paulus waited for the prearranged contact with Manstein. Now it was time. The device rattled and began to print: "Are the officers present?"

Paulus had a reply sent that they were.

"Please describe briefly your response to Eismann's proposal," came the message from Manstein.

Clearly and concisely, Paulus gave his opinion.

Case 1: Breakout from the pocket to link up with Hoth is only possible with tanks. Infantry forces inadequate. In this solution all armored reserves, which were used to close breaches in the front, leave the fortress.

Case 2: Breakthrough without making contact with Hoth is only possible in extreme emergency. The result would be the loss of a great deal of materiel. Prerequisite is delivery by air of sufficient fuel and provisions to increase the men's strength. This solution would be more easily carried out if Hoth could establish contact even temporarily and bring in transport. At present infantry divisions are virtually immobilized and will become even more so daily as horses will have to continue to be slaughtered.

Case 3: Continued holding out in present situation is dependent on supply and delivery of sufficient quantities. Deliveries of supplies so far totally inadequate.

And then he dictated into the teletype: "Unable to hold out much longer as things stand now." The teletype tapped out three crosses, signifying end of transmission.

Then the teletype machine clattered out the text of Manstein's reply: "When is the earliest you can initiate Solution 2?" (There it is, the key question, the risky solution; but a solution!)

Paulus answered: "Preparation time three to four days."

Manstein asked: "How much fuel and provisions are necessary?"

Paulus answered: "Reduced rations for ten days for 270,000 men."

The conversation was interrupted. It resumed a quarter of an hour later, at 1830, and once again Paulus and Manstein conversed via teletype. The device typed out the words on paper in a strangely anonymous way:

"*Generaloberst* Paulus here, *Herr Feldmarschall* † † †"

"Good day, Paulus † † †"

Manstein reported that Hoth's relief attack with *General* Kirchner's LVII Panzer Corps had reached the Mishkova.

Paulus reported that the Soviets had launched an attack against the forces assembled in the southwest corner of the pocket for an eventual breakout.

Manstein: "An order is to follow † † †" After a few minutes the order rattled over the teletype:

Order!

To the Sixth Army

(1) Fourth Panzer Army has smashed enemy in Werchne Kumski area with LVII Panzer Corps and reached the Mishkova. Attack initiated against strong enemy group in Kamenka area and north. Difficult fighting to be expected here. Situation on Chir front does not permit advance toward Stalingrad by forces west of the Don. Don bridge at Chirskaya in enemy hands.

(2) Sixth Army is to launch "Winter Storm" attack as soon as possible. If necessary, it is planned to establish contact with LVII Panzer Corps across the Donskaya Tsaritsa in order to get supply convoys through.

(3) Development of situation may compel us to expand the mission to breakthrough by the army to LVII Panzer Corps at the Mishkova. Codeword "Thunderclap." In this case everything will depend on quickly establishing contact with LVII Panzer Corps with tanks for the purpose of bringing in supply convoys. Thereupon the army will move forward toward the Mishkova, while guarding the flanks on the lower Karpovka and at the Chervlenaya, evacuating the fortress area sector by sector.

Operation "Thunderclap" may possibly have to follow immediately after the "Winter Storm" attack. In the main air supply will have to be continuous with no stockpiling of supplies. It is important that Pitomnik airfield be held as long as possible.

All movable weapons and artillery to be taken along, priority to the guns needed for the battle and for which there is ammunition, beyond that weapons and equipment which are difficult to replace. To this end these are to be moved into the southwest part of the pocket on a timely basis.

(4) Prepare for option in Subparagraph (3). Will take effect only on express order "Thunderclap."

(5) Report time and day of (2).

An historic document. The hour had arrived. The Sixth Army was to set out on its march to freedom. But still only "Winter Storm" was on, which meant smashing a corridor to Hoth's divisions; as Hitler ordered, Stalingrad was not yet to be abandoned.

That afternoon Manstein had tried once again to obtain permission from Hitler for an immediate, total breakout by the Sixth Army, for "Thunderclap." Hitler authorized "Winter Storm" but withheld permission for the big solution. Nevertheless, Manstein, as our document shows, gave the Sixth Army the order to prepare itself for "Thunderclap" and said in Subparagraph 3: "Development of the situation may compel us to expand the mission to breakthrough by the army." Therefore to break out.

The drama was at its high point. The fate of a quarter of a million soldiers hung on two code words: "Winter Storm" and "Thunderclap."

At 2040 the two Chiefs of Staff were back sitting at the teletype machines. *General* Schmidt advised that enemy attacks were tying up most of the tanks and part of the army's infantry strength.

Schmidt: "The breakout cannot begin until the forces are no longer pinned down on the defensive. Earliest date December 22." That was another three days. Three days!

The night was icy cold. In the bunkers near Gumrak there was feverish activity. By 0700 the next morning Paulus was already on his way to the crisis spots in the pocket. There were local battles in many sectors of the front throughout the day. That afternoon, when the two Chiefs of Staff, Schulz (von Manstein) and Schmidt, once again spoke by teletype, Schmidt reported: "Situation extremely tense on western front and in Stalingrad as the result of recent losses. Penetrations can only be eliminated by employing forces designated for 'Winter Storm.' In event of more serious penetration or even breakthrough, army reserves, especially the tanks, will have to be on the spot if the fortress is to hold at all."

"The situation may be assessed somewhat differently," added Schmidt, "if it is certain that 'Winter Storm' will be followed immediately by 'Thunderclap.' In this case we can put up with local penetrations on the remaining fronts provided they don't threaten the withdrawal of the entire army. We can then be significantly stronger for the breakout to the south, as we can assemble numerous local reserves from all fronts in the south."

There is the vicious circle again, which could only have been broken if the Sixth Army had had approval for "Thunderclap" – from Hitler or from Manstein on his own authority. But Manstein, too, had no intention of acting against Hitler's orders.

General Schulz answered – unfortunately through the medium of teletype, so that the entreating tone in which he dictated it to the Ia clerk was not transmitted: "Dear Schmidt, the Field Marshall is of the opinion that Sixth Army's attack for 'Winter Storm' must begin as early as possible. It cannot wait until Hoth is nearing Businovka. We are fully aware that your attack strength for 'Winter Storm' will be limited. *Feldmarschall* Manstein is therefore striving to obtain authorization to carry out 'Thunderclap.' In spite of our constant pressure the struggle with the OKH for this authorization has not yet been decided." (And then came the entreating sentence, behind which was hidden what the senior generals had some time ago termed 'the strategy behind the hand,' the directive between the lines, the creation of a situation where their was no choice but to act, so as not to disobey an order from Hitler.)

Irrespective of the decision for "Thunderclap," the *Feldmarschall* stressed emphatically that, "the start of 'Winter Storm' must take place as soon as possible. More than 3,000 tons of column space now stand ready behind the Hoth army, loaded and ready to convey fuel, provisions and munitions to you as soon as contact is established. Numerous gun tractors will be sent with the supply columns to restore mobility to the artillery. As well thirty buses are standing ready to evacuate the wounded."

Thirty buses! Even they were ready. It was fifty kilometers as the crow flies; that meant a march to freedom of sixty to seventy kilometers.

At this hour, in the midst of the discussions and deliberations, the studies and the fixing of deadlines, a fresh catastrophe struck Germany's Eastern Front: on December 16 three Soviet armies launched an attack against the Eighth Italian Army on the middle Don. Once again the Russians had selected a sector of the front held by the weak forces of a German ally.

The Soviets broke through following a brief, fierce battle and raced south. A tank army and two guards armies threw themselves against the weak German front at the Chir, which had just been established with great difficulty. If the Russians succeeded in rolling over the Chir front there would be nothing to stop them until they reached Rostov. And if the Russians took Rostov, then Manstein's Army Group Don would be cut off and Army Group Kleist in the Caucasus would be separated from its rear services: a super-Stalingrad loomed. It was no longer a question of 200,000 to 300,000 men, now one and a half million were at stake.

On December 23, while the soldiers of the Sixth Army were still waiting hopefully for their liberators, the enemy's armored spearheads were already approaching Morosovskaya airfield, 150 kilometers west of Stalingrad, from the north. The entire supply operation for the pocket hung on this airfield. The catastrophic situation was obvious. *Armeeabteilung* Hollidt, which was fighting at the Chir, no longer had any flanking cover.

In this situation Manstein had no other choice but to order Hoth to immediately send one of his three panzer divisions west to the lower Chir to prevent a further breakthrough by the Russians. Hoth did not hesitate and released his strongest unit for this important mission.

The 6th Panzer Division received the order to depart in the middle of the attack in the direction of Stalingrad. But with only two exhausted divisions it was now impossible for Hoth to continue his attack toward the pocket. On Christmas Eve, under pressure from the Second Soviet Guards Army, he was even forced to pull back beyond the Aksai.

Feldmarschall von Manstein was full of worry. He sent an urgent teletype message to Führer Headquarters and warned entreatingly: "The development of the situation on the army group's left wing makes necessary the immediate shifting of forces there. This measure means abandoning the relief of the Sixth Army in the long term with the consequence that it will have to be adequately supplied from the air indefinitely. In Richthofen's view we can reckon on an average of only 200 tons per day. If adequate air supply of the Sixth Army cannot be assured, all that remains is to force a breakout by the Sixth Army at the earliest possible date, while continuing to accept a high risk on the left wing of the army group. I am aware of the associated risk in view of the army's condition."

There it is, everything that there was to be said, expressed in military terms. Following the Russian breakthroughs at the Don and at the Chir the Sixth Army had to break out or it was lost!

Map 14: On December 22, 1942 the armored spearheads of Army Group Hoth were about fifty kilometers from the Soviet ring around Stalingrad. However, the Russian breakthrough in the sector of the front held by the Eighth Italian Army prevented the continuation of the relief offensive, because the Russian drive was aimed at Rostov and threatened to encircle both German Army Groups Kleist and Manstein. The Sixth Army had to be sacrificed to avert this tremendous threat.

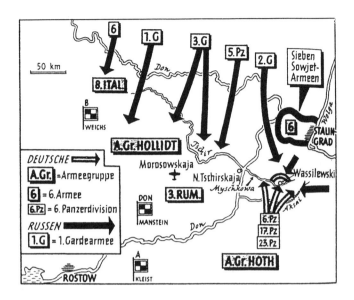

In Manstein's headquarters in Novo Cherkassk they waited tensely for the answer. Zeitzler sent it by teletype: the Führer authorizes the withdrawal of forces from Army Group Hoth to the Chir, but he orders that Hoth hold his jumping-off positions so as to be able to resume the relief attack as soon as possible.

This was optimism in a quandary, because Hitler had a convincing argument against authorizing "Thunderclap": "Paulus didn't have enough fuel to break through to Hoth." This theory was based on a report from the Sixth Army that the tanks had only enough fuel to cover twenty kilometers at most. This report has often been disputed. Whereas *General* Schmidt referred to his strong measures to get hold of the illicit stocks of fuel, Paulus later advanced the argument that no army could base an action which meant life or death on the suspicion of available illicit stocks of fuel.

In view of this situation, on the afternoon of December 23 Manstein once again established contact with Paulus by teletype and asked him to consider whether "Thunderclap" could still be carried out if there was no other choice.

Paulus asked: "Does this conversation give me the authority to initiate 'Thunderclap?"

Manstein: "I can't give you authority today, hope for a decision tomorrow." Then the Field Marshall added: "The crucial point is whether you believe the army capable of breaking through to Hoth if supply is not possible in the long run."

Paulus: "In that case there is no other choice."

Manstein: "How much fuel do you need?"

Paulus: "1,000 cubic meters."

But 1,000 cubic meters was 1,000 tons!

Why, in spite of all the risks and all the doubts, did Paulus not act? Why didn't he follow the order to launch "Winter Storm" in spite of the fuel and provisions available; after all, one way or another the existence of the army was at stake.

In his memoirs Manstein outlined the responsibility Paulus would have taken on with such an order: parts of the three divisions at the southwest corner of the pocket, where the breakout was to occur, were engaged in defensive fighting. Could he accept the risk of setting out with elements of these divisions alone in order to break the powerful encircling ring? Would the Soviet attacks even give him an opportunity to do so? Would he be able to hold the other fronts until the army group was able to give him the codeword "Thunderclap" and with it freedom of action for a complete breakout? Would there be enough fuel for the tanks to allow the assault force to be brought back into the pocket in the event that "Winter Storm" failed? What would become of the 6,000 sick and wounded?

And what would happen if the army's breakout failed and its units were destroyed? Freed from their role of encircling Stalingrad, the Soviet armies might bring about the collapse of the entire Caucasus Front with its one-million men.

The only possibility Paulus and Schmidt saw was to launch "Winter Storm" and "Thunderclap" simultaneously, and then only after sufficient quantities of fuel had been flown in.

On December 23, after scrupulous checking, it was found that the army had so little fuel that it would have had to abandon the tanks, assault guns, motor vehicles, artillery and heavy equipment necessary for the breakout after a few kilometers. From that point on the army would have been forced to fight its way across 50 kilometers of open steppe with rifles and spades against a superior enemy.

General Schmidt wrote in the margin of these documentary statements by Kehrig: "This was the decisive reason why we didn't launch 'Winter Storm.' We wanted to, but we couldn't."

The army wanted to initiate a total breakout with "Winter Storm" and proceeded on the assumption that the Soviet ring on the southwestern front had to be smashed before the pocket's fronts could be dismantled step by step, meaning that "Thunderclap" could be put in motion.

In addition to the military considerations, it was crucial for Manstein's time-table that Hitler would have submitted to the abandonment of Stalingrad only if faced with a development in the situation which left no other option and would no longer have been in a position to change his mind. This bore keeping in mind, and Manstein knew it: if the army group had ordered a total breakout and the abandonment of Stalingrad in advance, the order would have undoubtedly been countermanded immediately by Hitler.

A breakout by an entire army is a complicated process which would have involved numerous levels of command, including the Army High Command, simply because of the strategic reorganizations of other sectors of the front. It is impossible that Hitler would not have learned of it immediately and revoked the order. In that case Manstein could have expected not only his dismissal and replacement by a complaisant successor, but a court martial as well.

Paulus, tied down to his battlefield in the pocket and with every hour consumed by the necessary improvisations against the Soviet attacks, was a prisoner of the dramatic situation. And Manfred Kehrig was correct when he stated in his extensive study: "For Paulus and Schmidt to read between the lines of an order and interpret the 'meaning' of a superior, went against their military training as well as their nature."

These arguments show clearly that it is fruitless to try to trace the causes of the Stalingrad tragedy to the command of the Sixth Army and Army Group Don, or to seek the blame there.

Hitler's strategic errors, which were based on an underestimation of the enemy and an overestimation of his own forces, had led to a situation which no stopgap measure, no trick and no hold fast order could change. Only the timely withdrawal of the Sixth Army in October, on November 24 at the latest, could have prevented the catastrophe on the Volga.

In view of the Russian forces described in the Soviet history of the war, we now know that "Winter Storm" and "Thunderclap" would not have been able to bring an operationally capable army out of Stalingrad. At best they might have saved some of the soldiers.

There was a rarity in the sector of II Battalion, 64th Panzer-Grenadier Regiment. In a snow-covered wheat field the heads of grain were still sticking up through the snow. By night the soldiers crept out, cut off the heads, removed the kernels in their dugouts and cooked them with water and horse flesh, producing a wheat soup. The horse flesh came from the dead horses which lay everywhere, frozen stiff beneath mounds of snow.

On January 8 *Gefreiter* Fischer laboriously gathered the last few heads of grain and returned to the bunker, shivering from the cold. There was great excitement. News had filtered down from the battalion command post that the Russians had announced an offer of an honorable surrender in their propaganda broadcast.

The rumor spread through the pocket like wildfire. Then, in the Marinovka battle zone, a Russian Captain with a white flag appeared near the forward positions of *Kampfgruppe* Willig. The men summoned their commander. Courteously the Russian gave him a letter addressed to *Generaloberst der Panzertruppe* Paulus or his representative.

Major Willig thanked the Russian, and after checking with the army allowed him to leave with his flag. Then the telephones began ringing. A courier took the message to Gumrak. Paulus called personally and ordered: No one is to conduct surrender negotiations with Russian officers. In an order of the day he referred to the horrors of Russian captivity.

The next day every soldier in the pocket was able to read what Lieutenant General Rokossovski, the Russian Commander-in-Chief of the Don Front, had written to the Sixth Army: Russian aircraft dropped leaflets containing the Soviet offer of surrender over the entire pocket. There it was in black and white: signed, confirmed and sealed by General Voronov as the representative of the Red headquarters as well as by Rokossovski: "If all resistance ceases immediately and all the army's equipment is handed over undamaged and the troops surrender in an organized fashion, then (we) guarantee every officer, non-commissioned officer and man, who ceases resisting, life and safety as well as a return to Germany after the war or to another country of his choice if the prisoner so desires."

"All Wehrmacht members of the surrendering units may keep their uniforms, their badges of rank and decorations, their personal belongings and valuables. Senior officers will retain their swords and side-arms."

"The officers, non-commissioned officers and men who surrender will immediately be given normal rations. All wounded, sick and frostbite casualties will receive medical attention. We expect your answer in writing on January 9, 1943, at 1500 Moscow time, to be delivered by a representative personally authorized by you, who is to drive from the Konniy bypass to Kotluban station in a car marked with white flags. Authorized Russian officers will be expecting your representative at Rayon'8,' 0.5 kilometers southeast of bypass 564, on January 9, 1943, at 1500."

"Should our request for surrender be rejected by you, we advise you that the troops of the Red Army and the Red Air Force will be forced to take steps to destroy the surrounded German troops. You will bear the responsibility for their destruction."

The leaflets bearing the text of the letter also contained the following ominous sentence: "Whoever offers resistance will be killed without mercy."

Why didn't the Sixth Army accept this offer to surrender? Why did it not give up the hopeless battle before the troops were finished physically and morally? This question is asked with some bitterness to this day.

During his captivity Paulus repeatedly pointed out that he had not surrendered on his own authority because he still saw a strategic reason for continued resistance at the end of January: the tying down of strong Russian forces and with it the securing of the Eastern Front's threatened southern wing.

Feldmarschall Manstein expressed the same opinion. He said quite clearly: "The Sixth Army tied down sixty large Soviet units from the beginning of December. The situation of both Army Groups Don and Caucasus would have become catastrophic if Paulus had surrendered at the beginning of January."

One might have been able to explain and devaluate this thesis as "speaking on one's own behalf," but that is no longer possible: Soviet Marshalls Chuikov and Yeremenko fully confirmed Manstein's view in their memoirs. Chuikov wrote that in mid-January seven Soviet armies were still fully occupied by Paulus. Yeremenko stated openly that the offer to Paulus on January 9 promising him "honorable surrender" was based on the notion of freeing the seven Soviet armies in order to send them toward Rostov and bring about the collapse of the entire southern wing of the German Eastern Front. The last stand by the Sixth Army prevented this plan. Whether in retrospect the sacrifice was correct in the sense of a political evaluation of the war is another question.

But Paulus' position was reinforced by another factor: late in the afternoon of January 9 the capable *General* Hube returned to the pocket from an audience with Hitler and reported immediately what the Führer and officers of the OKH had said to him: they were planning a new relief offensive from the west. The movement of fresh panzer divisions was already under way, they were being assembled east of Kharkov. Since December 29 the airlifting of supplies had been placed on a new footing by *Generaloberst* von Richthofen. On orders from the Führer VIII

Fliegerkorps was relieved of all combat duties and committed solely to the airlifting of supplies to Stalingrad. Transport aircraft and other large-capacity machines were brought from the Reich, from other sectors of the front, even from Rommel's threatened front in Africa. On January 10, 1943, 490 machines of this type were at the front for "the supplying of fortress Stalingrad."

The Führer Order to the Luftwaffe read: "300 tons are to be flown in per day." The He 111 could haul 1.8 tons, the Ju 52 1.4 tons and the large-capacity Focke-Wulf Fw 200 6 tons. Strictly mathematically 300 tons could be flown in daily with only a 50% effort. Mathematically! But this calculation did not prove correct. The weather paid no heed to orders from the Führer. In many cases dense fog and blowing snow prevented aircraft from landing or taking off in the pocket. The makeshift airfields, far from Stalingrad, lacked the pre-heaters necessary to start aircraft engines in minus 40 degree temperatures. As well there was the concentrated Russian anti-aircraft fire and massed fighter operations against the unarmed transports, which finally forced the unarmed Junkers to fly only at night. As a result no more than 100 tons reached the pocket in any one day.

But *General* Hube's news had its effect nevertheless. The central point of his presentation was: in the view of Hitler and the OKH the Sixth Army had to hold on, if need be by reducing the pocket to the metropolitan area of Stalingrad, in order to allow the withdrawal of Army Group Caucasus and then to permit a new relief offensive to be launched from the west. It was a race against time.

Hube's statements correspond with what was reported by the Ia of the 71st Infantry Division, General Staff *Major* Below. Below, later an officer in the *Bundeswehr*, had become ill at Stalingrad in September 1942, was flown to Germany and after his recovery flew back into the pocket with Hube on January 9.

In late December, prior to his return flight, he had been in the OKH. There he was interviewed at length by the Chief of the Operations Department, *Generalmajor* Heusinger, as well as by *General* Zeitzler, as to the possibilities of a relief attack from the west, across the Don near Kalach. Below got the impression that those in the OKH still viewed the Sixth Army's situation optimistically and assessed favorably the possibility of a new relief attack. *General* Zeitzler dismissed the Major with the words: "There are enough general staff officers in the Stalingrad pocket already, but if I don't have you flown back they'll think that they've already been written off."

Seen from a military point of view, is it not understandable that Paulus rejected the Soviet offer of surrender on the basis of the strategic quandary and this glimmer of hope offered on January 9? The theory that Paulus was unaware of Hube's and Below's reports when he rejected the offer of surrender is refuted by Arthur Schmidt, who points out that Hube reported before noon on January 9 and that Paulus rejected the Soviet offer on the evening of the same day after consulting with the commanding generals.

This readiness to resist in the pocket had not yet been broken. Officers and soldiers believed, wanted to believe. In a letter dated January 11, 1943, *Hauptmann* Behr wrote: "We can hold here because we must, provided we receive the necessary supplies." He also wrote that Russian patrols made up of German-speaking soldiers in German uniforms were showing up at the pocket front.

The fortress propaganda office of the Sixth Army tried to counter the wearing-down tactics of the Russians. They produced trench newspapers and put on radio broadcasts in an effort to nullify the propaganda cleverly contrived by German communist emigrants and deserters.

CHAPTER VIII

The End

The Final Soviet Offensive – On the Road to Pitomnik – The End in the Southern Pocket – Paulus Goes into Captivity – Strecker Fights On – The Last Flight over the City – Last Bread for Stalingrad

As Rokossovski had announced in his leaflets, twenty-four hours after the German rejection of the surrender offer, on January 10, the Soviets launched their major offensive against the pocket. A 55-minute barrage from 7,000 guns opened the inferno. Then the infantry stormed the German positions, five Soviet armies against every front of the pocket. What followed has only happened to two armies in modern history: those of the Soviet Union and Germany.

Poorly-armed soldiers, cut off from the outside, hungry and plagued by chilblains, fought against a superior enemy with a dogged bravery which has rarely been equalled. Something similar had happened early in Operation "Barbarossa" in the Volkhov pocket, where the Second Soviet Army fought to the bitter end. The final battles for Stalingrad were as pitiless as any in the wintry forests of the Volkhov. Only the roles had changed. The suffering, the distress, the bravery and the misery were the same.

The Soviet attack against the positions of the pocket front was carried out with tremendous ferocity and concentrated on the sectors held by the 44th Infantry, the 29th Motorized Infantry and the 297th Infantry Divisions. Next the storm struck the 16th Panzer Division from the northeast, then the 44th and 76th Divisions on the western and southern fronts. What the Sixth Army had left in assault guns, tanks and anti-tank guns was thrown in to stop up the breaches in the lines. Detachments of *General* Pickert's 9th Flak Division, with their "eighty-eights" in the very front lines, tried to break the tank assault. They fought to the last round and knocked out over 100 Russian tanks. But it was of no use. The German infantry were smashed in their positions. The Russians broke through in many places. The loss figures of the exhausted battle groups climbed rapidly, as did the number of frostbite casualties. A blizzard howled across the steppe with temperatures of 35 degrees below zero. The men of the veteran 16th Panzer Division had no more fuel for their tanks and no ammunition. They fought as infantry "with small arms."

Isolated battalions of the divisions deployed on the western front fought like islands in the sea. Such was the case with the Austrian 44th Infantry Division in the approaches to the vital airfield at Pitomnik. Anyone who sees only misery, suffering, error, hubris and folly in the Battle of Stalingrad should take a look at these battalions. One of many was I Battalion of the 134th Infantry Regiment.

The battalion's emaciated companies clung firmly to their positions before Baburkin. In mid-December *Major* Pohl, the battalion commander, had received the Knight's Cross. As well as the decoration *General* Paulus sent him a small package. On it in the General's hand was "warmest greetings." Inside was a loaf of army bread and a tin of herring in tomato sauce. At that time in Stalingrad it was a precious prize for the highest award for bravery.

Pohl lay in his foxhole with a rifle like his men. At the northern tip of the pocket the last heavy machine-gun fired belt after belt. A few days earlier an *Unteroffizier* had said to Pohl: "*Herr Major*, no one will get me out of here." There was another burst and then the gun fell silent. They saw Russians leap into the position. There was a flurry of rifle butts and spades, then nothing. The battalion held on the whole night, backed up by the 46th Anti-tank Battalion with a few 20mm anti-aircraft guns and three captured Soviet 76.2mm guns.

When the battalion was forced to pull back the next morning the guns stayed where they were; there was no fuel for the captured Jeeps to tow them away. Each step back was a Waterloo for the gunners: they were forced to spike one gun after another. And in the cases where they laboriously dragged the guns by hand, they were unable to find ammunition for them. The idea of retreating into the ruins of the city of Stalingrad and continuing resistance there was illusory.

The next night the Major drove to Pitomnik to get a picture of the current situation from the senior Luftwaffe signals officer in the pocket, his friend *Major* Freudenfeld. The drive was a nightmarish one. To better mark the roadway in the desert of snow, frozen legs of horses, which had been hacked from the dead animals, had been stuck in the snow with the hoofs up: terrible road markers in a terrible battle.

At the airfield itself things looked bad. The army's life center was a field of wreckage. The airfield was littered with damaged and destroyed aircraft. The two casualty tents were filled to overflowing. And more aircraft were guided into this chaos. They landed, were unloaded, loaded and then took off again.

In the period from the 10th to the 17th of January the transport units brought 736 tons of supplies into the pocket. 736 tons instead of 300 tons per day! *General* Schmidt angrily radioed to Army Group Don: "Have we been written off?"

On the evening of January 11 *General* Paulus radioed to Manstein: "No reserves left. Enough ammunition for three days. Heavy weapons immobilized by lack of fuel. Can hold pocket front for only a few more days."

Nevertheless on the 12th battle groups of VII Army Corps held on behind Kolkhoz 1 and elements of XIV Panzer Corps defended with infantry weapons on the west bank of the Rossoshka.

The army sent a radio message to Manstein requesting that several battalions with heavy weapons be flown in to allow the defenders to continue to hold. But nowhere was a battalion available. And on January 13 the Sixth Army's battles were not mentioned in the Wehrmacht communique. Strangely enough, that same day Chief of Staff Zeitzler approved the operations section's plans for Operation "Dietrich" – the relief of the Sixth Army in February-March!

Pitomnik fell three days later, on January 16. The loss of the airfield delivered the final blow to the trickle of supplies still arriving, as well as to the evacuation of the wounded.

Now everything went downhill quickly. The last battle groups, now without heavy weapons, fell back in the direction of Stalingrad. *Major* Pohl and his men, too, moved through this hell. By the wayside lay a group of German soldiers who had been felled by an aerial bomb. They were still alive, but many had lost limbs and the spilled blood had turned to ice. No one had dressed their wounds, no one had moved them off the road. All the retreating columns had passed by them, each man engrossed in his own depressed hopelessness. Pohl had the wounded men tended to, laid them together and left a medic with them to wait for a truck to come by and pick them up. No more trucks came.

Tens of thousands lived through similar experiences in the last days of Stalingrad. The terrible hunger and defenselessness in the midst of the great Soviet offensive caused fighting strength and morale to sink rapidly. The sacrifices were tremendous. The divisions reported 70 to 80 percent "bloody losses." Congestion at the aid stations was fearful. Medicines and dressings ran out. Marauders roamed about.

At 1645 on January 24 the Army Ia sent a message to Manstein; its matter-of-fact language was shocking:

"Attacks of undiminished intensity against the entire western front, which since early on the 24th has been conducting a fighting withdrawal toward the east in the area of Gorodicze in order to establish a hedgehog position in the tractor works. As of 1600 western front in southern part of Stalingrad holding on line 45.8 western and southern edges of Minina. Local penetrations there. Volga and northeastern fronts unchanged. Horrible conditions in inner city area, where about 20,000 wounded are seeking shelter in ruins. With them an equal number of starving, frostbite casualties and stragglers, most without weapons which were lost in battle. Entire metropolitan area under heavy artillery fire. Last stand will be made at the southern edge of Stalingrad on 25. 1. under command of energetic Generals and courageous officers who have assembled around them those still able to fight. Tractor works may possibly be able to hold out somewhat longer. AOK 6/Ia."

Energetic generals. Courageous officers – indeed!

At the railway embankment south of the Tsaritsa Ravine the commander of the 71st Infantry Division from Lower Saxony, *Generalleutnant* Hartmann, stood and fired freehand with a rifle into the attacking Russians until he was mown down by a burst of machine-gun fire.

When *Feldmarschall* von Manstein read the radio message from the Sixth Army's Ia he knew that there could be no more talk of a military mission for the Sixth Army. "On January 24, when the army was no longer able to tie down enemy forces worthy of mention," said the Field Marshall, "I tried in the course of a lengthy telephone discussion to secure from Hitler the order to surrender, unfortunately without success. At this point in time, but only then, the army's containing role ended. It had saved five German armies."

What Manstein tried by telephone, *Major* von Zitzewitz was supposed to bring about through a personal report to Hitler.

Zitzewitz had flown out of the pocket on January 20 on orders from the OKH. On January 24 *General* Zeitzler brought him to Hitler. This meeting is of shocking symbolism. Zitzewitz described it:

"When we arrived at Führer Headquarters, General Zeitzler was shown in immediately while I had to wait in the anteroom. After some time the door opened and I was called in. I reported myself present. Hitler came up to me and took my right hand in both of his. 'You come from a wretched situation,' he said. The spacious room was dimly lit. Before a fireplace sat a large, round table, surrounded by club chairs. To the right was a long table, lit from above, on which was a huge situation map of the entire Eastern Front. In the background sat two stenographers who took down every word. Other than General Zeitzler, only General Schmundt and two personal adjutants of the Army and the Luftwaffe were present. Hitler gestured for me to take my place on a stool at the map table and then sat down across from me. The other officers sat down on the armchairs in the dark. Only the army adjutant stood on the other side of the map table. Hitler spoke, in the course of which he repeatedly pointed to the map. He talked of the consideration being given to launching an attack through to Stalingrad with a battalion of new 'Panther' tanks, in order to channel supplies to the Sixth Army and reinforce it with tanks. I was speechless. A single panzer battalion was to carry out a successful attack through several hundred kilometers of heavily-occupied enemy territory where an entire panzer army had failed. I took advantage of the first pause in Hitler's presentation to began describing the Sixth Army's troubles, citing examples and reading him numbers from my prepared notes. I spoke of the hunger, the cold, the inadequate supplies and the feeling of being abandoned, of the wounded and the lack of medicines. I closed with the words: '*Mein Führer*, I wish to report that we cannot order the soldiers of Stalingrad to fight to the last round, because they are no longer physically able to do so and because they no longer have a last round.' He looked at me in astonishment, but it was if he was looking right through me. Then I was dismissed."

On the 25th *General* von Seydlitz asked Paulus to order an end to the fighting. He argued correctly that they couldn't burden the individual man with the decision of when to stop fighting. Paulus refused. At 2300, on his own, Seydlitz ordered his corps' divisions to fire off the rest of their ammunition and then cease fighting.

On the other hand *General* Heitz, commander of VIII Corps, to which belonged the well-tried 76th Infantry Division, forbade any formal surrender, in particular the hoisting of white flags.

On January 26 Paulus moved his staff into the *Univermag* department store, around which were the remnants of the 71st Division from Lower Saxony. More and more commanders requested permission to stop the fighting.

Paulus drove through heavy artillery fire to the GPU prison, where a number of generals had installed their staffs. He explained his reasons for his refusal to authorize a surrender: every day they tied down Soviet forces was of vital importance in enabling Army Group Caucasus to make an orderly withdrawal.

But pathetic aspects no longer had any effect. Even the bravest officers had lost hope. In the cellar of the GPU prison lay staff officers and regimental and company commanders; dirty, wounded, feverish from furunculosis and dysentery, unsure of what to do. They had no regiments, no battalions, no weapons, no bread, and often only a single round left in their pistols. The last round – just in case. Some used this last round to shoot themselves in the head.

On the 27th the highly-decorated commander of the famed and much-lauded *Hoch- und Deutschmeister* Regiment, *Oberst* Boje, stepped before his men in the GPU cellar and said: "We have no more bread and no weapons. I propose that we surrender." The men nodded. Feverish and wounded, the *Oberst* walked with them out of the rubble of the GPU prison.

It was fifty meters to the front line at the railway embankment. At the mouth of the Tsaritsa ravine stood the remnants of *Generalleutnant* Edler von Daniels' division. The CO was with them. All were unarmed. They, too, were ready to surrender. It was a sad procession. Red Army troops lined both sides of the street, submachine-guns at the ready. The Germans were filmed and photographed, loaded into trucks and driven away. Then the steppe swallowed them up.

One Russian who witnessed this pitiful march was General Chuikov. He wrote in his memoirs: "We watched hundreds of prisoners of war march past. They were taken to the Volga and then across the river for which they had fought for months. The prisoners included Italian, Hungarian and Romanian soldiers. The men and NCOs were emaciated, their uniforms full of vermin. The Romanian soldiers made the most pitiable impression; they were so poorly clothed that it was hard to look at. They walked in bare feet even though we had a temperature of 30 degrees below zero."

General von Seydlitz surrendered in his bunker to the leader of a Russian assault squad at about 1400 on January 31, and began his dramatic and tragic role in Soviet captivity.

Meanwhile elements of XI Corps under *General* Strecker continued to hold their last positions in the split-off northern pocket.

The worst message of all those sent from Stalingrad passed through the ether:

"To Army Group Don. Forced by food situation to withhold rations from wounded and sick so that fighting men can survive. AOK 6/Ia."

Nevertheless at 0130 on January 31 Hitler had the Chief of the General Staff send another message to Stalingrad: "The Führer has pointed out that each day the fortress continues to hold out is of vital importance."

The final tragedy of the last days is founded in the attitude of Paulus, who wanted to avoid entering into a "formal surrender." As a result individual commanding generals and commanders completed surrender negotiations with local Russian commanders on their own. And when, late in the afternoon of January 30, it became clear that the headquarters in the department store could no longer be defended, *General* Schmidt gave *Oberst* Roske and *Sonderführer* Neidhardt the task of making contact with the Russians and initiating a sort of "unofficial surrender" by the Commander-in-Chief of the Sixth Army. Roske's opposite number in the negotiations was the Soviet General Laskin, Chief of Staff of the Sixty-fourth Army.

Care of the wounded was a main concern during the negotiations. Laskin agreed to this. He confirmed all the promises made in Rokossovski's surrender offer of early January, which he repeated "solemnly."

At exactly 1130 on January 30 the *Oberleutnant* of the officers guard stepped into the department store in Stalingrad's Red Square and announced: "The Russians are at the door."

Paulus had been up since six o'clock, speaking with his Ia, *Oberstleutnant* von Below. He was tired and disillusioned, but determined to make an end of it. But "without ceremony," as he said, meaning without a surrender document and without ceremony.

This was probably the reason for the often misinterpreted way in which Paulus went into captivity. He held to the order not to surrender with his army. He went into captivity with just his staff, while the individual sector commanders arranged the cessation of fighting with the Russians. When General Laskin and his interpreter entered the room, Paulus stood up and said: "Feldmarschall Paulus."

Through his interpreter Laskin said: "*Herr Feldmarschall*, I declare you my prisoner; I request you hand over your weapon."

Paulus gave his pistol to *Oberst* Adam, who handed it to General Laskin. Then the Commander-in-Chief of the Sixth Army drove through a lane of German officers and soldiers into captivity.

In the northern pocket, in the infamous tractor works and in the "Red

Barricade" gun factory, where the first shots had been fired in the Battle of Stalingrad the previous summer, strongpoints of XI Corps continued to hold out on February 1. It ended where it had begun.

Although this battle in the ruins had no military significance whatsoever, Hitler radioed to *General* Strecker: "I expect that the northern Stalingrad pocket will hold on to the end. Every day, every hour won in this way is of decisive advantage to the remaining fronts."

But resistance by XI Corps died away too. *General* Strecker spent the night of February 1/2 in the command post of the battle group under the command of *Oberstleutnant* Julius Müller.

At 4 o'clock in the morning two of his Generals pressed him to call an end to the fighting. They had already arranged with the Russian General for a cessation of hostilities at 0430.

Strecker said: "Do what you think is right." Then he walked out into the night. The battle in the northern pocket ended when it became light.

The Battle of Stalingrad was over.

At 0840 Strecker radioed Führer Headquarters: "XI Army Corps with its six divisions has done its duty." With six divisions! That was once 80,000 men.

In the northern pocket, too, the hollow-cheeked, starving men of well-tried and honored divisions stepped out of the trenches and rubble and assembled into grey columns. Then they were led off into the steppe: seemingly endless processions. How many?

The question of how many is still disputed. But arguments cannot change the face of suffering, bravery and death. Based on the war diaries of the Sixth Army and the daily reports of the corps, and according to a report made on the 22nd of the rations strength on December 18, there were 249,600 German and allied personnel in the pocket, including 13,000 Romanians. The reports also show 19,300 Russian prisoners, including *Hiwis*.

Of these 249,600 officers and soldiers, 42,000 sick and wounded and specialist personnel were flown out of the pocket by January 24, 1943. According to Soviet reports 16,800 were taken prisoner by the Soviets between January 10 and 29. Based on Soviet sources 91,000 men surrendered in the period January 31-February 3, other sources put the figure at 130,000.

85,000 lay dead on the Stalingrad battlefield: many of them had been badly wounded, defenseless and without food or medical attention in the final days, and were not recovered when the surrender came. The Russians claim to have buried

147,200 on the battlefield. This figure can only be accepted if those who died after the surrender and the wounded are numbered with the fallen.

Of the 107,800 to 120,000 who went into captivity after the surrender, only about 6,000 returned.

Manfred Kehrig's documentation puts the number of Sixth Army soldiers who went into captivity in early February at just over 200,000, including wounded. In his margin comments *General* Arthur Schmidt disputed this number, which was reached in part through estimates because, for example, men on leave and other army elements not in the pocket – 70,000 to 80,000 men – were not taken into consideration.

On February 3, 1943, *Leutnant* Herbert Kuntz of *Kampfgruppe* 100 made the last flight over Stalingrad by a German pilot in his He 111.

His commanding officer, *Hauptmann* Bätcher, had told him: "See if there's still fighting anywhere, or if there are any groups trying to escape. Then drop your load." The load consisted of bread, chocolate, bandages and some ammunition.

Kuntz circled over the city at 2,000 meters. There was no anti-aircraft fire. Dense fog hung over the steppe. Observer Hans Annen looked at Walter Krebs, the radio operator, and shook his head: "Nothing."

Kuntz dropped the machine lower. The altimeter showed 100 meters. Eighty. Flight engineer Paske strained to see something. Then the fog fluttered away: not sixty meters high, they streaked over the furrowed, rugged battlefield. Kuntz climbed to a safe altitude and continued searching. There – wasn't that men in the patchy fog? "Release!" he shouted. The load of supplies dropped into the depths. Bread fell in the snow of Stalingrad. Fell beside the dead, the frozen and those few waiting for death.

Perhaps it was found by one of the small groups of men trying to break through to the German lines. Many set out: staff officers with entire companies, like those from the headquarters of XI Corps and the 71st Infantry Division. Lieutenants and Sergeants set out with platoons under cover of night. Corporals and Privates stalked out of the rubble in twos and threes or even alone. Isolated groups were spotted in the steppe by pilots as late as mid-February. Then they lost track of them. Only one man, an NCO with a flak battery, *Unteroffizier* Nieweg, is reported to have got through. But forty-eight hours after reaching safety he was killed by a stray mortar round at a dressing station of the 11th Panzer Division.

PART III

THE MARCH TO STALINGRAD •
PHOTOGRAPHS BY THE SOLDIERS

This photo shows the Lower Don with its wide, wooded river valley near Konstantinovka. In the foreground Rasdorskaya. The summer of 1942 saw many German divisions fording the river, driving towards the Caucasus.

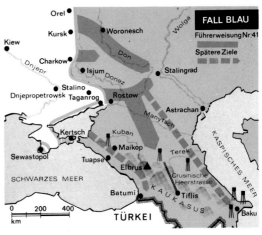

FALL BLAU
Führerweisung Nr: 41
Spätere Ziele

216/217

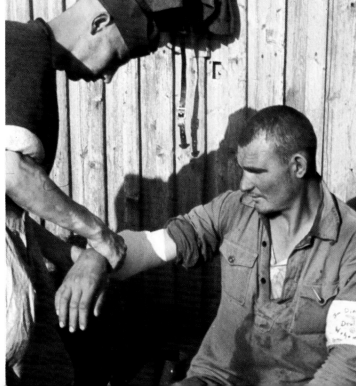

When Alfred Ott took this picture, he saw the men crying from the cold: Italian soldiers from the warm south of Europe, in the merciless hell of a blizzard. ● This phot of the industrial surroundings of Krivoy Rog, taken by Günther Thiem, shows clearly that the burden of rebuilding rested on the shoulders of the Russian woman.

German Armies of Army Group South marching over the Pruth (Above), over Dneiper and Don.

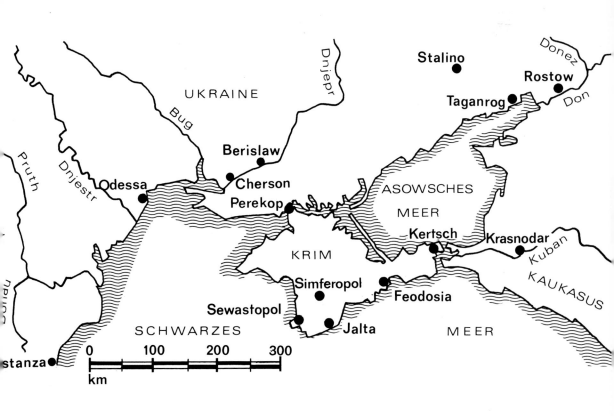

Unguri

230/231

-Podolsk

Bronita

Into the Boats

Rivers are not insurmountable objects. Imbued with
the precision of a fine clockwork, even if the bridges
were blown. The troops had instructive photos with
marked enemy positions (Above) (E = Attention -
enemy bunkers with casemats). • Divisions of the 11th
Army cross the Dnestr. Well camouflaged infantry and
engineers wait for their order: into the boats (Right).
The inflatable rafts hold twelve men.

Over the Dnieper
Almost three and a half Kilometers wide, the second
largest river of Eastern Europe. German Grenadiers
crossing on July 10-11 were not aware of the decisive
role the river played in the outcome of the war.
(*Operation Barbarossa*, pages 67-80).

Motorcycle Detachments to the Front
Hussars of the motorized Divisions liked the
Southern Wing for its ideal battlefields. Side-
cars marked with the "Jumping Horse",
tactical emblem of the 24th Division, the
battalion races into the steppe. Meets the
enemy. "Get down." Attacks with machine
gun and small arms. This photo was taken
during the summer battles of 1942 on the way
to the Don.

Inside, Outside
No soldier has a permanent quarter during any
given war. He only has a temporary stay. A witness:
the "Berliner Morgenpost" in the quarters of a
Berlin Division (Below)

240/241

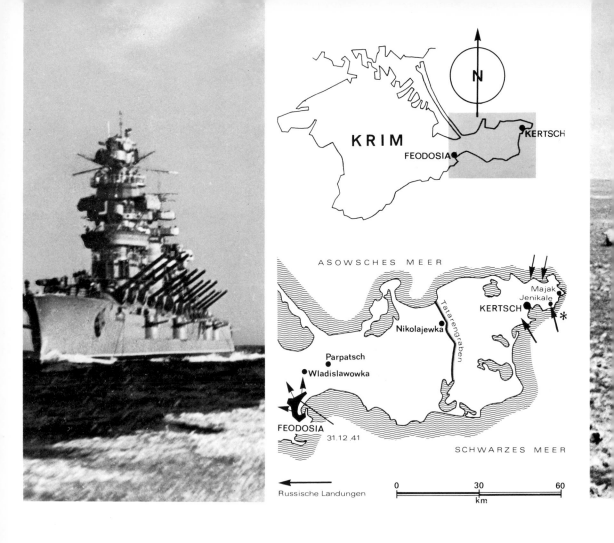

KRIM

KERTSCH

FEODOSIA

ASOWSCHES MEER

Majak
Jenikale

KERTSCH

Nikolajewka

Tatarengraben

Parpatsch

Wladislawowka

FEODOSIA
31.12.41

SCHWARZES MEER

Russische Landungen

0   30   60
km

Jenikale

Opassnaja

Russische Landung

The Bloody Coast
The peninsula of Kertch held a key-point of German strategy: 1941/1942-springboard to the Caucasus; 1943-backbone of the Kuban bridgehead. (left) Battleship "Sevastopol." Supported by naval forces, Soviet landing troops tried again and again to gain a foothold.

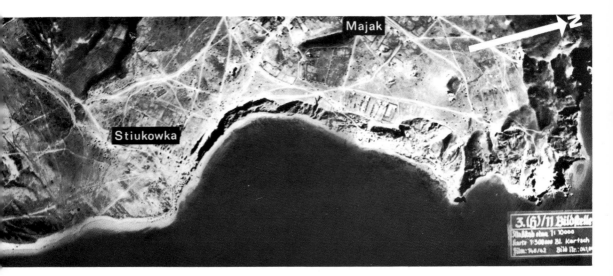

"What you obliterate now, is no obstacle later on."
Hitler explains to General von Salmuth. Visit by the Führer at the Headquarters of Army Group South near Poltawa, June 1, 1942. The military heads of the Southern Wing meet in front of the situation map. Favorable development south of Kharkov compels Hitler to change the timetable of "Operation Blue." (*Operation Barbarossa*, pages 400-408). • (Left to right) General Schmundt, *Generaloberst* von Weichs; Hitler talking to General von Salmuth; in front of the map: General von Sodenstern, General von Mackensen, *Generaloberst* von Kleist; (half way covered) *Feldmarschall* Keitel conversing with General Paulus; *Generaloberst* of the Air Force Löhr.

Storming Rostov
Rostov was blitzed by units of Panzer Group Kleist on November 21, 1941. It took the Russians only one week to take the doorway to the Caucasus back (Left), and throw the Germans out. Eight months later, July 25, 1942 the Germans are back again. *Oberst* Reinhardt with 421st Infantry Regiment during the street-fighting.
(*Operation Barbarossa*, pages 268-272).

254/255

The White "K"
Taking revenge on July 25, 1942, for November 28,
1941, the 1st Panzer Army, the old Panzer Group
Kleist, snatched the city again. Soviet Artillery tried
without success to smash the jump-off positions of
the German Panzers. • Combat engineers mounted
on Panzers advance to the city center (Right). •
Pockets of resistance in the ruins are mopped up by
Panzer-grenadiers (Above).

To the south . . .
Passage to the Caucasus is forced wide open.
Crossings over the Lower Don are gained.
Divisions of Army Group A and B storm to the
south,and east to the Volga.

258/259

Over the Chir, Over the Kshen

Are the Russians surrounded? The march on Stalingrad begins. First goal: Voronezh. Gun crew member 1 shoulders his machine gun again. ● Platoon leader points out the direction. ● Grenadiere, engineers and motorcycle riflemen attack. ● In the center of it General Kempf, 48th Panzer Corps, in his command vehicle bearing the insignia of the Corps.

In the Land of the Circassians
Parching heat and pouring rain sees the Gebirgsjäger moving over the passes and through the valleys of the Caucasus. ● Pyatigorsk on the Kuma in the northern Caucasus, resembles a gold mining town of America.
(*Operation Barbarossa*, pages 443-457).

ad to Asia

e gleaming panorama of the Elbrus
untains, is the background for the columns of
40th Panzer Corps driving through the
lmyk steppes to the Terek. ● This was the last
tacle before the oil region of Groznyy and the
Army road to Tiflis, Kutaissi and Baku was
behind on August 25, 1942. ● Supplies for the
al thrust roll over the Terek bridge. But the
rman forces were not strong enough and
viet resistance on the inclines of the Caucasus
he vicinity of Ordchonikidse demonstrated its
wer (Left).

peration Barbarossa, pages 472-475).

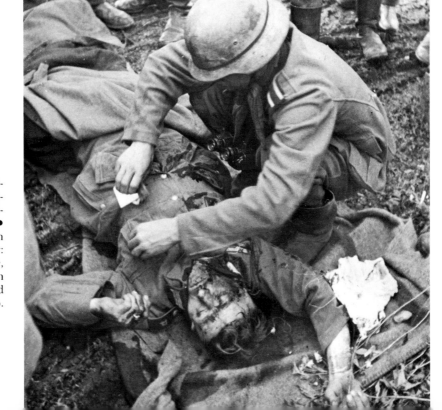

-time: 5 O'clock

minutes to go. Light anti-
ank gun ready to give cover-
ge. The company leader al-
eady on top of the ditch. ●
Now it's time! ● Someone in
he 3rd platoon keels over:
"Medics"! ● They are there,
elping. If the man had been
ne step closer, there would
ave been nothing left to help.

Kharkov
More than twenty German Divisions took part in the four battles for Kharkov. At least one million of them set foot into the fourth largest city of the Soviet Union. Pyramids of signposts guided them. ● They admired the monuments and buildings of Red Square. ● Trains and canals fulfilled important necessities in the economic structure of the country. Magnificent buildings stood beside hovels and beautiful churches.

Rossosch Falls

Anyone who marched with the troops of the 6th Army south of Woronesch, remembers Windmill Hill and the dusty highways on the passage to the Don. ● Second part of "Operation Blue" started July 6th with a rapid advance into the bend of the Don to encircle the Russians (Right); Windmill Hill appears again in the background.
(*Operation Barbarossa*, pages 433-435).

292/293

Over the Chir to the Don
General Paulus outmaneuvered the Soviet forces in front of the Don. His Panzer Divisions gain passage over the Chir (Left). ● The Russians are badly hit by Stukas of 8th Air Force Corps. ● July 26, and German advance units are on the river within the wide Don bend.
(*Operation Barbarossa*, pages 479-482).

The Steppe of the Don
Two Panzer Corps spearhead the 6th Army. Infantry, horse-drawn artillery and equipment behind them. Objective: Kalatsch on the Don.
(*Operation Barbarossa*, pages 477-479).

The Bridges Over the Don
The technical machinery of the bridge-building combat engineers worked excellently. Colorful signposts of the Don heights were famous. ● Attacked 67 times in one night by Russian planes, the Luchensky bridge led into the bridge-head of the 11th Corps (Lower Right).

Donhöhenstrasse

Donbrücke
Akatow

8 km Donbrücke
Akimowskij

5 km Donbrücke
Lutschenskij

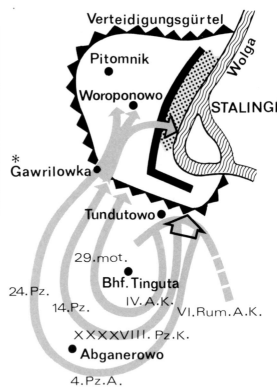

Breakthrough at Gavrilovka

Abganerovo on the outer defense ring of Stalingrad was reached on August 19, 1942 by the 4th Panzer Army. (Below) ● Grenadiers of the 29th I.D. storm positions of the 64th Soviet Army (Right). ● Then it stops. Hoth gambles on a bold regrouping, and eleven days later, tears into the inner defenses from the south-west. Still 13 Kilometers to Stalingrad.
(*Operation Barbarossa*, pages 486-493).

Durchbruch bei Gawrilowka am 30.8.194

STALINGRAD: Verlustliste der 6. Armee

👤 = 6 000 Mann

18.12.1942

Verpflegungsstärke der im Kessel befindlichen deutschen und verbün = deten Truppen

230 300 Mann

Bis zum 24.1.1943

werden ausgeflogen (Verwundete und Spe = zialisten) 42 000

Bis zum 29.1.1943

gefangen * 16 800

171 500 Mann

31.1.1943 – 3.2.1943

* 91 000 gehen in Gefangenschaft 80 500

Tote und Verwundete bleiben auf dem Schlachtfeld

Gefangene

107 800 Mann

Heimkehrer

6 000 Mann

* Sowjetische Angaben

324

Appendixes

APPENDIX A

Führer Directive No. 41

The Führer and Supreme Commander   F.H.Qu., 5. 4. 1942
    of the Wehrmacht   14 copies
OKW/WFSt No. 55/616/42 g. K. Chefs   4th copy
SECRET COMMAND MATTER / COMMANDER MATTER
OFFICERS ONLY

Directive 41

The winter battle in Russia is approaching its end.

A defensive success of the greatest magnitude has been achieved for German arms through the outstanding bravery and selfless actions of the soldiers of the Eastern Front.

The enemy has suffered the heaviest losses in men and materiel. In endeavoring to exploit apparent initial success he has this winter also largely used up the bulk of his reserves earmarked for later operations.

As soon as weather and terrain conditions provide the necessary pre-conditions, the superiority of the German command and troops must regain the initiative in order to impose their will upon the enemy.

The objective is to finally destroy the remaining military power of the Soviets and to the extent possible deprive them of their most important military-economical sources of strength.

To this end all available forces of the German Wehrmacht and our allies will be mobilized. However it must be assured that the occupied areas in western and northern Europe, especially the coasts, remain secure in any event.

I. General Aim

Adhering to the original basic concepts of the eastern campaign, we must bring about the fall of Leningrad and establish land communication with the Finns in the north and on the southern wing of the army front force a breakthrough into the Caucasus area, while holding in the army center.

In view of the situation following the conclusion of the winter battle, the available means and forces and the transport situation, this objective will have to be achieved in stages.

Therefore, initially all available forces are to be assembled for the main operation in the southern sector with the objective of destroying the enemy forces forward of the Don, in order to capture the oil region in the Caucasus area and the crossings over the Caucasus itself.

The final isolation of Leningrad and the capture of the Ingermann Land will have to wait until developments in the situation in the area of the encirclement or the availability of other, sufficient forces make them possible.

II. Conduct of Operations

(A) The first task of the army and the air force following the conclusion of the muddy period is to create the conditions necessary for the carrying-out of the main operation.

This will require the mopping-up and consolidation of the entire Eastern Front and the rear army areas with the objective of obtaining the maximum possible forces for the main operation, while at the same time allowing the remaining fronts to meet any attack with minimum effort. However where attack operations with limited objectives are carried out for this purpose on my order, it is to be ensured that all available army and air force resources are employed in overwhelming strength so as to ensure quick and decisive success. Only in this way will our troops' unconditional confidence in victory be reinforced, in particular before the start of the big spring operations, while at the same time we hammer into the enemy how hopelessly inferior he is.

(B) The next tasks within this framework are to clear the Kerch Peninsula in the Crimea and bring about the fall of Sevastopol. The air force and later the navy will have the task of ruthlessly stopping enemy supply traffic on the Black Sea and in the Straits of Kerch in preparation for these operations.

In the southern area the enemy forces which have advanced on both sides of Izyum along the course of the Don are to be cut off and destroyed. Necessary adjustments in the central and northern sectors of the Eastern Front can be finally examined and decided upon following the conclusion of combat operations and the muddy period.

But in addition to this, the necessary forces will have to be obtained by diluting the front – as soon as the situation permits.

(C) The Main Operation on the Eastern Front:

Its objective – as already stated – is to decisively smash and destroy the Russian forces located in the Voronezh area to the north, west or south of the Don, so as to facilitate the capture of the Caucasus front. Due to the arrival of available units, the operation will have to consist of a series of attacks carried out one after another but which are interconnected or supplement one another. They are therefore to be coordinated as to time from north to south so that a high degree of concentration of ground and especially air forces can be assured in each of these attacks.

Given the now sufficiently demonstrated Russian resistance to strategic encirclements, it is of decisive importance to turn the individual breakthroughs into close encirclements, as in the double battle of Vyazma-Briansk.

The enemy must not be given an opportunity to escape destruction as the result of the encircling units turning inward too late.

The panzer and motorized units *must not be allowed* to lose contact with the following infantry as a result of stepping out too fast and too far, nor may the panzer and motorized units be placed in a position where they are unable to help the army's infantry forces as they fight their way forward, through their direct effect in the rear of the encircled Russian armies.

With the exception of the overall strategic objective, in each individual case the destruction of the enemy is to be ensured by the manner of the attack and the method of command of our units.

The initial stage of the total operation is to begin with an enveloping attack or breakthrough from the area south of Orel in the direction of Voronezh. Of the panzer and motorized units committed, the northern is to be stronger than the southern. The objective of this breakthrough is the occupation of Voronezh itself. While it is the mission of part of the infantry divisions to immediately establish a strong defensive position between the attack's Orel starting position and Voronezh, it is the mission of the panzer and motorized units to continuing the attack southward from Voronezh along the Don with their left wing to support a second breakthrough toward the east, which is to be made from the general area of Kharkov. Here too the primary objective is not to crush the Russian front as such, rather to destroy the Russian forces in conjunction with the motorized units advancing down the Don.

The third attack of this operation is to be carried out so that the forces advancing down the Don link up in the Stalingrad area with the forces advancing out of the Taganrog-Artemovsk area between the lower course of the Don and Voroshilovgrad. These are to finally link up with the panzer army moving toward Stalingrad.

Should opportunities to establish bridgeheads east or south of the Don arise during the course of these operations, especially through the capture of undamaged bridges, such opportunities are to be seized. In any case the attempt must be made to reach Stalingrad itself or at least to so bring it under the effect of our weapons that is eliminated as an armaments and transportation center.

It would be especially desirable to succeed in capturing either undamaged bridges, be it in Rostov itself, or otherwise secured bridgeheads south of the Don for the resumption of operations planned later.

In order to prevent significant elements of the Russian forces located north of the Don from escaping south across the river, it is important that the forces advancing east from the area of Taganrog receive a strengthening of their right wing through the addition of panzers and fast troops, which – if necessary – are to be made up of improvised formations.

As the attack progresses consideration must be given, not only to strong guarding of the attack operation's northeast flank, but to the immediate strengthening of the defensive positions along the Don as well. In doing so great emphasis is to be placed on the strongest possible anti-tank defense. From the beginning the positions are to be laid down with a view to their possible use in the winter and are to be prepared accordingly with all means.

Primarily allied units will be used to occupy the Don front as it lengthens in the course of this operation, with the understanding that German units are to be employed as a strong back-up between Orel and the Don as well as on the Stalingrad isthmus. However, individual German divisions are to remain behind the Don front as a mobile reserve.

The allied units are to be largely used in their own sectors and positioned so that the Hungarians are employed farthest north, then the Italians and farthest southeast the Romanians.

(D) The rapid continuation of the movements across the Don to the south toward the operational objectives must be ensured in regard to the seasonal conditions.

signed Adolf Hitler

APPENDIX B

Observations and Documents on the Outbreak of War Between Germany and the Soviet Union in 1941

"There are an abundance of opinions concerning the German-Soviet war (1941-1945), some erroneous and misleading. Many authors, especially in West Germany, are inclined to take the one-sided view that only Hitler was pursuing aggressive objectives in 1939, while Stalin's Soviet Union was a peace-loving nation, interested only in its 'building of socialism'. . . Usually this portrayal culminates in the theory of the 'German surprise attack on the peace-loving Soviet Union'. . . . The argument just outlined is frequently characterized by a conscious veiling of facts and a suppression of key texts. It then tries to cite Soviet archives, the majority of which are not yet accessible, without acknowledging the abundance of conclusive sources already available which today permit a relatively clear assessment."[1]

On the August 23, 1939 conclusion of the Hitler-Stalin pact which contained secret clauses on zones of interest and a partitioning of Poland.

"Stalin's main concern (in the pact), was that war should now finally break out between the two camps into which capitalism had split. Stalin had calculated that Hitler, compelled by reasonable security assessments, would only enter into a passage of arms if his rear was free as the result of an alliance with the Soviet Union."
"It was therefore Stalin who initiated the rapprochement and . . . brought it over the final hurdle."[2]

On August 19, 1939, four days before an agreement was reached on the Hitler-Stalin pact, Stalin made a speech before a secret sitting of the Politburo in which he described the motives behind his policies. In his speech he said: "If the Soviets conclude an alliance treaty with France and Great Britain, Germany will see herself forced to step back from Poland and seek a modus *vivendi* with the western powers. In this way war could be avoided and the later development of the situation would have a dangerous character for us. If, on the other hand, we accept Germany's proposal, it will surely lead to a war with Poland, and the intervention of England and France will be unavoidable. We will then have great opportunities . . . and we can advantageously wait for our moment. Our interests demand that we follow the latter course."[3]

On August 24, 1939, the day after the Hitler-Stalin pact had been concluded, Hitler said to Krushchev: "I've outwitted him (Hitler), duped him."[4]

June 16-22, 1940: While Germany was occupied with the French Campaign, the Soviet Union occupied the Baltic States and declared them Soviet republics.

June 24, 1940: Stalin issued an ultimatum to Romania demanding Bessarabia and Northern Bukovina and then occupied these areas with the Red Army. Russia had thus moved closer to the Romanian oil fields necessary for Germany's conduct of the war.

By the end of July 1940 the Soviet Union increased its forces on its western front, from the Bay of Finland to the Black Sea, to 113 divisions and 28 motorized brigades. On the German side there were six security divisions and 27 Romanian divisions.[5]

On November 12-13, 1940, during his visit to Berlin, Stalin's Foreign Minister Molotov made demands – virtually ultimatums – for territorial influence in the Balkans, in Finland, at the Dardanelles and the outlets from the Baltic. Hitler rejected these demands.

On May 1, 1941 the Red Army called up 800,000 reservists and the corps and divisions in the western frontier military districts received orders to move closer to the front and set up front-line command posts. The ratio of strength on the German eastern, or Russian western, border was as follows:

On the Russian side: 118 rifle divisions, 20 cavalry divisions, 49 tank brigades.

On the German side: 77 infantry divisions, 3 panzer divisions. Given the German forces, in particular the limited armored forces, an attack by Germany was practically out of the question.

On May 15, 1941, in a secret report to Stalin, People's Commissar Timoshenko and Head of the Soviet General Staff Zhukov requested the order to attack Germany. The report stated: "When we take into account that Germany is mobilizing her army at the present time and has in position an extensive rear guard, it gives her the opportunity to beat us to the punch and launch a sudden attack. In order to avoid this we consider it imperative that we deny the German command the initiative, strike before the enemy and attack the German army at the moment when it is in the act of deploying . . ." The Red Army was therefore in position on Germany's eastern frontier on May 15, 1941, ready to strike, and could obviously have gone on the offensive in a very short time.[6]

On June 21, 1942 Germany attacked the Soviet Union. German forces: three army groups with 123 divisions, including 17 panzer divisions and 35 divisions of the allied nations. 3,300 tanks, 2,000 Luftwaffe aircraft.

Based on the information available today, the following is known of the Russian side: the first echelon consisting of five army groups with 170 divisions, 46 motorized units, 10,000 tanks, including 1,475 T-34 and KV types, which were superior to the German tanks. Behind it was the second echelon with 70 divisions and 8,000 tanks. These forces began moving toward the Russian western front on June 13; they were supposed to arrive at their positions on July 10. Had the German attack not taken place, on July 10 the Red Army would have been standing ready in its positions with 240 divisions, 29 motorized corps, 20,000 tanks and 10,000 aircraft. Standing ready for what?[7]

The answer was provided on May 9, 1991 by PRAVDA, the official organ of the Russian Communist Party. On the anniversary of the German surrender it made public that the German "Barbarossa" attack had driven into the midst of an offensive buildup being carried out by the Red Army. PRAVDA's wording: "Unrealistic plans of an offensive nature were drawn up before the war as a result of an overestimation of our own possibilities and an underestimation of the enemy. In accordance with these plans we began grouping forces on the western frontier. But the enemy beat us to it."[8]

Thus PRAVDA confirmed what it had long been possible to conclude from the assessments of German military historians and Soviet memoirs: the German attack on June 21, 1941 was objectively a preventive strike.

Notes:

1. Prof. Klaus Hornung, Das Signum des *Jahrhunderts*, 1992. From: a pre-publication manuscript.

2. Konrad Guthardt, *Präventivschlag oder Überfall*, unpublished file study, 1992. From: Gottfried Schramm: *Grundmuster deutscher Ostpolitik 1918-1939*, Page 16.

3. Victor Suvorov, *Der Eisbrecher*, 1989. Georg F. Willing, *Der Zweite Weltkrieg*, 1988, Page 139.

4. Nikita Krushchev, *Vospominanija*, New York 1981, Page 69.

5. *Vergleichsübersicht über die Verstärkung der Roten Armee seit dem 1.9.1929*, OKW to the Foreign Office, attached to 944/41-9 GKDOS.

6. Dr. Walter Post, *Zur Vorgeschichte des deutsches-russischen Krieges unter Würdigung der sowjetischen Geschichtsschreibung*, CRITICON.

7. May/June 1991. From Victor Suvorov where cited, OKW Diary, Dimitri Volkoganov, *Stalin, Triumph and Tragedy*, 1989, Page 557; Marshall Zhukov, "Recollections and Thoughts," 1969, Pages 195-201.

8. PRAVDA, Moscow, May 8, 1991. Text from Prof. Topitsch in DIE WELT 7.12.1991.

APPENDIX C

Statements on the Tragedy of Stalingrad

Adolf Hitler to *Feldmarschall* von Manstein on February 5, 1943:

"I alone bear the responsibility for Stalingrad! I could perhaps say that Göring gave me an incorrect picture of the feasibility of supply by the Luftwaffe and thus lay at least part of the blame on him. But he is my designated successor and therefore I can't burden him with responsibility for Stalingrad."

General von Seydlitz, commander of the Sixth Army's LI Corps, in his memoirs:

"It would never have come to this catastrophe of the collapse of the relief attempt if Hitler had not clung to Stalingrad like a maniac from the beginning to the end."

Feldmarschall von Manstein, Commander-in-Chief of Army Group Don:

"The encirclement of the Sixth Army could only have been prevented if the army had initiated a breakthrough in the very first days of the enemy offensive. Issuing the necessary orders was a matter for the supreme command. Certainly *General* Paulus could have made the decision to withdraw from Stalingrad on his own. But he was not in a position to make it as early as the OKH would have been, as he had no way of knowing the situations of the neighboring armies. When on November 22 or 23 he requested permission to be allowed to break out to the southwest with the army . . . the decisive hour had already passed. *General* Paulus knew Hitler and was aware that he credited himself with saving the German Army from a Napoleonic catastrophe that winter (1941) through his order to hold at all costs. He must have told himself that Hitler would never allow

the evacuation of the city after his speech (in the Münchner Löwenbräukeller) . . . The only possibility would thus have been to present Hitler with the *fait accompli* of the army's departure from Stalingrad, especially if the supreme command shrouded itself in silence for 36 hours, as in fact happened. It is of course possible that such a course of action would have cost Paulus, among others, his head. One can assume, however, that it was not worry over such an outcome that prevented Paulus from doing unilaterally what he saw as correct. Rather it was his loyalty to Hitler that led him to seek permission for the army to break out."

Generalmajor Hans Doerr, general staff officer and the commander of a division in Russia, in his book *Der Feldzug nach Stalingrad*:

"When Hitler forbade a breakout on November 24 the army was still fully combat capable. Even if the commanders at the front were of the opinion that there was no other solution but to break out, there was no available proof that the relief offensive which had been ordered would not succeed and that the promised airlift would fail. A breach of obedience on that November 24 could not and cannot be readily sanctioned; only history can judge the success or failure of such acts. By December 12 the situation had worsened decisively for the Sixth Army. The relief offensive by Army Group Hoth had failed and the promised air supply had not arrived. In spite of this the army was still a considerable fighting force and was only 65 kilometers from nearest German front. Given the overall situation at that time it could have saved the majority of its resources. As it was obvious that this opportunity would disappear within a few days and never return, an action against Hitler's orders would have been justified. By January 8 the conditions for a breakout no longer existed, because the army was no longer capable of conducting combat operations and the front held by Germany and its allies was 200 kilometers away."

Retired *Bundeswehr General* Franz Uhle-Wettler in his book *Deutsche Militärgeschichte*:

"A voluntary retreat from the Caucasus or from Stalingrad . . . would have enabled the Germans...backed up by strong reserves, to wait calmly for the Russian winter offensive. But the German command didn't know enough about its enemy to make such a difficult decision . . . Indeed, where in history is there an example of a powerful army, looking back on brilliant victories, guaranteeing a defeat. Such a decision would have demanded more wisdom and more modesty than was possessed by most, and certainly by Hitler. But a different outcome in the Battle of Stalingrad could scarcely have changed the end result of the war . . . Because of its tremendous size, spaces and distances Russia could only be conquered by Russians . . . More than a million Russians served on the German side in the Second World War, an unheard of event in the history of warfare. More than 20,000 of them fought and died at Stalingrad. Only a few of these Russians had a desire to fight for Hitler or a nationalist-socialist Germany, but most of them wanted to see the defeat of the hammer and sickle."

Marshall Chuikov, the defender of Stalingrad, on January 31, 1942 (according to the Seydlitz memoirs):

Question to the captured German generals: Why didn't you break out? We were very fearful of this at the beginning."

Marshall Zhukov, Deputy Soviet Commander-in-Chief, in his memoirs:

"What circumstances contributed to the catastrophic collapse of the German troops and to our historic victory? The failure of all of Hitler's strategic plans in 1942 was the result of the underestimation of the forces and potential of the Soviet state, the moral strength of its people and the overestimation of their own forces and military capabilities by the Hitler fascists."

Manfred Kehrig in *Stalingrad, Beiträge zur Militär- und Kriegsgeschichte des militärgeschichtlichen Forschungsamtes*:

"The conquest of Stalingrad failed for three reasons: the necessary strong infantry forces were missing, the unusually strong artillery lacked sufficient ammunition and, not least, there was a lack of training in fighting in built-up areas. More than anything the high German losses are attributable to the latter shortcoming. Not until toward the end of the war were steps taken to adapt the training program to include this style of modern warfare."

In his book *Stalingrad und die Verantwortung des Soldaten*, Joachim Wieder, operations officer of an army corps of the Sixth Army, elevates the problem from the military-historical into the moral dimension, and in support of this quotes from the will of *General* Ludwig Beck, prewar head of the General Staff:

"It is a shortcoming of greatness and understanding of duty, when in such times a soldier in the highest position sees his duties and responsibilities only within the limited framework of his military missions, without being conscious of his greatest responsibility, to the entire nation. Extraordinary times require extraordinary actions."

General Arthur Schmidt, Chief of Staff of the Sixth Army, in the notes he left behind:

"Outwardly we had to show confidence, so that the will to hold on didn't wane. It was only thanks to this policy that the army fought on for another four weeks. This had nothing to do with ideology (faith in Hitler). 'Faith in Hitler' or 'defiant reaction' were not the reason for the position we took then, rather it was the expression of fulfillment of duty to Germany which dictated our position: even if the army was destroyed, the war could and had to be won. We could contribute to this by holding out for a long time, occupying Russian forces. – Only in this way can our appeals to the troops and teletypes to Manstein or to Hitler be understood."

Walter Görlitz in the introduction to his book *Paulus – Ich stehe hier auf Befehl*, literary bequest of the Field Marshall:

"Whoever follows military history will always ask the question whether Paulus ought not to have acted in those days (Christmas 1942) for his army, which still possessed great strength, which was hoping for a breakout, which would have fought like a lion – without asking Manstein or Hitler any further? Especially since Manstein, the old-style Prussian, would probably have supported such an action? Perhaps a Karl the Twelfth of Sweden would have acted this way, or perhaps Field Marshall von Reichenau or Field Marshall Model, the latter two in accordance with their tactic of informing the Führer that they believed they had to act as he would have done and had therefore ordered this or that. Reichenau acted thus when, contrary to Hitler's orders, he withdrew Army Group South to the Mius in December 1941. Paulus, the thorough, soldierly thinker, who coolly weighed each decision two or three times, was cut from different cloth."

And *Feldmarschall* Paulus:

". . . what convincing and solid arguments could have been brought forward by the Commander-in-Chief of the Sixth Army for his conduct contrary to orders in the face of the enemy, especially when he had no way of knowing the eventual outcome? The fundamental question is, does a hopeless situation, perceived or subjectively identifified, give a commander the right to disobey orders? In the case of Stalingrad the question of hopelessness could definitely not be answered in the absolute affirmative, therefore there could be no question of it being identified subjectively, if one disregards the final stages of the battle. How could I later have demanded obedience from any subordinate in a similar – or in his opinion – more difficult situation?

"Does the prospect of one's own death or probable destruction or the capture of one's troops relieve one of the responsibility of soldierly obedience?

"Today each person may find the answer to this question for himself and for his own conscience.

"At that time the Wehrmacht and the nation would not have understood such conduct on my part. In its effect it would have been a decidedly revolutionary, political act against Hitler. It also remained to be seen whether by acting contrary to orders and abandoning the position at Stalingrad I wouldn't have played the argument into Hitler's hand, exposing publicly the cowardice and disobedience of the Generals and shifting onto them the entire blame for the military defeat which was clearly coming . . .

"The revolutionary objective of consciously causing the defeat, so as to bring about the fall of Hitler and national socialism, which were hindrances to ending the war, was neither considered by me, nor did I become aware of it in any form anywhere in my command.

"Such ideas were beyond the realm of my considerations at that time. They were also not in keeping with my character. I was a soldier and I believed then that

I was serving my nation through obedience.

"As far as the responsibility of the officers under my command is concerned, seen tactically, they had to carry out my orders in a difficult situation, just as I had to follow the orders given me within the framework of the overall strategic situation.

"Before the troops and officers of the Sixth Army as well as before the German nation I bear the responsibility that I carried out the orders to hold on issued by the supreme command until the collapse."

Abbreviations

3 = III.	24 = XXIV.	47 = XXXXVII.
4 = IV.	30 = XXX.	48 = XXXXVIII.
7 = VII.	40 = XXXX.	49 = XXXXIX.
8 = VIII.	41 = XXXXI.	51 = LI.
11 = Xl.	42 = XXXXII.	54 = LIV.
14 = XIV.	46 = XXXXVI.	57 = LVII.

A. K.	Armeekorps, several infantry divisions under the command of a corps headquarters
Pz K.	Panzerkorps, several panzer divisions or panzer and infantry divisions under the command of a corps head quarters for mobile troops
Geb. K.	Gebirgskorps, several mountain divisions or several mountain divisions and other divisions under the com mand of a corps headquarters for mountain troops
AOK	Armeeoberkommando - Army headquarters
Arko	Artilleriekommandeur
Chef	Chief of the General staff
Ia	First General staff officer (Command)
Ib	Second General staff officer (Supply)
Ic	Third General staff officer (Intelligence and Security)
Fla	Fliegerabwehr des Heeres
Flak	Flugabwehrkanone
F. HQu	Führerhauptquartier - Hitler's field headquarters
G. R.	Grenadierregiment
He	Heinkel

H. Gr.	Heeresgruppe, an army group, several armies
HKL	Hauptkampflinie
Hornisse	Panzerjäger with 88mm Pak
Hummel	Heavy Self-propelled howitzer
I. D.	Infanteriedivision
i. G.	im Generalstab, Denotes officer with General staff training
I. R.	Infanterieregiment
I-Trupp	Instandsetzungstrupp
Ju	Junkers
Krad	Kraftrad
KTB	Kriegstagebuch
Kwk	Kampfwagenkanone
Me	Messerschmitt
Mech. K.	Mechanized Corps, Soviet designation for a fully motorized corps with tank and rifle brigades
MG	Maschinengewehr, machine gun
sMG	schweres Maschinengewehr, heavy MG
mot.	Motorized
MPi	Maschinenpistole
MTW	Mannschaftstransportwagen
OB	Oberbefehlshaber
OKH	Oberkommando des Heeres - High command of the Army
OKW	Oberkommando der Wehrmacht - High command of the Armed Forces
OT	Organisation Todt
Pak	Panzerabwehrkanone - (Pak) anti-tank gun
Pz. D.	Panzerdivision
Pz. Gren. R.	Panzergrenadierregiment
RAD	Reichsarbeitsdienst - Reich Labor Service
S. Br.	Schützenbrigade
Schtz. Div.	Schützendivision, rifle division, Russian infantry division
Schtz. Rgt.	Schützenregiment
SPW	Schützenpanzerwagen

SS-Kav. D.	SS-Kavalleriedivision
STAVKA	Stalin's military command staff
Stoss. A.	Stoßarmee, (Shock Army), Soviet designation for an army especially well equipped with offensive weapons
Stuka	Sturzkampfbomber
V. P.	Vorausbefördertes Personal eines höheren Stabes
z. b. V.	zur besonderen Verwendung

Bibliography

Benary, Albert: *Die Berliner 257. Bären Division*, Podzun Verlag, Bad Nauheim, 1957

Bereshkov, Valentin: *In diplomatischer Mission*, Frankfurt-Main, 1967

Böhmler, Rudolf: *Fallschirmjäger*, Podzun Verlag, Bad Nauheim, 1961

Braun, J: *Enzian und Edelweiss, 4. Geb. Div.*, Podzun Verlag, Bad Nauheim, 1955

Buchner, Alex: *Gebirgsjäger an allen Fronten*, Adolf Sponholz Verlag, Hannover, 1954

Carell, Paul: *Die Wüstenfüchse*, Nannen Verlag, Hamburg, 1954

Carell, Paul: *Sie kommen*, Stalling Verlag, Oldenburg, East Germany, 1961

Carell, Paul: *Unternehmen Barbarossa*, Ullstein Verlag, Frankfurt-Main-Berlin, 1963

Carell, Paul: *Verbrannte Erde*, Ullstein Verlag, Berlin, 1966

Carell, Paul: *Unternehmen Barbarossa im Bild*, Ullstein Verlag, Berlin 1966

Carell, Paul/Böddecker, Günter: *Die Gefangenen*, Ullstein Verlag, Berlin 1980.

Carnes, James D.: *General zwischen Hitler und Stalin*, Droste Verlag, Düsseldorf, 1980

Chuikov, V.I.: *At the Beginning of the Road*, Moscow, 1959 (Russian)

Dallin, Alexander: *Die Sowjetspionage*, Verlag für Politik und Wirtschaft, Cologne, 1956

Dieckhoff, G.: *Die 3. I.D. (mot.)*, Erich Börries Druck und Verlag, Göttingen, 1960

Doerr, Hans: *Der Feldzug nach Stalingrad*, E.S. Mittler & Sohn, Darmstadt, 1955

Document collection on the main war criminals before the Nuremburg International Tribunal, Volume 34.

Ernsthausen, A. von: *Wende im Caucasus*, Vowinckel Verlag, Neckargemünd, 1958

Esteban-Infantes, General: *Blaue Division*, Druffel Verlag, Leoni, 1958

Fabry, Philipp W.: *Die Sowjetunion und das Dritte Reich*, Busse-Seewald Verlag, Herford, 1971

Fischer, Johannes: *Über den Entschluss zur Luftversorgung Stalingrads*, Militärgeschichtliche Mitteilungen, Volume 2, 1969

Förster, Jürgen: *Hitlers Entscheidung für den Krieg gegen die Sowjetunion*, quoted by Topitsch.

Fretter-Pico, M.: *Missbrauchte Infanterie*, Verlag für Wehrwesen Bernard & Graefe, Frankfurt-Main, 1957

Fuller, J.F., General: *Der zweite Weltkrieg 1939-1945*, Humboldt Verlag, Vienna-Stuttgart, 1952

Garthoff, R.I.: *Die Sowjet-Armee*, markus Verlag GmbH, Cologne, 1955

Görlitz, Walter: *Keitel, Verbrecher oder Offizier?*, Musterschmidt Verlag, Göttingen, 1961

Görlitz, Walter: *Paulus: Ich stehe hier auf Befehl*, Verlag für Wehrwesen Bernard & Graefe, Frankfurt, 1960

Grams, Rolf: *14. Panzer-Division*, Podzun Verlag, Bad Nauheim, 1957

Graser, G.: *Zwischen Kattegat und Kaukasus, 198. I.D.*, private publication, 1961

Guderian, Heinz: *Erinnerungen eines Soldatens*, Kurt Vowinckel Verlag, Heidelberg, 1951

Halder, Hitler's Chief of General Staff: War Diary, W. Kohlhammer, Stuttgart, 1962

Halder: *Hitler als Feldherr*, Münchner Dom-Verlag, Munich 1949

Herhudt von Rohden, H.D.: *Die Luftwaffe ringt um Stalingrad*, Limes Verlag, Wiesbaden, 1950

Hillgruber, Andreas: *Der Zweite Weltkrieg 1939-1945*, W. Kohlhammer, Stuttgart, 1983

Hoffmann, Joachim, in: *Der Angriff auf die Sowjetunion*, omnibus volume of the Military Historical Research Department, Freiburg

Hoth, Hermann: *Panzer Operationen*, Scharnhorst Buchkameradschaft, Heidelberg, 1956

Hubatsch, Walter: *Hitlers Weisungen für die Kriegführung*, Verlag für Wehrwesen, Bernard & Graefe, Frankfurt-Main, 1962

Hughes, Emryn: *Churchill – Ein Mann im Widerspruch*, Tübingen, 1959

Jacobsen, Hans-Adolf: *1939-1945, Der zweite Weltkrieg in Chroniken und Dokumenten*, Wehr und Wissen Verlagsgesellschaft, Darmstadt, 1959

Kalinov, Kyrill D.: *Sowjetmarschälle haben das Wort*, Hansa Verlag, Hamburg, 1952

Kardel, Hennecke: *Geschichte der 170. I.D.*, Podzun Verlag, Bad Nauheim, 1952

Keesing: *Archiv der Gegenwart, 1941/42*

Kehrig, Manfred: *Stalingrad: Analyse und Dokumentation einer Schlacht*, Deutsche Verlags-Anstalt, Stuttgart, 1974

Keilig, Wolf: *Das deutsche Heer 1939-1945*, Podzun Verlag, Bad Nauheim

Kesselring, Albert: *Soldat bis zum letzten Tage*, Athenäum Verlag, Bonn, 1953

Konrad, R.: *Kampf um den Kaukasus*, Copress Verlag, Munich, year unknown

Kunert, Dirk: *Ein Weltkrieg wird programmiert*, Arndt Verlag, Kiel, 1984

Kunert, Dirk: *Hitlers Kalter Krieg...*, Arndt Verlag, Kiel 1992

Lanz, Hubert: *Gebirgsjäger*, Podzun Verlag, Bad Nauheim, 1954

Lemelsen, Joachim: *29. I.D. (mot.)*, Podzun Verlag, Bad Nauheim, 1960

Liddell, Hart/ Basil, Henry: *Die Rote Armee*, Verlag WEU Offene Worte, Bonn, year unknown

Lusar, Rudolf: *Die deutschen Waffen und Geheimwaffen des zweiten Weltkrieges*, J.F. Lehmanns Verlag, Munich, 1962

Mackensen, Eberhard von: *Das III. Panzer-Korps im Feldzug 1941/42 gegen die Sowjetunion*, 23rd Panzer Division publication, April 1959

Mannerheim, Marshall: *Erinnerungen*, Atlantis Verlag, Zurich, 1952

Manstein, Erich von: *Verlorene Siege*, Athenäum Verlag, Bonn, 1955

Martini, Winfried: *Der Sieger schreibt die Geschichte*, Universitas Verlag, Munich, 1991

Mellenthin, F.W. von: *Panzerschlachten*, Kurt Vowinckel Verlag, Heidelberg, 1963

Middeldorf, Eike: *Taktik im Russlandfeldzug*, E.S. Mittler & Sohn, Berlin, 1956

Munzel: *Panzer-Taktik*, Kurt Vowinckel Verlag, Neckargemünd, 1959

Nehring, Walther K.: *Geschichte der Deutschen Panzerwaffe 1916-1945*, Propyläen Verlag, Frankfurt-Main-Berlin, 1969

Philippi, A./Heim, F: *Der Feldzug gegen Sowjetrussland*, W. Kohlhammer Verlag, Stuttgart, 1962

Platanov, S.P./Pavlenko, N.G/Parotkin, I.W.: *History of the Second World War*, three volumes, Moscow, 1958 (Russian)

Ploetz, A.G.: *Geschichte des zweiten Weltkrieges*, A.G. Ploetz Verlag, Würzburg, 1960

Röhricht, Edgar: *Probleme der Kesselschlacht*, Condor Verlag, Karlsruhe, 1958

Samyalov, A.S./Kalyadin T.J.: *The Battle of the Caucasus*, Moscow, 1956 (Russian)

Selle, H.: *Die Tragödie von Stalingrad*, Verlag das andere Deutschland, Hannover, 1948

Senger, U. von/Etterlin jr., Dr. F.M.: *24. Panzer-Division, vormals 1. Kavalleriedivision*, Kurt Vowinckel Verlag, Neckargemünd, 1962

Seydlitz, Walter von: *Stalingrad Konflikt und Konsequenz*, Stalling Verlag, Oldenburg, East Germany, 1977

Shilin, P.A.: *The Most Important Operations of the Great Patriotic War 1941 to 1945*, Moscow, 1956 (Russian)

Spaeter, Helmuth: *Die Geschichte des Panzerkorps Großdeutschland*, published privately

Speidel, Helm: *Reichswehr und Rote Armee*, Quarterly for Contemporary His tory, 1/1953

Scheibert, Horst: *Nach Stalingrad – 48 Kilometer*, Kurt Vowinckel Verlag, Neckargemünd, 1956

Schramm, W. von/Drechsler, H.: *Deutschland im zweiten Weltkrieg*, Berlin, 1976

Schröter, Heinz: *Stalingrad bis zur letzten Patrone*, Kleins Druck- und verlagsanstalt, Lengerich, year unknown

Streets, Hans: *Gebirgsjäger in der Nogaischen Steppe*, Kurt Vowinckel Verlag, Neckargemünd, 1956

Suworow, Viktor: *Der Eisbrecher*, Klett-Cotta Verlag, Stuttgart, 1989

Tippelskirch, Kurt von: Gesch*ichte des zweiten Weltkrieges*, Athenäum Verlag, Bonn, 1951

Toepke, Günter: *Stalingrad wie es wirklich war*, Kogge Verlag, Stuttgart, 1989

Topitsch, Ernst: *Stalins Krieg*, Busse-Seewald Verlag, Herford, 1990

Uhle-Wetter, F.: *Höhe und Wendepunkt deutscher Militärgeschichte*, Hase & Köhler, Mainz, 1984

Voyetekov, Boris: *The Last Days of Sevastopol*, Cassel, London, 1943

Wagener, Carl: *Der Vorstoss des XXXX Pz.Korps von Kharkov zum Kaukasus*, in Military History Review, Sept./Oct. 1955

Wegner, Bernd: *Zwei Wege nach Moskau – vom Hitler-Stalin-Pakt zum Unternehmen Barbarossa*, produced by Military History Research Office, Freiburg

Werthen, Wolfgang: *Geschichte der 16. Panzerdivision*, Podzun Verlag, Bad Nauheim, 1958 and photo album 1956

Wieder, Joachim: *Stalingrad*, Nymphenburger Verlagshandlung, Munich, 1962

Yeremenko, A.I.: *Direction West*, Moscow, 1959 (Russian)

Yeremenko, A.I.: *Stalingrad*, Moscow, 1961 (Russian)

Zeitzler, Kurt: "The Battle of Stalingrad", in: *The Fatal Decisions*, Michael Joseph, London, 1956

Zhukov, Georgi K.: *Erinnerungen und Gedanken*, Deutsche Verlagsanstalt, Stuttgart, 1969

Separate print and private publications:

Geschichte der 24. Infanteriedivision, division working group, 1956
Panzerkeil im Osten, Verlag "Die Wehrmacht," Berlin, 1941

The following made available unpublished manuscripts, studies and articles and answered questions:

General Staff Oberst von Below, Oberst Arthur Boje (rtd.), General der Flieger Paul Deichmann (rtd.), Oberst Joachim Hesse (rtd.), Generaloberst Hermann

Hoth (rtd.), Major Hermann Kandutsch (rtd.), General der Panzertruppe Hasso von Manteuffel (rtd.), General der Panzertruppe Walther K. Nehring (rtd.), Generalmajor Herman von Oppeln-Bronikowski (rtd.), General der Flakartillerie Wolfgang Pickert (rtd.), Oberstleutnant Eberhardt Pohl (rtd.), Dr. Helmut K.G. Rönnefarth, Generalleutnant Alfred Reinhardt (rtd.), Generalleutnant Arthur Schmidt (rtd.), Oberst Herbert Selle (rtd.), Generaloberst Strecker (rtd.), General der Panzertruppe Walter Wenck (rtd.), Oberstleutnant Coelestin von Zitzewitz (rtd.).

Also from the publisher

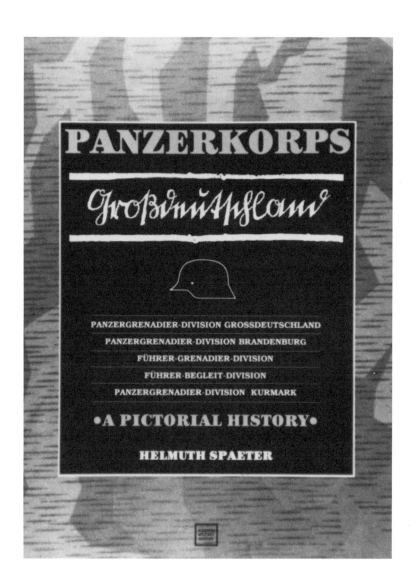

PANZERKORPS
GROßDEUTSCHLAND

Helmut Spaeter

Size: 7 3/4"x 10 1/2" 248 pages hard cover $29.95

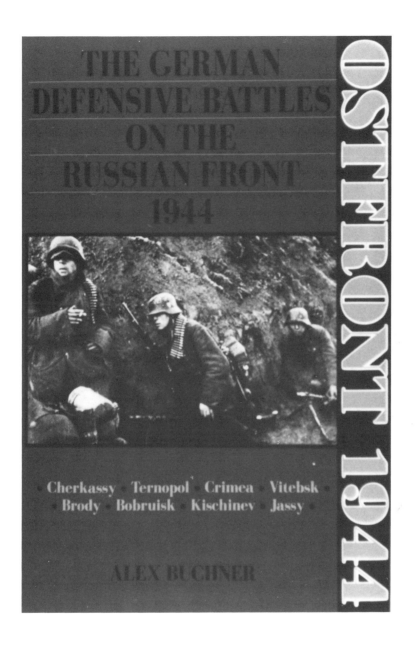

OSTFRONT 1944

Alex Buchner

Size: 6" x 9"   336 pages   hard cover $29.95

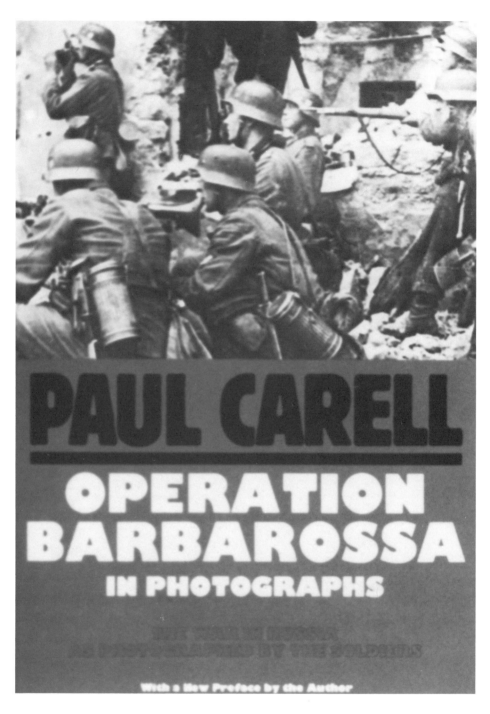

OPERATION BARBAROSSA
Paul Carell

Size: 7" x 10"   460 pages   hard cover $44.95